Fighting the
Fuzzy-Wuzzy

So 'ere's to you, Fuzzy-Wuzzy, 'at your 'ome in the Soudan;
You're a pore benighted 'eathen but a first-class fightin' man

1. Lieut.-General Sir Gerald Graham, VC, KCB. (ILN 21 February 1885)

Fighting the Fuzzy-Wuzzy

Days and Nights of Service with Sir Gerald Graham's Field Force at Suakin

by

Major E. A. De Cosson, FRGS

Greenhill Books, London
Presidio Press, California

Greenhill
Books

This edition of *Fighting the Fuzzy-Wuzzy*
first published in 1990 by Greenhill Books, Lionel Leventhal Limited,
Park House, 1 Russell Gardens, London NW11 9NN
and
Presidio Press,
31 Pamaron Way, Novato, Ca.94947, U.S.A.

British Library Cataloguing in Publication Data
De Cosson, E. A. (Emilius Albert)
Fighting the Fuzzy-Wuzzy – Days and Nights of Service
with Sir Gerald Graham's Field Force at Suakin. – New ed.
1. Sudan. Army operations by Great Britain. Army, 1820–1956
I. Title   II. Days and Nights of Service
962.403

ISBN 1–85367–066–9

Publishing History
Fighting the Fuzzy-Wuzzy was first published in 1886 as
*Days and Nights of Service with Sir Gerald Graham's
Field Force at Suakin* (John Murray). The text in the original volume
is reproduced now exactly, complete and unabridged. For this edition
8 pages of illustrations have been added.

Printed in Great Britain by
Billing & Sons Ltd, Worcester

PREFACE

I HAVE endeavoured to sketch in the following pages the events that both gladdened and saddened our lives during the brief Suakin Campaign of 1885, trusting that those English men and women who, perforce, have to sit at home at ease, may feel a kindly interest in knowing how the troops, who go out to fight for Queen and country, pass their days and nights on active service.

My notes were written during the brief intervals of almost continuous duty; often in the saddle when events were actually happening around me, at other times when they had subsequently come to my knowledge ; and I must trust to the good-nature of my readers to pardon their literary shortcomings. Perhaps there are few things more perplexing to the writer of a daily journal than the persistency with which he finds his own personality and opinions cropping up on every page. His narrative bristles with I, and my, till he feels heartily ashamed of the egotism that seems to pervade its whole structure ; but to elevate a rough field diary into a regular history, would be to change its character altogether ; and, if I have had somewhat frequently to allude to the particular duties with which I was entrusted, I can only plead in excuse, that Sir Gerald Graham said in his despatch of the 30th May, "the main difficulty of this campaign has been the want of water."

The opinions I have advanced are perhaps crudely expressed, but they serve to illustrate the impressions made by events that were fresh in my mind at the time I jotted them down, and for this reason may, I trust, contain some suggestiveness to those better able to judge than myself.

The sources from which my information is derived are of three kinds—personal observation, for the accuracy of which I am responsible, despatches (now public property) which may be taken as official, and common report, in which latter category I include the accounts of newspaper correspondents, for which I cannot, of course, be responsible, though they are of undoubted value as being the testimony of men enjoying special facilities for observation, which a soldier engaged on his duty does not always possess ; but where not writing from personal experience, I have always endeavoured to give my authority.

If I have occasionally ventured to criticize, I trust it has been in no unkindly spirit, and only on subjects that are open to fair discussion. Sir William Napier's remark on Lord Wellington, at the end of his Peninsular war, "To say that he committed errors is to say that he made war," applies to all who embark on the vicissitudes of a campaign ; but I believe also, that the errors of past campaigns, if carefully studied, are the surest foundation on which to build up the glorious successes of the future ; and in pointing out where a different plan of action might have been pursued, it must be understood that I am only following the principle that it is unfair to criticize unless you have an alternative to propose, and that nothing can be further from my wish than to cast the slightest imputation on the ability, energy, and devotion to duty of the officers who conducted the operations. That they displayed those qualities in a marked degree is now a matter of history, and if the campaign led to no immediate or very definite result, I believe it was solely owing to the conditions under which it was undertaken, and the necessity which arose for the recall of the troops at the very moment the principal difficulties of the advance had been successfully overcome. With regard to the Nile Expedition, though I have always doubted the expediency of choosing that route, I can only speak as one who was not on the spot, and has, therefore, drawn his conclusions from the writings of those who were.

The campaign I have endeavoured to describe was memorable, in that it was the first occasion on which English, Australian, and Indian troops, have met together in the common brotherhood of arms, while the foe they contended against was possessed of a courage and cunning that has perhaps not been surpassed even in the annals of Red Indian warfare.

As Sir Gerald Graham said in his last despatch, —" It is necessary to bear in mind not only the nature of the country, but also the style of warfare practised by the enemy, which consists in long range firing from cover, combined with desperate hand to hand assaults from the bush, through and under which they can steal unobserved."

Those who have only seen soldiers in garrison at home, may perhaps think they lead a somewhat idle and frivolous life, but if they could behold them on active service, they would find that when called upon to maintain the honour of their country, English soldiers are capable of performing daily acts of unostentatious heroism which, could they be all recorded, would excite the most profound admiration. During the wearisome march under a burning sun, the dreary hours passed on laborious fatigue duty, the long watches of the night that too frequently follow a day of toil, when the sentry is responsible for the safety of his comrades, the still more trying time when sickness stalks invisible through the camp, or in that supreme moment of battle, when death or mutilation in its most terrible forms stare them in the face,—our soldiers display a cheerful and unselfish devotion to duty which must endear them to the hearts of all who move among them, and, if in the following pages I have been able to present to the minds of my readers even an imperfect picture of the way they passed their days and nights during the late Suakin Expedition, I do not think I shall have written in vain.

WHADDON HOUSE, BRUTON, SOMERSET,
February 23, 1886.

CONTENTS

CHAPTER VIII.

CHAPTER IX.

CHAPTER X.

CHAPTER XI.

CHAPTER XII.

Fighting the Fuzzy-Wuzzy: Days and Nights of Service with Sir Gerald Graham's Field Force at Suakin was originally published as *Days and Nights of Service with Sir Gerald Graham's Field Force at Suakin.*

LIST OF ILLUSTRATIONS

All illustrations from *The Illustrated London News*.

"Fuzzy-Wuzzy"

(SOUDAN EXPEDITIONARY FORCE)

We've fought with many men acrost the seas,
   An' some of 'em was brave an' some was not:
The Paythan an' the Zulu an' Burmese;
   But the Fuzzy was the finest o' the lot.
We never got a ha'porth's change of 'im:
   'E squatted in the scrub an' 'ocked our 'orses,
'E cut our sentries up at Sua*kim,*
   An' 'e played the cat an' banjo with our forces.
        So 'ere's *to* you, Fuzzy-Wuzzy, at your 'ome in the
           Soudan;
        You're a pore benighted 'eathen but a first-class
           fightin' man;
        We gives you your certificate, an' if you want it
           signed
        We'll come an' 'ave a romp with you whenever
           you're inclined.

We took our chanst among the Kyber 'ills,
   The Boers knocked us silly at a mile,
The Burman give us Irriwaddy chills,
   An' a Zulu *impi* dished us up in style:
But all we ever got from such as they
   Was pop to what the Fuzzy made us swaller;
We 'eld our bloomin' own, the papers say,
   But man for man the Fuzzy knocked us 'oller.
        Then 'ere's *to* you, Fuzzy-Wuzzy, an' the missis
           and the kid;
        Our orders was to break you, an' of course we
           went an' did.
        We sloshed you with Martinis, an' it wasn't
           'ardly fair;
        But for all the odds agin' you, Fuzzy-Wuz, you
           broke the square.

'E 'asn't got no papers of 'is own,
    'E 'asn't got no medals nor rewards,
So we must certify the skill 'e's shown
    In usin' of 'is long two-'anded swords:
When 'e's 'oppin' in an' out among the bush
    With 'is coffin-'eaded shield an' shovel-spear,
An 'appy day with Fuzzy on the rush
    Will last an 'ealthy Tommy for a year.
            So 'ere's *to* you, Fuzzy-Wuzzy, an' your
                friends which are no more,
            If we 'adn't lost some messmates we would
                'elp you to deplore;
            But give an' take's the gospel, an' we'll call
                the bargain fair,
            For if you 'ave lost more than us, you
                crumpled up the square!

'E rushes at the smoke when we let drive,
    An', before we know, 'e's 'ackin' at our 'ead;
'E's all 'ot sand an' ginger when alive,
    An' 'e's generally shammin' when 'e's dead.
'E's a daisy, 'e's a ducky, 'e's a lamb!
    'E's a injia-rubber idiot on the spree,
'E's the on'y thing that doesn't give a damn
    For a Regiment o' British Infantree!
            So 'ere's *to* you, Fuzzy-Wuzzy, at your 'ome
                in the Soudan;
            You're a pore benighted 'eathen but a first-
                class fightin' man;
            An' 'ere's *to* you, Fuzzy-Wuzzy, with your
                'ayrick 'ead of 'air –
            You big black boundin' beggar – for you broke
                a British square!

RUDYARD KIPLING

1890

2. "Zereba and Advanced Redoubt near Souakim". (ILN 21 March 1885)

3. "War in the Desert: A Runni

ht". (ILN 7 February 1885)

4. "A Night Attack on the C

Souakin". (ILN 4 April 1885)

5. "The Fight of Sunday, March 22,

Niell's Zereba". (ILN 18 April 1885)

6. The late Captain F. J. Romilly. (ILN 11 April 1885)

DAYS AND NIGHTS OF SERVICE

CHAPTER I.

ON BOARD A TROOPER.

FEBRUARY 17, 1885.—A dull wet morning at Aldershot, the gray overcast sky hanging low with water-laden clouds, a fine drifting rain beating in the faces of all abroad, and the sodden ground glistening with small lagoons and rivulets through which the men splash heavily as they form up on parade ; their dripping greatcoats seething and steaming as though resenting the steady downpour. In the wooden Orderly Room hut, a group of officers, booted and spurred, are standing before a bright coal fire chatting and smoking cigarettes ; punctually, as the hand of the clock points to half-past eight, they don their greatcoats and step out into the rain ; then follows a brief inspection, and the men march off amid the cheers of their comrades ; for they are under orders to proceed to the seat of war, and will this afternoon be on their way to Suakin, to open a new Campaign. A band marches in front playing "The Girl I Leave Behind Me," " Auld Lang Syne," etc.—familiar tunes that for generations have greeted the ears of British troops when they leave their native land.

Every now and then a soldier steps out of the little crowd of sight-seers, who, regardless of the rain, have come to see us start, and wrings the hand of a comrade as he passes. " Good-bye, good luck," is the usual formula of these adieux, both with officers and men, but commonplace though the words may be, there is a touching ring in the tone with which they are delivered, for who can tell when the friends will meet again ?

Tramp, tramp, through the cheerless rain and slush, with a short halt on an open space, while other companies join us, and some dripping staff officers ride up to exchange a few words ; then on again past the permanent barracks through the narrow streets of the town, where convivial civilians strive to press mugs of beer into the not unwilling hands of the passing private, and the small boys set up a shrill cheer ; then a long halt at the little station, where the special train is shunted. Mr. Smith's newsboy drives a brisk trade at the book-stall, for the officers buy plenty of papers to dis-tribute among the men, their scabbards tracing quaint watery zig-zags along the platform, as they trail through the little pools that have collected wherever they stood ; but at last everybody is seated, the whistle sounds, and we are off.

Off, rolling swiftly on our way to an unknown future, and gazing our last at the pleasant English scenery ; past green fields fringed with graceful elm-trees, now in their winter bareness, but full of promise of fat brown buds that will burst into delicate green leaves in the spring to come, and expand into glorious shady foliage as May ripens into June. Past shady steep-banked lanes and russet hedgerows, where the sportsman with his dogs and gun is now watch-ing for rabbits, but which will presently be gay with

a wild luxuriance of sweet, homely, country flowers,
bright and innocent as childhood's laughter, to gladden
the heart with their simple beauty. Past cosy farm-
steads nestling in sheltered places, with a dreamy
sound of bleating lambs coming from their well-
stocked folds. Past pretty rustic villages where
women standing at their cottage windows wave dish-
cloths and aprons as they see the troops go by.
Past stately mansions and noble parks, and many a
delicate church spire pointing silently to heaven
from among the clustering trees that surround
its quiet graveyard. The rain has ceased, and the
pale winter sun disperses the clouds with its kindly
rays, the refreshed meadows give forth a pleasant
fragrance, the incense offered by a grateful earth, and
the blithe call of the blackbirds is heard from copse
and hedgerow ;—in short, it is a thoroughly English
landscape, the memory of which will dwell in our
hearts during the hot and weary months to come,—
a landscape which some of us in the train are looking on for the last time in this life, and which many
a poor fever-stricken fellow will think of, with a wild
longing to behold its sweet home freshness once
again, as he gazes on the terrible monotony of the
burning gravel plains round Suakin.

But no premonition of these things seems to weigh
on the minds of those within the comfortable carriage
where we are smoking and discussing the future,
the tongues are wagging freely, and my brother
officers eagerly reviewing the means by which they
propose to make the winged moments fly when once
we reach our destination ; some have telegraphed
to Cyprus for ponies, and it is generally agreed that
we are to get up a polo team that shall challenge
the whole Field Force ; then there is to be lawn-
tennis, racing, and cricket ;—in fact the camp at Suakin

is to be a second Curragh, with the additional charm
of an occasional fight with the enemy thrown in.   It
is natural that the spirits of Englishmen should rise,
when approaching the field where that great match
between death and duty, called war, is to be played
out ; but it strikes me that our spirits may perhaps
be a little forced, and meant to conceal hearts that
are sad at the thought of those they have left sorrow-
ing behind only a few hours before.   However this
may be, no man shows his wounds, and all *seem*
in high spirits, with the exception of a young
army doctor, whose face is what Washington Irving
calls "a title-page to tribulation," and wears an
expression of immovable gloom which it is to be
hoped, for the sake of his patients, he will manage
to shake off in the hospital ward ; perhaps he will
brighten up when he gets the chance of an operation.

A little after one, we reach Southampton, and
there is more cheering from the crowd and waving
of handkerchiefs from house windows.   " Give it 'em
'ot," shouts a sturdy Hampshire man as the train runs
into the dockyard enclosure, to which an officer
promptly replies, " All right," and we prepare to embark on the hired transport *Arab*, bound for Suakin.

It is needless to describe how on board that good
vessel, chaos soon reduces itself to order beneath the
magic touch of discipline.   How the last stores are
shipped and the moorings cast loose.   Presently
the tug comes alongside to take off visitors, the final
grip of the hand is exchanged which means so much
though the lips say little, the screw revolves, and the
great vessel with its living freight of over seven
hundred souls slowly steams on her way to Africa.

February 18.—The day dawns fair and clear, and
we are soon grouped on the quarterdeck eagerly
discussing the red books, maps, and Arabic vocabu-

laries, with which a generous Government has provided us.   How high are our hopes, how wide
winged our ambition !   Too late, it is true, to save
Gordon, we may still rescue our gallant comrades
from their perilous position on the Nile, and, joining
hands with Wolseley, deliver a crushing blow to the
power of the Mahdi.   By opening up a great trade
route to equatorial Africa, shall we not be laying the
foundation of a civilization which will spread over
the length and breadth of that vast Continent,
destined, one of these days, to be the granary of
Europe ?   Will not the slave-trade, with all its
unspeakable horrors, vanish before the establishment
of European commerce ; and may not unborn generations hereafter, learn to bless the memory of the
sturdy English soldiers who carried the iron road to
the banks of the Nile, and opened the heart of
Africa to the missionary and the colonist ?

Is it not a new crusade to strike a death-blow to
Mahdism, that growing power embodying all the dark
and ferocious bigotry which actuated the earlier followers of the Prophet, when they swept in their countless hordes over Europe, till checked by the iron front
of Charles Martel ?   True, they cannot sweep over
Europe now, but how will it be with our brothers
and sisters in India, if the furious spirit of fanaticism
which actuates these barbarous warriors of the desert
spreads into Asia, and the millions of Mahommedans
under our rule, maddened by fanatic rage, the scent
of blood, and the lust of plunder, should rally to the
old war-cry of " Death to the Christians ? "   Is it not
an honourable service, to break down once for all,
this last great effort of savage barbarism and brute
force to turn back the advancing wave of Western
civilization from the " Dark Continent ? "   And have
we not cheerfully left fathers and mothers, wives

and families, to follow the path of duty ; trusting that in our double capacity of soldiers and pioneers, we shall dispel a present danger, and lay the foundation of the future happiness and prosperity of millions of fellow-creatures?

So we thought, full of high hopes and honourable ambition, and though some of us knew that the task was no light one, and that during four of the summer months at least, active operations would have to be suspended, we argued that no Government would dare to embark the flower of our army and millions of money on such an enterprise, unless it was honestly resolved to carry out the task to which it had set its hand. Well, we were mistaken. I have looked on the lonely desert graves beneath which lie all that remains of many a gallant English soldier, who did not believe that he was giving his life in vain. I have seen the sick and wounded brought back in hundreds to their native country, shattered in health and spirit. I have known of friendly tribes who have lost their wives, their children, and their cattle, because they trusted in our honour ; and I have seen a country, through which twelve years ago I travelled with a single servant, almost as safely as one can now travel through Scotland, given back to bloodshed and barbarism ; all because our Government never honestly worked with a definite purpose—indeed, I have wondered bitterly when looking on these sights, whether it was ever really intended that the Suakin expedition should achieve the ostensible object for which it was sent out ; and whether the lives and the money expended on it were not deliberately sacrificed to political exigencies.

Did the Liberal Government ever seriously mean to carry the undertaking through? No doubt it was hoped that a brilliant victory might be obtained and

public feeling thereby conciliated.   But the story of
the three English expeditions that have been despatched to the Soudan, has a painful sameness.
They have all been sent out too late, in order to
allay popular excitement when the Government was
threatened with censure ; that danger averted, they
have all been withdrawn before they could achieve
any object honourable to England or beneficial to the
cause of humanity.   If the consensus of military
opinion at Suakin had been taken, I believe it would
have been found that three-fourths of Sir Gerald
Graham's force were Conservatives.   We were, in
fact, the strange anomaly of a Conservative army
making a political demonstration to keep a Liberal
Government in power.   Of course soldiers on service
must have no politics, and gallantly did those who
fought and those who fell strive to perform their
duty to their country.   The British forces, both on
the Nile and at Suakin, cheerfully encountered the
hardships and hard blows of a serious campaign ;
but the reward was denied them of carrying to a
successful conclusion an achievement that would
have redounded to the national honour, and led to
the pacification of a country, now thrown back from
its early promise of civilization into hopeless barbarism.   The graves of hundreds of our countrymen,
and of thousands of hapless Soudanese, cry aloud to
ask why this should be.   And whether it is right
that British soldiers should be turned into party
agents for political purposes ;—it is the duty of the
country to require, that when her forces are placed
in the field and her sons lay down their lives in her
service, it shall be with the distinct object of their
being led to victory.   In every one of the Soudan
campaigns, the soldiers have nobly fulfilled their part
and proved ever victorious under the most trying

circumstances ; it is not, therefore, the fault of the army, if these campaigns have ended in nothing but a lamentable waste of life.

February 19. —Strong wind blowing, no more books or maps, officers and men very sea-sick, heavy seas breaking over the vessel, and sailors hardly able to keep their feet on deck ; even the Naval Transport officer confides to me that, when he gets into this sort of weather, he thinks what a fool he must be to be a sailor !

February 20.—It is not my intention to chronicle the monotony of a sea-voyage day by day—I have endeavoured to sketch the martial enthusiasm that fired our souls at starting.   Alas for the frailty of our bodies, we were now in the " Bay," and all such lofty thoughts had been swept away by a mere capful of wind.   " Whatever I may be as a soldier, I am a wretched bad sailor," said Sir Frederick Roberts to the Mayor of Dover, when he returned from Candahar ; and many of my companions lying prostrate in their berths would have echoed his words.   The heroism that will cheerfully face death on land, is not always proof against a severe attack of sea-sickness, and I fear they were thinking of anything but glory.

As for the men, they were in a state of abject misery, and when I forced myself to go down and have a look at them after breakfast, I found the greatest kindness was to leave them alone ; they were lying helplessly about in the stifling atmosphere of the lower decks, green and wretched, too young, most of them, to have much stamina, and looking hardly up to the work before them.   When C——, our quartermaster, spoke kindly to one, he burst into tears—poor fellow, he was little more than a boy, and perhaps thinking of home !   The first voyage of

a private soldier must indeed be a wretched experience, if he is a bad sailor.   Most of these men were
under three years' service, some hardly of one, and
yet they were going to a climate, which, last year,
had so tried the hardy and seasoned Marines, that I
was told, it took 1500 men to keep up an efficient
force of 500.

Towards evening the rain, which had fallen without intermission all day, cleared off, and two bright
spirits produced a concertina and a banjo, (it is
wonderful how many miscellaneous musical instru-
ments found their way to the Soudan) and commenced
singing ; this did a lot of good and brought many a
pale face up on deck.   All honour to these merry
fellows who used their little accomplishment so well
to cheer the hearts of their comrades.

Sunday, February 22.—We reached Gibraltar at
1.30, and were soon moored alongside the new
Mole.   Here a telegram came on board telling of
General Stewart's death and the retreat from
Matammeh, which was received both with sorrow
and indignation,—sorrow that so gallant an officer
should have fallen, indignation that our troops
should have been placed in a position where they
would have to retreat one step, after their brilliant
victories.

The first time I saw Gibraltar, I was a boy
travelling with my tutor before going to College,
and fresh from witnessing an insurrection at Cadiz,
where the hardy mountaineers, who dwell in the
Sierras and spend their lives in smuggling, had used
their carbines with deadly effect from window and
housetop on the Government troops below.   The
change from the turmoil of barricades and street
fighting in the Spanish town, to the quiet order and
discipline which reign supreme at Gibraltar, made a

profound impression on my mind, and, when I beheld the mighty strength of her defences almost hidden among the bright flowers that deck the glorious gardens of the Alhameda, our great rock fortress raising its lofty crest proudly between two seas, calm and peaceful in the knowledge of its impregnable strength, seemed to me the very type and symbol of England's power and glory.

I remember standing at the top of the broad flight of stone steps that leads down from the public gardens to the parade ground, and seeing a portion of the garrison drawn up in Review Order, while a solitary man, a soldier who had committed some disgraceful action, stood motionless in the centre of the open space. As I watched, a non-commissioned officer stepped up to him with a knife in his hand, and ripped the buttons and facings from off his tunic, then he was marched once up and down before his old comrades to the strains of " The Rogue's March," and drummed off the ground. Anon the music changed and the grand strains of " God Save the Queen," pealed through the air, and I pitied the poor wretch who had been thus dismissed with ignominy from the service of his country.[1]

On this my third visit to Gibraltar, the place exercised its old fascination over me, and, after lunching at the hotel, I escaped from my companions, who, in wild spirits at the prospect of a few hours on shore, were rushing about making last purchases at the various stores, and found my way to a shady seat on the Alhameda, where I could enjoy undisturbed the fragrance of a meditative cigar. " A pipe," says Lord Lytton, " is a great soother!—a pleasant comforter! Blue devils fly before its honest breath! It ripens the brain—it

---

[1] The order of this parade is described from memory.

opens the heart; and the man who smokes, thinks like a sage and acts like a Samaritan!" I cannot pretend that tobacco does all this for me, but I can testify that there are few things more conducive to a peaceful flow of pleasant reflection, than a good cigar enjoyed in a clear balmy atmosphere and the vicinity of a lovely view. Above and around, the fragrant stone pines cast their broad cool shadows across the path; behind them rose the weather-worn rock, its sides clothed with the delicate gray green of the cacti and prickly pears that grow in every crevice; the sloping banks of the gardens, even at this early season of the year, were gorgeous with scarlet and yellow flowers, which sparkled like gems among the dark shadows of the trees, and beyond lay the blue Mediterranean sea gently heaving beneath the declining sun. "It is indeed a lovely spot," I said to myself as I slowly strolled back to the ship, where the first words that caught my ears were—"Isn't it beastly hard lines to be left cooped up in this stinking hole?" We were going to the possibility of death, the probability of sickness, and the certainty of discomfort and hardship; yet the soldiers living in the quiet security of this beautiful spot, envied us from the bottom of their hearts!

As we steamed away in the deepening twilight, the familiar strains of "Auld Lang Syne," were wafted to us from the Gunners' barracks at Europa Point, and the faint echo of a farewell cheer stole softly across the water.

February 26.—Something burst in our boilers last night, so we have been going very slowly and there is no chance of our reaching Malta till late this evening; I fear we shall not stop there, as they are able to patch up the machinery on board, but it will be false economy, for Malta is only half-way to

Suakin, and should we break down again it may delay us for days.   Of course a Government Board inspected the ship before she was sent out, but somebody must have blundered, for it now appears that a number of her boiler tubes are quite unfit for service.

All the morning we have been hard at work putting the men through their carbine exercise, and organizing sports for the afternoon to keep them in health and spirits.   At nightfall we pass the island of Gozo, and sight the lights of Malta, but, though we have sent a rocket into the starlight sky to let them know we are here, no signal comes off for us to put in, and we are unable either to receive or post letters.   More than one officer has already complained to me of feeling home-sick, and to all I have replied—" My dear fellow, I should feel so too if it would do any good, but it won't ; so you must fight down the thought."   Indeed, how *dare* we let our minds dwell on such thoughts with the work we have before us.   I confess I often feel profoundly sad when I look at our men, so young and so unfitted for the climate they are going to ; they do not know what it is, but I do, and I keep wondering how many amongst them will never see home and friends again ; for too certainly I know that in a few months' time many of those eyes which now shine so brightly will be closed for ever.   It is like walking in a company of ghosts.   In vain I look for some sign that may mark out the doomed ones, but I can see none.—There were two who sat and laughed with me daily at the officers' mess, but no voice whispered to them that before a month was over, they would both be lying beneath the desert sand.—Indeed, we are mercifully precluded from knowing whose turn it will be to be called first,— mine perhaps, but I think I can honestly say that no feeling of anxiety touches my heart, only I feel sad sometimes to think of all the sorrow in store for many a loving heart at home ; for I suppose there is not one of all these seven hundred men who has not left some one who loves him behind, and in many a peaceful English village and homestead good women are praying for their absent ones this night.

After supper the men hold a concert on deck, and some sing wonderfully well ; one man, of the Bearer Company, has a fine tenor voice, and sings " So Near and yet so Far," " Where is Now that Merry Party," etc., with great feeling ; others have a turn for the humorous, and one man, who is also very proficient with the bones, has sung, I am sûre, with a blacked face on many a racecourse, before he enlisted ; some are exceedingly comic from their utter inability to sing at all ; there is also an impromptu poet, who has composed a song about the " May-di," as he calls him, and the unfortunate musician who plays the piano has a hard time of it, for he is expected, after hearing a few muffled notes hummed into his ear, to strike out an accompaniment without the slightest hesitation to the most diverse kinds of song. Of course songs with a chorus are most popular, and the effect of over seven hundred voices swelling into the still evening air is very impressive.

It is a lovely moonlight night, and every curling wave as it breaks gleams and sparkles with the pale phosphorescent light so often seen in these waters, while a shoal of shadowy porpoises dash gamboling round the bows. Decks, spars, and rigging are crowded with the dark forms of the soldiers and sailors, the light of the hurricane lanterns gleaming on their tanned faces with Rembrandt-like effect. How fast the thoughts crowd through the mind as the familiar old songs, breathing of home, of love, and brave deeds ring through the still air, and the hardy features of the soldiers flush and glow in the lamplight under the awning, every note stirring some thought of home and kindred different to each man, but appealing to all! You can read the power of the music in their changing expression as in a mirror. Now every eye kindles and flashes in response to the stirring strains of some patriotic song ; again, as the singer strikes some tender chord of feeling, the eyes that glanced so proudly a few minutes before, melt and glisten with the softer light of memory, carrying them back to kindred and home. To-morrow, the officers will give a return concert to the men.

I may here remark that I think our military authorities will act wisely to provide our soldiers with music whenever it is possible ; and more especially during the trials of a campaign, for music is a very important factor in military economy, exercising both a powerful influence over the men's minds to incite them to gallant deeds, and a humanizing influence over their hearts, the true value of which cannot be over-estimated when large bodies of men are separated from the companionship of the gentler sex. Men fight for different causes, but the love of home and kindred underlies the heroism for which English soldiers have ever been conspicuous ;[1] music tends to strengthen that love, and can do much to keep the wearied soldier from seeking relaxation in drink and vice. There is a tendency, I know, to consider the band of a regiment a useless encumbrance when it proceeds on active service ; I doubt very much if its value to the *morale* of the

---

[1] "England expects every man to do his duty," "The eyes of your country are upon you," etc., are the watchwords that have stirred English hearts most deeply,—the memory of home, not the abstract love of glory.

men does not fully compensate for any encumbrance it may prove ; but, even if there be objections to a noncombatant band, it would be easy to hold out inducements to men serving in the rank and file to practice part-singing and the use of some instrument, the carriage of which would not materially add to the transport ; and I am quite certain the gain to the health and spirits of the troops by giving them frequent musical entertainments during their hours of relaxation, would fully repay the cost and trouble involved. What if the sweet notes of " The Blue-bells of Scotland," or " Annie Laurie," carry the Highlander's thoughts with passionate affection to his heather-clad hills and the wife or sweetheart he has left behind ? He will be a better man and fight none the worse for the tender emotion. What if the Irishman's eyes swim when he hears " Kathleen Mavourneen " in a foreign land, or the Englishman feels his heart beat strangely when five hundred voices join in the simple old song of " Home, Sweet Home," carrying him back to his schooldays : will their arms be weaker in the day of battle ? Nay, they will rather be nerved by these sacred memories to do deeds that England shall be proud of. I cannot better conclude these observations than by quoting the words of one of our most sagacious statesmen. " Oh, music, miraculous art !" exclaims Lord Beaconsfield, " that makes the poet's skill a jest ; revealing to the soul inexpressible feelings, by the aid of inexplicable sounds ! a blast of thy trumpet, and millions rush forward to die ; the peal of thy organ, and uncounted nations sink down to pray. Mighty is thy threefold power !"

February 28.—One more scene at sea. It is the last day of the men's sports, for to-morrow night we expect to reach Port Said. The sun shines brightly overhead, around us the blue expanse of sea leaps and dances beneath a light breeze which just crisps its surface with little curling waves, there is not a sail in sight. Every available sitting and standing space on the bulwarks, spars, and rigging, is crowded with human forms eagerly watching the sports on the deck below ; for to-day the prizes are to be distributed, and those of the competitors who have been ties in the previous contests, are to compete against each other in the final heats. A "tug of war" between soldiers and sailors is about to come off ; the position of the teams, whether facing the bows or stern, has been tossed for, as, owing to the pitching of the vessel, there is a slight advantage on one side. The officers, Naval and Military, stand by to encourage their men, who, with bare arms and feet, are holding on to the rope ready to heave. In the centre stands the umpire over the chalk line, which one or other side will have to be pulled across before the tug can be decided ; he is steadying the rope before he lifts his hand and gives the word, " lay on ; " when clang, crash, clang, the great bell of the ship rings out a wild note of alarm, and a whisper runs through the densely-packed crowd of men, swift as an electric flash—" The vessel is on fire !"

On fire ! What terrible visions does not that cry conjure up when heard at sea—a burning prison from which there may be no escape, especially when, as in our case, the boats are equal to holding less than two-thirds of the passengers ; a desperate struggle between man and an all-devouring element, in which, even the most desperate pluck sometimes fails to win the victory, and step by step the crew of the doomed vessel are forced back along the red-hot decks amid falling spars and suffocating smoke, till even the cruel, relentless waves seem merciful in their cold embrace!

In a moment the sailors have run forward, and before the heavy tongue of the alarm bell has smitten its quivering sides a dozen times, the men in obedience to the brief authoritative order of their officers are on the way to their posts, not rushing or scrambling, but marching steadily and in good order, as becomes British soldiers. So quietly and quickly is every movement executed, that not five minutes have elapsed since the first alarm before they are all drawn up on their respective parades with their company officers, the sentries posted on the boats and spirit room, the fire-gangs with their hose uncoiled at the pumps, the stewards waiting with blankets over their arms, the cutter manned, etc., and the Adjutant is able to report every soul of the seven hundred officers and men on the ship in his proper place and ready for orders. There is no noise or confusion, and the quiet tones of the Captain's voice can be heard the whole length of the vessel, while the men stand at ease in their ranks as steady as if they were in the barrack-yard. After a few moments of suspense, during which a brother officer confides to me in a whisper that the fire has broken out in the coal-hole, for he heard the pumps working down there, the bugle sounds, and we are dismissed ; the whole thing is, in fact, nothing but a fire parade, but so well has the Captain kept his counsel, that not even the officer commanding the troops on board, had the slightest idea that it was a false alarm. It was a truly pleasant sight to see the behaviour of our young soldiers in such an emergency.

I have said that there was not a vessel in sight, and that the *Arab* did not carry boats sufficient to hold more than two-thirds of the human beings on board. When ————, a brother officer on special service, mentioned this in a letter home, his father

asked a question in the House on the subject. The
answer was that the facts as stated by him were
substantially correct, but that the *Arab* fulfilled all
the requirements of the Transport regulations. If
this was so, surely there is something wrong about
the regulations, for what catastrophe could be more
awful than that, say 200 English soldiers should
perish in the sea, because a transport, allowed to
carry over 700 soldiers and sailors, was provided by
regulation with boats only sufficient to hold 500?
Yet this is clearly what may happen if such a state
of things is permitted to continue.

March 2.—We entered the Suez Canal at mid-day,
passing an English gunboat, and large Italian iron-
clad anchored at Port Said, which both cheered us
to the echo, the Italian dipping her flag again and
again, the friendship of Italy for England being very
warm just now. Poor T——, a young gunner, has
got a touch of fever and fainted as he was getting
into his berth ; C—— has also fever hanging about
him and looks wretched, the doctors had given him
strong doses of quinine while the attack was on him,
which of course affected his head. I gave him seven
drops of muriatic acid in a tumbler of water, and two
hours afterwards found him playing the piano with
his headache killed, as he expressed it.

Nothing can be more lovely than the nights in
the Suez Canal after the heat and glare of the day ;
the monotonous stretches of arid sand become transformed into a mysterious undulating vista of purple
shadows and frosted silver lights, with here and there
a ghostlike jackal stealing noiselessly across, or a
flock of white pelicans sleeping tranquilly on the
placid bosom of some shining lake. The filthy
water of the great ditch gleams like crystal beneath
the rays of the glorious Eastern moon, the heavy

splash of the fish with which it abounds, breaking it
every now and then into a thousand tiny mirrors as
they rise at some passing fly or locust, and above all,
is the curious velvety softness of the Egyptian sky,
almost purple in its tint, and different from anything
one sees in Europe. But I fear these beautiful
African nights are often treacherous to the unac-
climatized, and I would advise all my countrywomen
who may have to go through the Suez Canal to be
well provided with warm wraps.

The men are again singing. Not a fortnight
ago they were in England among green fields, now
they are 3000 miles from home in mysterious
Egypt, a country which for the last 4000 years has
been troubling the heads of mankind. Her cities
may perish and her monuments vanish beneath the
drifting sands of the desert, she may sleep for
centuries, but Egypt never dies : Pharaoh, Cleopatra,
Napoleon, Arabi, the Mahdi,—a strange admixture of
names ! Yet all have marshalled their armies on this
monotonous tract of mud and sand, the offspring of
the mighty Nile, which has played a part in the
world's history from the days when history and the
world were young together, until now, that not Baby-
lon, Athens, or Imperial Rome can equal. Far into
the archives of the past as her great memories extend,
the future of Egypt is yet a vital, ever-present
question, threatening alike the peace of Europe and
of Asia. We may speak as disparagingly as we
choose of her degenerate and bankrupt peasantry, her
corrupt governing classes, her waste and waterless
deserts, but she makes her presence *felt.* Her
sands are still thirsting for more blood, and it is
English statesmen alone who can prevent the sacrifice, by taking such decisive measures as shall give
to her in the future, the security, justice, and pros-

perity, which are the birthright of our English possessions.

March 3.—Two large P. and O. steamers passed us to-day ; the ladies all ran on deck to wave their handkerchiefs and everybody shouted ; it is pleasant to see the bright faces of our countrywomen and to hear the hearty English voices wishing us God-speed, as we pass. We happen to be the first trooper through the canal, which perhaps accounts for all the enthusiasm, but not far behind us is the *Manora* with the Guards, and following her the *Queen*, with the Balloon Detachment and some of the Commissariat and Transport Staff. Presently a great French troopship returning from Tonkin also passes, but in dead silence, a great contrast to the Italian and English vessels, for our relations with France are a little strained, and the crew stare gloomily at us, while our men remark," Them's the Johnny Crappos, ain't they ?" It is strange what a delicate thing the pulse of a nation is, and how quickly popular feeling can be aroused.

What most strikes the casual observer in the Suez Canal, is not the vast engineering skill displayed in its construction, but the apparent absence of it. It is simply a gigantic monument to the power of manual labour, we feel painfully what thousands of human hands must have toiled under the Egyptian sun to dig this great ditch ; that is all. There is nothing visible to denote a triumph of mechanical skill, and few means have been employed to prevent the banks from falling in. Lesseps seems to have gone on the principle, that, as the Nile is able to remain a river through endless deserts of shifting sand, so if he dug a deep ditch between two seas, and let a never-failing supply of water into it, it would remain a ditch without further trouble than occasional dredging here and there to keep it from silting up into shallows.   This was true, and the only strange thing is that nobody did it before, but it certainly appears that more ingenuity might have been employed to support the banks ; for instance, had young mangrove trees been planted along them ten years ago, it is probable that by this time their interlacing roots would have protected the sides of the canal against the shifting of the sand more effectually than any masonry, while their verdure would certainly have afforded a pleasant rest to the eye, yet the experiment does not appear to have been tried.

In many parts of the canal the high rising ground on either side, completely commands the decks of vessels passing through, and it is at once evident what serious damage an enemy in possession of the land would have it in his power to inflict, even without blocking the canal, were he to place guns at these points, for the vessels would be helpless to retaliate.   There is a story, I do not know if it is true, that just before our war-ships entered the canal in 1882, the Governor of Port Said awoke one night to find his bedroom full of English sailors, who politely requested the key of his bureau and the key of his cipher.   The unpleasant proximity of a revolver to his right temple produced prompt compliance on the part of the worthy official, and a telegram to Arabi was found in his desk ready for instant despatch saying, "The English are approaching, send ten thousand men;" this was presently altered to "Send no men ; the English are in possession of the canal," and forwarded to Arabi in the Governor's cipher.   Shortly afterwards our war-vessels steamed through without opposition or accident, though they did not trouble M. de Lesseps for pilots.

March 4.——We reached Suez and steamed out the same evening, the *Manora*, which had anchored near

us, burning blue lights, and the bugles sounding the
"advance," and the "charge," when we passed. Picketed
along the shore at Suez, were hundreds of camels
and mules waiting to be shipped to Suakin, and the
Transport officers seemed very hard worked. We
were told we must 'not leave the ship for more than
half an hour, and nobody could tell us where our
letters were likely to be found ; at last we discovered
one at the Transport office docketed " *S.S. Arab*
gone forward."   This was very provoking, for there
is nothing that men proceeding on service look
forward to so much as the receipt of their letters,
and it would display more kindly feeling and give
little extra trouble if the mails for troopships were
sent on board immediately they reach the ports of
call—Gibraltar, Malta, Port Said, Suez, etc. ; yet
this is rarely done, and it is sometimes a toss up
whether the letters will be found at the post-office,
one of the many military departmental offices, or in
some forgotten pigeon-hole nobody knows where.
The staff officers who meet the vessels are generally
able to give little or no information on the subject ;
this cannot be affectation, and if it is ignorance, it
should be made the duty of some particular one to
attend to the matter and have the mails got ready
to forward on board each troopship as soon as she
is signalled, and at all events, to know which have
passed through and which not.

The next two days passed uneventfully in the
steaming atmosphere of the Red Sea, our progress
being much delayed by the periodical breaking down
of our engines, owing to the rotten boiler pipes before
mentioned.   We took advantage of the time on our
hands to give the men some ball practice at a wooden
target towed behind the ship, which they stood much
in need of, as some of them had never fired ball

cartridge before. It seems a strange idea to send armed men on active service who have never been taught to use the beautiful weapon that is placed in their hands ; but it is a lamentable fact that even after he has been through a course of musketry, the British soldier is generally a very bad marksman. If he has the distance measured out for him and is allowed to take his own position and his own time, he may succeed in hitting an iron target fairly well, knowing, as he does, that the target will not fire back at him. But ask him to find his own range in an unfamiliar country, to hit a moving object, or to shoot at a mark after running a hundred yards, and you will not find ten men in a hundred who will hit a haystack ; simply because our soldiers have no opportunity of practising the kind of shooting which will be most useful to them in the field.

These things are easy to the deerstalker, but they require practice, and that is precisely what our soldiers do not get ; the present allowance of ball cartridge to each man in the course of the year is ridiculously insufficient, and the consequence is that I have known a hundredweight of lead expended before a single man of the enemy was hit. Now it is evident that if we can teach our soldiers to make, say only two hits where now they make one, we double their power of injuring an enemy in the field, and materially add to the effective strength of our army ; for each man who is a " marksman " becomes worth two who are not, so far as his shooting power is concerned ; and it, therefore, is a false economy to grudge an extra issue of ammunition in time of peace, if such a result can be obtained in time of war.[1]

[1] The question of how to improve the firing of the army is now occupying serious attention, and since these lines were written, an increased allowance of ammunition has been authorized from the 1st April 1886.

The methods by which the standard of effective marksmanship in our army might be raised, are simple enough.   In the first place, at military butts all stones or platforms marking the exact length of the range should be done away with ; the men should be marched up to unknown and uneven distances from the butts, such as 375 yards, 550, etc., and taught to find their own range and make the necessary allowance for the odd number of yards. They should also be frequently practised in shooting at portable wooden dummies, placed at various distances and moved from time to time, lest they become too familiar with the aspect of the fixed butts ; this practice should be performed in *every* kind of weather, and in no case should the men be allowed to fire from artificially levelled platforms, for they will assuredly find none prepared for them in the field of battle.   They should also be exercised in volley or independent firing after they have been moving at the double ; and where practicable at firing up and down hill.   In our frequent wars with savage nations, our soldiers, who are generally exposed to the charges of overwhelming numbers, have almost always to fire with bayonets ready fixed ; yet this is a practice which is much neglected at home, though it is a most important one, the balance of the rifle being considerably altered when the bayonet is attached to it.

Such exercises as these are absolutely necessary to make a man a good practical marksman in the field, which is the only place where his marksmanship is of value.   The next point is to consider the best means for encouraging competition among the men themselves.   This may be achieved by giving greater encouragement to weekly and monthly Regimental matches, at which small money gratuities allowed by Government will be competed for ; care being taken to handicap the best shots, so that they may not carry off all the prizes, and the bad shots may be encouraged to compete ; by establishing a shooting-shed at every barrack, where in bad weather and during hours of recreation men may compete among themselves with Morris's tubes at a nominal cost, for their own amusement, as in a shooting-gallery ; and by having one company in every Battalion composed entirely of "marksmen," who have passed a certain standard and wear a distinctive badge. The school system, in fact, of higher and lower forms should be introduced into shooting, so as to make it the ambition of every young soldier to advance step by step till he reaches the "marksmen's company." By these means the Colonel of a Regiment would always have at his command a company of picked marksmen, who could be depended on in time of need to disorganize the enemy, harass a reconnaissance, or silence a field battery, by their accurate shooting. The system I have advocated for Regiments, might with advantage be extended to the whole army, and our Rifle Battalions converted into something more than mere line Regiments with green jackets and short rifles. None who could not pass the higher standard of practical marksmanship should be permitted to remain in them, and a small addition of pay might be granted to the men who qualified for these favoured Battalions, in order to make it the interest of all good shots to pass the higher standard and belong to them. The value of a Battalion of reliable marksmen to a General in the field would be incalculable, and every army we send out should be accompanied by at least one Battalion of Rifles.

The Germans are able to produce a large number

of fine marksmen from among the Imperial rangers who act as keepers in the forests of Nassau and other wooded districts, and have frequent practice in shooting at roebuck, boar, and even hares and foxes, with the rifle; but we have no such class in England, and our soldiers have no opportunity of practising rapid firing. However, I believe that if they were trained on the lines I have roughly sketched, the marksmanship of our army would soon reach a very high standard, and the increased skill our men acquired with the rifle would render them a terror to foreign nations. In former days English bowmen were the best marksmen in the world; our men still possess their old qualities of coolness, pluck, and keen sight, and with a much superior weapon and intelligent training, these gifts should render them superior as marksmen not only to the shortsighted Germans, but to any adversary that could be brought against them; even the Boers.

After spending the morning in teaching the men how to inflict wounds, some of us devoted part of the day to studying their cure, one of the "Linseed Lancers," as the army doctors, who mustered strong on the ship, were familiarly called, having very kindly offered to give all of us who chose a course of lessons in the first dressing of gunshot wounds, etc. The antiseptic treatment is now in great favour with army doctors, and their main object is to cover up the wound from the air as soon as possible after the ordinary means have been employed for stopping the hemorrhage. We were told it was intended that every man of this expedition should carry a bandage, some lint, and a piece of carbolised wool, pinned inside his jacket ready for use, but I very much doubt if this wise order was ever carried out. No doubt it is useful for officers to have a practical knowledge of surgery, as it may enable them to save some valuable lives, but when you are proceeding on a campaign the study is certainly not an exhilarating one, and, as few sights are more ghastly than that of a hale man swathed in surgical bandages, some of us had little appetite left for lunch by the time the lecture was over. But I have already digressed too much, and must now proceed to our arrival at Suakin, the haven, though not of rest, to which we have been looking forward as the scene of our future exploits. One worldly-minded officer has already calculated how many decorations it will be possible for him to win, if rewards are given on the scale of the Tel-el-Kebir campaign, and has come to the conclusion that if he gets the V.C., C.B., medal, bronze star, and medijeh, he will be fairly content. Let us leave him to his pleasant dreams.

CHAPTER II.

THE SEAT OF WAR.

MARCH 7, noon.—At last Suakin is in sight, and every glass is turned towards the broad plain lying between it and the Waratab mountains, on which our first battle with Osman Digma's wild hordes will probably be fought ; as I happen to be the only officer with the expedition who has traversed the desert between Suakin and Berber, I am asked many questions as to the nature of the country through which we shall have to pass before we can reach the Nile. At present the Hamsin, or wind of fifty days, is blowing, and a dense cloud of fine sand sweeping across the plain, which makes it difficult to distinguish distant objects ; this wind is enervating in its effects, like the Levante and Sirocco, of Spain and Italy. Many of our people are suffering from relaxed sore throat and swollen glands, probably owing to the foul air of the ship, which is badly ventilated, and more suited to the rough North sea than a tropical climate, as she has no raised deck, and her solid bulwarks are so high that when the awning is up hardly a breath of air can be obtained. She is, however, a fine-sea boat, though of a somewhat lively nature which induces her to roll and pitch on the slightest provocation ; the cook, after the time-honoured custom of sea-cooks, has done his best to tempt our jaded palates with boiled bullock's heart and other delicacies unknown to Vatel, the peculiar toughness of which is only surpassed by their oily richness, but, in spite of these attentions, after twenty days at sea, we are all possessed with a longing to eat a meal on shore again, though it consist only of "bully beef," as the tinned meat provided by Government is familiarly called, and we are therefore somewhat disappointed at lying for five hours tossing and pitching unnoticed outside the line of pale blue water, hardly three feet deep, that covers the dangerous coral reefs which extend for miles along the coast.

Through these reefs a narrow channel runs back to the small lagoon, in the centre of which stands the little island of Suakin, with its coronal, of white flat-topped houses gleaming in the sun ; another small island nearer the mouth of the lagoon is covered with English tents, and many a vessel flying the British flag is anchored near it in the narrow roadstead.   This is Quarantine Island, the terminus of the proposed railway, where all the stores for the expedition are being unladen, and it looks like an ants' nest, so busy are the little figures moving about on it.   Behind stretches the great level dun-coloured plain some ten miles broad, at first barren and sandy, but presently thinly dotted with mimosa bushes which cluster thicker as the mountains are approached ; on the nearer side of this plain many portions of the English camp are already standing, but without any apparent order, and a few small forts may be seen dotted here and there, our most advanced posts on the desert.   Up a creek to the right the *Dolphin* lies moored, with her long range guns ever pointed at the plain ready to open fire, should any of the enemy appear from among the dark basaltic chain of mountains which bound the horizon, their sharp gray peaks and spurs presenting a bold and picturesque outline.   Everything is quiet now, and there is nothing to show that the white town and camp sleeping in the quivering sunlight are not as secure a habitation as Aldershot, or the Curragh.

At last a tiny steam launch comes puffing towards us, now lost in the hollow of a wave, now gallantly topping it, and soon a naval officer swings himself on deck and with a brief—" How are you all ? " walks to the bridge and proceeds to pilot the vessel through the channel between the coral reefs, a work which he performs with considerable skill.—The native pilots were not trusted to handle any English ship, and so well did our naval officers do this duty, that, notwithstanding the great number of vessels of large tonnage which they had to bring in and pack as close as herrings in a small harbour, not a single accident occurred to any of them during the whole course of the campaign.—Presently we are moored near a little Christian cemetery already fast filling with simple crosses, and, borrowing the captain's gig, seek the town.

The small square houses built of rough blocks of coral without any pretence to architectural beauty, but relieved by picturesque windows of carved and fretted lattice-work ; the narrow dusty lanes and ruinous squares, littered with piles of loose stones and rubbish ; the squalid bazaar, darkened by heavy matting stretched from house to house ; the rough kraals of the Arabs planted on every piece of waste ground, with their high fence of twisting mimosa stakes enclosing low round huts covered with skins and mats, in which dusky women are grinding flour between two stones, while little brown, bright-eyed children run in and out like mice ; the mingled odour of seaweed and decaying offal which pervades the air,

—are all unchanged since I landed here twelve years
ago, a sportsman eager to shoot big game.   But outside the town there is a mighty change.   In the harbour, where formerly a few native "dhows," painted
in gaudy colours, with high carved sterns, low-pointed
bows, and masts raking forward, which had borne
many a poor slave to Arabia, were the only vessels ;
a fleet of stately English transports is now riding at
anchor.   On Quarantine Island and the mainland,
where once a string of weary camels coming in from
Berber, or an aged Arab sleepily tending a flock of
small white sheep with black heads, were the only
living things that broke the monotony of the scene,
our tents now spread far and wide, and the notes of
the bugle, the tramp of armed men, and the neighing
of chargers, are all eloquent of what Mr. Gladstone
calls the resources of civilization, with which Osman
Digma is to be converted from the error of his ways
It seems like employing a Nasmyth's hammer to
crack a nut—this mighty display of strength put
forward by a powerful nation to subdue a few
thousand lean-shanked savages armed with shields
and spears.   But Osman had the laugh on his side
when three months later the nut still remained un-
cracked.   In the meantime the native population
evinced no surprise at all that was going on around
them.   They skimmed over the blue waters of the
bay in their little "dug-outs" composed of the
hollowed trunk of a tree and propelled by a single
rude paddle, or a triangular cotton sail, one corner
of which they held in their teeth, as contentedly as
if there were no steam launches, or smart men-of-war's
gigs flying past them with levelled oars.   The
whistle of the locomotive, or the ascent even of a
war-balloon, produced no outward sign of emotion,
save, perhaps, a brighter twinkle in their dark brown

eyes and a broader grin of their white teeth. It is true that a few of the fighting men were wont to stride along with knitted brows and stately tread, their long cross-handled swords slung over their shoulders, their round giraffe hide shields on their arms, and spears in their hands, looking as if, though tolerating our presence, they would love nothing so much as to drive the crooked bladed knife that hung at their girdles up to the hilt in the entrails of a Christian. But for the most part the people of Suakin were always smiling, as if they thought our presence there a good joke, and I have seen the lower class of native women draw themselves up and mimic the stiff salute of the British soldier, when an officer was passing, with a roguish grin on their blubber lips which certainly showed they had some sense of humour. The little children picked up a smattering of English with extraordinary facility, and they called us all " Johnny," from the General downwards, a trick they no doubt caught from our men, to whom the whole population of Egypt and the Soudan are known as " Johnnies," and nothing else.

I had not been long on shore before I was captured by a Brigade Major, who requested me to take the orders on board, which were to the effect that the men were not to disembark till the morrow. In fact it was clear that things were in a state of rather wild confusion on shore, and little preparation had yet been made for camping the troops who were now rapidly pouring into the place, though it is only fair to say that the Engineers had provided some excellent piers for disembarkation.

Sunday, March 8.—This morning we heard the first shot fired, the *Dolphin* having sighted a small party of the enemy on camels crossing the plain, about five

miles distant, and opened fire on them.   This was
practically the first shot of the new campaign, as for
some time past the rebels had given up their practice
of making night attacks on the town, and there had
been little or no firing ; though they still displayed
wonderful pluck and audacity in creeping down the
gullies at night and silently filling up the trenches
of our advanced works, after the fatigue parties had
been withdrawn.   An attempt was made to give
them a lesson by mining the ground shortly before
we arrived, but in the morning it was found that by
some marvellous instinct they had managed to enter
the works without exploding the mines, which, indeed,
proved more fatal to *us* than to them, for poor
Askwith, of the Engineers, was literally blown to
pieces the next day, (Feb. 27) by one of the mines,
which he was examining, suddenly exploding for
some reason that can never now be ascertained.
This deplorable accident cast a great gloom over
the camp, for so strangely is the human mind
constituted, that the loss of a hundred men in battle
does not shock us so much as one sudden and
unforeseen death of this kind.

The Arabs are now reported to be in force near
the Wells of Hasheen, at the foot of the Waratab
range West of Suakin, where they are supposed to
be digging trenches and rifle pits for our reception ;
probably the party sighted by the *Dolphin*, were on
their way there, but after receiving two or three
shells in their midst, they quickly dispersed.
Those who have only heard guns fired on Field days
or at practice, do not know the peculiar thrill with
which the heart responds to " the cannon's roar,"
when it is a messenger of death.

Being Captain of the day, my duty required me
to be up at 5.30 A.M. to superintend the counting

of some seven hundred hammocks and blankets, previous to the disembarkation of the men, in a small dark well on the lowest deck, whence they were flung into the hold, and the stifling hot atmosphere of which was so laden with flue that it was thicker than a December fog, and anything but pleasant to a fasting man. I could not leave the ship until it had been inspected, and had to content myself with watching through a field-glass a short reconnaissance made by the Cavalry, who trotted out on to the plain in gallant array amid a cloud of dust, and appeared soon to get touch of the enemy; for there was some sharp firing along the line, the little white puffs of smoke being clearly visible, though we could hear no sound. It is a strange and unenviable sensation to have to sit quiet and safe on the deck of a ship watching one's comrades fighting in the distance, like puppets in a dummy show; but I afterwards learned that only one man was wounded in this little skirmish.

Last night some of the enemy actually succeeded in creeping into the lines of the Headquarter camp and stealing the horse of the Provost Marshal, after stabbing his servant in five places; the poor fellow was carried past our men on a stretcher covered with blood, as they were disembarking. This was the first of those night assassinations for which the camp was soon to become notorious. I was told that when the Headquarter camp was alarmed by the screams of the wretched man, the Staff turned out to defend their lines in the most Spartan simplicity of costume; the garrison, of course, consisting almost entirely of Generals and Field officers, who, with a sprinkling of A.D.C.'s, rushed out in many-hued pyjamas with drawn swords and revolvers, prepared to hold the position like a second Thermopylæ,

if need be. Everybody was issuing orders at
the same time, in English, Irish, and broad Scotch,
especially the latter. Here an officer connected
with the Balloon Detachment, which may perhaps
have accounted for the lightness of his apparel, was
running wildly about with a sword in one hand and
a brandy bottle in the other, searching for the
wounded man. There stood a General, usually
celebrated for the size of his solar-topè and the
amplitude of his pantaloons, exposing himself to the
breeze divested of both these adjuncts, but not of
his voice and a fine command of the more forcible
idioms of our language for which he was famous.
Short and tall, broad and thin, the fantastic night-
capped figures flitted about in the electric light,
presenting a grand subject for the pen of the poet
or the brush of the battle painter, who rarely gets a
chance nowadays of introducing such classic variety
of costume into his pieces.

It was late in the afternoon before I had completed
my wearisome duty on board the ship, and was able
to join my comrades, whom I discovered encamped
in the midst of a solitary waste of sand about a mile
and a half West of Suakin. An old Arab graveyard close by reminded us unpleasantly of human
corruption, by the effluvia it sent forth when the
heavy dews fell at sunset, and the sand underfoot
was wet and clammy, being strongly impregnated
with salt ; but the tents provided for our use were
exceedingly good, being what are known as E. P.
tents, large marquees with standing walls, double
roofs, and four doors that render it possible to let
a current of air through, whichever way the breeze
is blowing.

Three of the Amarar tribe, a section of whom
have joined the rebels, though the remainder under

Mahmoud Ali, are still friendly to us, brought a letter from Osman Digma to the camp this evening ; in which, after recalling the defeat of General Hicks, Baker Pasha, the capture of Sinkat, Tokar, the fall of Khartoum, death of Gordon, and the retreat of Wolseley before the forces of the Mahdi, he solemnly warns us not to advance beyond the walls of Suakin, as, if we do, our whole army will be driven into the sea, and none spared who do not embrace Mohammedanism and become soldiers of the Madhi. He is said to have 7000 men, massed at Tamai, and 2000, or 3000, at Hasheen, which is good news, as we may now hope soon to meet the stubborn old slave-dealer face to face.

The first Battalion Coldstream Guards, first Battalion Shropshire Regiment, and Royal Marines, disembarked in the course of the afternoon. The first Battalion Berkshire Regiment, the second Battalion East Surrey, the Loodhiana Sikhs, and 17th Bengal N.I., are already here ; and fresh batches of white tents are springing up from the plain like mushrooms every few hours, transforming the barren desert into a scene of life and animation. Some of the Medical Staff have been placed near us in single bell tents, which seems rather hard on them, considering the fierce anger of the sun ; and the Bearer Company are encamped in their rear, which caused an officer sarcastically to remark that he supposed the wounded were expected to be brought in from *that* direction.

I afterwards heard a rather good story about these bell tents. They soon attracted the eagle eye of one of the special correspondents roaming about in search of copy, and he put them into his telegram home ; this brought the Press Censor down on him at once, and he was promptly summoned to Headquarters, where it was sought to prove to him by the help of elaborate figures that he had been wrong, and that such things as single bell tents did not exist in this model camp; further that it was quite impossible in the interests of discipline, to permit such wanton assertions to be made. "I don't know about the figures," said the unfortunate correspondent, under this sudden douche of official cold water, "but I saw the tents with my *own eyes.*" "Ah, well, Mr. —— you had better go back; I think you will find you are mistaken" : and true enough, when he returned to the scene of his discovery, there were nothing but E. P. tents visible; the little error having already been corrected. It is by calling attention to things of this sort, that the special correspondent sometimes exercises an unacknowledged but most beneficial influence in camp, representing as he does public opinion. Occasionally, of course, he may be betrayed into mistakes, and no doubt he often sorely tries official patience; but his presence is a distinct benefit, not only to the public whom he supplies with a consecutive narrative of events, but to the General himself, and every officer and man in camp, for he is a direct check on any attempt at injudicious parsimony on the part of the home Government.

Armies can no longer be badly equipped in the field, or the services of distinguished officers unjustly ignored, when it is known that public attention will at once be drawn to the fact, and the voice of the press find an echo in Parliament. I had some friendly discussions afterwards with the head of the Intelligence Branch on this subject, and, while freely admitting the value of the correspondents, he pointed out that they occasionally caused much inconvenience, the object of the General being usually to keep his army as much as possible in the dark concerning the exact nature of his future movements, lest they should leak out, while the correspondent has the diametrically opposite aim of obtaining the earliest information he can. It is no wonder, therefore, if the interests of the two are rather antagonistic ; moreover, by going from the General to the Chief of the Staff, from the Chief of the Staff to the Military Secretary, and from the Military Secretary to the head of the Intelligence Branch, etc., pumping each in turn as much as he dare, and comparing their statements together, unless he be a very scrupulous man, the correspondent may place those officers in an unpleasant position, as they cannot always tell exactly what their colleagues may have said, especially if one of them has thought it advisable to circulate a false report, intended to reach the enemy.

A case of this kind came under my observation. A correspondent went to a Staff officer one day, and asked him if a certain thing was true; the officer, who had not heard the report before, and knew it must be false, said it was not ; considering he was safe in denying information, though he might not be safe in confirming it. " Oh, but," said the correspondent, " I had it from So-and-so," mentioning a senior officer. " In that case," replied the other, " if So-and-so told you, it *must* be true ;" but he naturally felt very sore at being placed in a position where he either had to tell a lie himself, or infer that his senior had told one. It is only just, however, to say that generally correspondents fulfil their difficult task with great tact, and not unfrequently refrain from making use of information that would be valuable to them, from a high-minded desire not to betray trust ; for in a large camp it is almost impossible to prevent some secret information from

leaking out or falling into wrong hands, however
careful the Staff may be.

I think the knowledge of this responsibility,
occasionally induces Staff officers to assume an air
of needless official mystery and reserve towards the
correspondents, concerning matters which are well
known throughout the camp, and about which it is
not in the least necessary to the interests of the
service that there should be any concealment ; and
such reticence conduces to bitterness of feeling, for
the correspondent does not care to be treated like a
child by a man who may perhaps be his inferior in
mental capacity. His position is always a very
delicate one, for he has his trust to the public to
fulfil, as well as his duty to his employers, to whom
the first issue of " the special edition " may represent
a value of several thousand pounds, at the same
time he must work with tied hands, for every
telegram he sends has to pass through the Censor's
office ; while, should he express his opinions too
frankly in his private letters to the paper, he runs
the risk of being removed from his post. He must
be a man of unimpeachable honour, and honestly
desire the good of the service, yet submit to be
treated with a certain amount of distrust ; and, therefore, I say, every care should be taken to render
his position as little irksome as possible, by frankly
furnishing him with every particle of information
that can be useful, and which it is not absolutely
necessary in the interests of the campaign to withhold.
Of course, correspondents, being merely the agents
of a mercantile firm, have no technical *right* to
accompany an army in the field ; but they are
something more than this,—they are the ears, nose,
eyes, and mouthpiece of the English people ; and
it is utterly useless for officers to regard them

as interlopers, for the public, which pays for the maintenance of the army, will never in the present day consent to a British Force being unaccompanied by them, any more than it would consent to the proceedings in our courts of law, or even in Parliament itself, remaining unreported.

It strikes me that some of the difficulties I have hinted at, might be removed by intelligent regulations. In the first place, each paper should be strictly limited to one correspondent at the seat of war, and the correspondents should all be stationed at the Headquarter camp, where they can be brought into friendly contact with the Staff, from whom they will gain a truer insight into the real working of the campaign than they can from the ordinary run of regimental officers, many of whom are confirmed grumblers. Their presence in camp should be frankly recognised, not as a necessary nuisance, but as beneficial alike to the country and the army ; none but men of the highest character should be admitted to their ranks, and those who have had previous military training should always be preferred, as being best able to comprehend the necessities of the service. There should be only one Press Censor entrusted with the power of passing telegrams, and a Staff officer under him should be detailed to collect and reduce to a written form all the official information that can be given to the correspondents each day, and this should be communicated to them in identical terms, in time for their telegrams to be forwarded home, so that none should have an advantage over the other. The information should be as frank, full, and comprehensive as the exigencies of the service will permit, but, once given, no permission should be accorded to correspondents to interview heads of departments with the object of obtaining more. They should be required to wear a special uniform, easily distinguished, which would ensure their being treated with courtesy and honour, and on which they could show the medals of those campaigns, the hardships and perils of which they have shared with British troops.

March 9.—Owing to the isolated position of our camp, we had double sentries posted with twenty-four rounds each, and slept with our drawn swords beside us, but, though we heard a few shots fired in another portion of the camp, the enemy were kind enough to leave our lines alone, and let us enjoy our first night on shore in comparative peace. We heard, however, in the morning, that the first Battalion Berkshire Regiment, encamped a little beyond, had not been so fortunate, three of their men having been fearfully stabbed by the Arabs during the night.

Reveille sounded at 5 A.M. and we were soon astir. At 6.30, Col. —— rode up to visit the camp and speak to the officers. He said we should need to be up early and in bed late, the work to be got through in organizing the Transport being simply enormous, before the army could be put in a position to advance, and he ended by giving us a short lecture on the treatment of natives : telling us to regard them as children, who should be ruled by gentle measures and patient investigation into their wants and grievances; though they might show a little waywardness at times, this was not to be reproved too sternly, and we were rather to lead than to drive them, and on *no* account were they to be struck. Now, theoretically, this exactly coincided with my own views, and when I formerly travelled through Abyssinia and the Soudan, I did so without once having recourse to blows ; but I recalled the Uncle Tom's Cabin style of this discourse a week later with some amusement, when I beheld the same officer vainly struggling at the entrance to Suakin with a number of obstinate camel-drivers who were blocking up the gate, and pathetically calling for somebody to lend him a *big stick*, with which he presently dispersed them like a second son of Anak.

Immediately after breakfast, Colonel —— asked me to walk with him to the camel depôt, which was situated on the mainland, in the corner of a large but squalid suburb that has now outgrown the old town on the island. In this suburb are many large open spaces which were crowded with oxen, sheep, mules, horses, camels, etc., and the whole is enclosed by a strong wall of mud and coral, some two miles in length, which, roughly speaking, forms an arc with both ends resting on the lagoon, and is protected by a few redoubts mounted with guns.

We found the camel depôt one roaring mass of camels all bemoaning their fate as only camels can, groaning at being made to kneel down, groaning at being made to get up, groaning at being laden, groaning at being unladen, groaning at being left alone, and all smelling in a way which would have made the forty stenches of Cologne appear a vague and pleasant fragrance by comparison. There were also long lines of mules, and some horses, picketed in another part of the enclosure, and great numbers of drivers ; Bengalees, Punjaubees, Somalis, Maltese, Cyprians, and others, who had been engaged for the expedition, and were adorned with round tin badges stamped with their numbers. I was ordered to select from among the Cyprians eighteen mule-drivers and eight leaders of good character for the Royal Marine Artillery, and proceeded to inspect as forbidding a set of countenances as the Island of Cythera could well produce. Having from a physiognomist's

point of view chosen the least repulsive, with the
assistance of an interpreter, who pretended to have a
particular knowledge of the private history and
character of each, I entered their classical-sounding
names in my pocket-book, and proceeded to select
sixty-four mules, also for the Artillery : thirty-six of
which were for draught, and the remainder pack or
saddle animals ; this entailed a good deal of dodging
about between lines of kicking heels and vicious-
looking heads and teeth, amid a cloud of dust that
soon covered face and hands like plaister, for the air
was as hot as a Turkish bath, and the sun nearly
vertical.   It was two o'clock before I was able to
leave the dépôt, having at last collected sixty-four
mules fit for the work required, and carefully rejected
some hundred sore-backed, weedy, unsound, or otherwise objectionable beasts, which might answer at a
pinch for ordinary work, but were hardly up to the
requirements of Artillery.

Weary and faint, after the long morning in
the sun and two miles' trudge home through the
deep sand, I was glad to reach the cool shelter of
our tent, offering a pleasing prospect of rest and
lunch, and still more rejoiced to find lying on the
table, that most pleasant of sights on foreign service—
a bundle of letters from home ; but I had hardly
time to stretch out an expectant hand for them,
when the shadow of a horseman fell across the
bright patch of sunlight in the doorway, and a voice
called out, " I say, De Cosson, I am glad I caught
sight of you ; I am just going to the camel dépôt,
and want you to come with me."   The gladness is all
on one side, my friend, I thought; however I replied,
as in duty bound, " All right, Major, I'll be ready as
soon as they have saddled my horse ; come in for five
minutes," and, giving the necessary order, thrust the

precious letters unread into my pocket, and hastily swallowed a few mouthfuls; five minutes later my bâtman brought the horse, and jumping into the saddle we started for the camel depôt. My companion was riding a Cyprian pony used to camels, but the moment my English steed caught sight of one of those ungainly animals plodding slowly towards him, like some colossal four-legged ostrich of antediluvian times, he reared up and commenced a waltzing movement which bid fair to last all the afternoon; at last by a vigorous use of knee and spur, I got him to make a terrified bolt past the first batch of camels, only to be brought sharp up by the next, when the waltzing commenced again, varied occasionally by violent plunges which scattered the natives, who were looking on, in all directions. In fact the poor beast was mad with terror, and did not know which way to turn, for there were soon camels all round him, roaring hideously, gigantic, big-eyed, with long swaying necks and projecting yellow teeth,—a sight, in truth, to alarm the stoutest-hearted horse that had never seen them before; even the sheep, with their curious black heads and necks, stuck on pure white bodies, as if they had belonged to another animal, and balanced by enormous cushion-like tails; the oxen, with their long straight horns and humped backs, and the people, with their brown skins and fuzzy heads, on which one portion of the hair was combed straight up like a mop, while the rest hung round their ears in a sort of fringe, were all unfamiliar to him, and it was no wonder that he burst into a cold sweat, and by his violent struggles put me into a hot one; however, at last our destination was reached, and I learned that two or three hundredweight of coal was urgently needed to heat the branding irons for marking the camels; this I was requested to get without delay, rather vague instructions being given me that if I proceeded to a place I had never heard of before, I should probably find a cart and horse, and that at another place in a diametrically opposite direction, there ought to be some coal.   It seems at first a strange thing to bring an officer a couple of miles to go and fetch a few hundredweight of coal, but on a campaign there is only one rule to follow, and that is to be ready to turn your hand at once to *anything* that is useful, no matter what, and however trivial the task, to perform it to the very best of your ability.   That is the advice I would give to young officers, and as it turned out, it was fortunate I went for the coal.

After some little difficulty I found my way through the winding and frequently blind lanes of Suakin, to the places I had been directed to, only to learn that there were no carts, horses, or coal, at either of them, and that nobody knew where I should be able to get what I wanted, though one or two other places were suggested, which I visited with as little success.   At last it occurred to my mind that I had seen a large stack of coal on Quarantine Island, when I landed, and, as it was clear that no carts or horses were forthcoming, I rode back to the camel depôt to secure a couple of camels and some old sacks, provided with which, and taking care to arm myself with a written order, I started for Quarantine Island, a ride of some two miles along the sea-shore, from whence the island is reached by means of a long causeway where new terrors awaited my horse, in the shape of a little railway engine which puffed busily along beside the footway.   Narrowly escaping a jump into the waters of the lagoon, I proceeded in search of the officer in charge of the stores, but not a soul knew anything about the coal or had anything to do with it. In fact, it was supposed to belong to a private firm, probably the railway contractors; however, there the coal was, and an Engineer officer superintending some soldiers who were making a cutting, said that if I liked to take the responsibility of carrying off the coal *vi et armis*, he would lend me a couple of men to fill my sacks. Necessity has no law, the coal was needed, so I had my camels laden and returned in triumph.

The second Battalion Scots Guards landed during the afternoon, and presented a very fine spectacle as they marched to their camping ground in rear of the Coldstreams; most of the officers carried walking-sticks, and some of them had a Christmas-tree-like collection of knives, tobacco pouches, and pipe-cases hanging to their belts. It was quite dark before I reached home and found my comrades, who had been employed in a somewhat similar manner, pretty well exhausted with their day's work. Indeed, I have only described my adventures at such length, as a specimen of the daily duties of officers attached to the Transport, at this time; fortunately for myself, I was soon to be transferred to Headquarters, and saw little more of the camel depôt, the most hot and pestilential spot in Suakin. When I was returning to England in the *Ganges*, both the A.C.G. at the base, and his Adjutant, were brought on board dangerously ill from continuous residence there, the one owing to heat exhaustion, which seemed to have sapped every drop of blood out of him, and the other from a serious sunstroke caught, not from exposure in the open air, but while he was sitting in his own tent.

During the night there was again firing, and two wretched grass-cutters were speared in the camp of

the Indian Contingent, by some of the Arabs who
had crawled into their lines under cover of the
darkness. We had double sentries posted on all
sides, but, owing to our isolated position, the ninety-
seven men who composed the company, would have
been quite powerless to save our camp from being
rushed, had the enemy paid us a visit ; we,
however, took the precaution to place our reserve
close to the horses, so that in case of alarm we
could rally round them and prevent a stampede. A
heavy shower fell during the night, which brought
out the scent of the graveyard most unpleasantly,
and in the morning all our clothes were wringing
wet from the exhalations of the ground.

March 10.—I rode over early to the Headquarter
camp, to call on Sir George Greaves, and Sir John
M'Neill, who had both served with an uncle of mine
in the New Zealand war, and I was just inquiring
of an orderly the position of the latter officer's tent,
when I heard a sharp clear voice saying at my elbow,
" Here you are, I am Sir John M'Neill, but I wouldn't
ride down that street if I were you." Indeed, in my
search for some one to direct me, I had committed
the heinous offence of riding into the " street," or
open space in front of the General's tent, facing
which were the tents of the principal officers of his
Staff. When afterwards I lived in the " street "
myself, I learned to appreciate the luxury of its
being held sacred from the dust-provoking hoofs of
passing horses. The speaker was a rather short,
firmly-knit man, dressed in a flannel shirt, boots, and
breeches ; he wore neither coat nor cap, having just
stepped out of his tent, and his resolute glance,
square well-cut features, and a peculiar, rather
defiant way he had of carrying his head, stamped
him at once as a man of daring temperament, whose

courage might perhaps approach foolhardiness, but who would assuredly not lose his presence of mind in the moment of peril. It was little wonder that such a man had won that proudest of all decorations, the Victoria Cross. An unmistakable gentleman, he yet had a quick abruptness of manner, which savoured more of the camp than of the Court, though he is equally familiar with both, and I believe very popular with those officers who have been brought into immediate contact with him.

I found I could not see Sir George Greaves, till the afternoon, so paid another visit to Headquarters, after lunch ; my horse, which was a young unbroken trooper that I was riding for the first time, backed and sidled with me a few yards up the sacred street, when I promptly heard Sir J. M'Neill's sharp but not unkindly voice saying, " I wouldn't ride up that street if I were you ; you'll catch it if you do." He had evidently constituted himself the guardian of the street, and in future I refrained from trespassing, and always carried a light picketing rope attached to the headstall of my horse, so that I could strap him to the nearest tent-peg or water-cart. I would recommend mounted officers never to go unprovided with rope of this kind, as it saves much trouble, and, even if an orderly can be found to hold the horse, it is hardly fair in a climate like the Soudan, to keep him for perhaps an hour or more standing in the sun looking after it, while one is awaiting the leisure of some overworked head of a department.

Sir George Greaves was a contrast to Sir J. M'Neill, small and wiry, with gray hair, and a heavy white moustache, he looked the type of an officer who has been much in India, as indeed he has. It was reported in camp that he was given to using

rather more vigorous language than his officers quite
liked ; but, if quick-tempered, I think he was kind-
hearted, and so far as my own personal experience
went, I always found him courteous, and even con-
siderate in his manner.

I never saw a man with a greater aptitude for
hard work ; as Chief of the Staff, he had not only
the gravest but often the most trivial and absurd
questions brought to him to settle, but he never sent
any one away ; always ready to take responsibility,
always ready to give advice, he disposed of every
matter in a plain, sensible, straightforward way,
completely free from red tapeism, which was of
immense service in clearing away difficulties. At
sunrise in the morning his was the first voice I
heard ; all day long he was either in his office or
galloping over the plain in an enormous solar-topè
organizing, inspecting, and directing. He suffered
frightfully from prickly heat, as indeed we all did,
and many a time have two voices of the night
broken the silence of the camp, the one deep
and slow, saying, " ——, are you there ?" the other,
sharp and alert, replying, " All right, I am here,
lying on my back in the dark, scratching like
the d——." But otherwise he seemed always in
good health and spirits, notwithstanding the weight
of responsibility that rested on his shoulders ;
and the amount of business he disposed of during
the campaign must have been prodigious. He told
me to put myself in communication with the Intelligence Branch, and said that the men were full
of fight, but that everything now depended on the
Transport, as though there were plenty of troops
they had no means of moving them.

After my return to camp, I walked with a friend
to the wells of Suakin ; these are situated more

than a mile from the town, between the Right and
Left Water Forts, which protect them from attack ;
they consist of several round holes, some thirty feet
deep, and most of them are curbed with wood, the
water—which, though slightly brackish, is not un-
wholesome—being drawn from them by means of
pumps, though some are left open for the use of the
Arab population, who still follow the primitive fashion
of drawing their water in a goat-skin attached to a
cord.   Here, at this time, most of the horses were
brought to be watered, long troughs having been
erected for their use, and numbers of native women
with water-skins and donkeys were constantly passing
to and fro between the wells and the town, for it is
still the special duty of the Arab women to draw
water as in days of old.   But there was no Ruth at
these wells, the maidens of Suakin being of an
ugliness peculiar to themselves, even among African
races.   I believe it used to be the custom in H.M.
Navy to present an old knife to the ugliest man on
board ship, which knife he was obliged to retain until
he could discover a man more ill-favoured than himself
to pass it on to ; but if the ladies of Suakin were
drawn up in line, it would puzzle even Paris to decide
which ought to be the holder of the knife, they are
all so painfully plain, each in her own way.

Just beyond the wells, on the fringe of the desert, as
it were, is a garden—an unfenced wilderness of stunted
palms, aloes, wild cotton, and other shrubs, which the
vicinity of water has enabled to spring from the
sandy soil with some appearance of healthy verdure.
It is not extensive, but there are a couple of fair-
sized sycamore trees in it, the broad leafy boughs
of which offer the only cool and pleasant shade near
Suakin ; the rough bark of these trees is scored
with many an Arabic name, among which, for aught

I know, may be that of Osman Digma himself; for it is a spot where the rich slave-dealer must have loved to sit and smoke his chibook in more peaceful days, when the evening breeze was blowing from the sea, and his caravans could be seen winding their tedious way across the plain from the Western Mountains, laden with ivory, ebony, ostrich feathers, coffee, potash, senna, bee's-wax, skins, aromatic woods, spices, etc., and accompanied by many a sad and weary slave-girl from Abyssinia, or the Galla country, destined to be presently smuggled across the Red Sea and sold at a profit in the markets of Arabia, from whence she would never return to behold again the thatched huts of her native village in the green pasture lands beside the lake ; where the hippopotami came out on moonlight nights to crop the young grass, after the cattle had been gathered to the fold safe from lions and panthers, and where all the sunny day long, regiments of white storks, scarlet flamingos, and gray spoonbills, stood on one leg solemnly gazing at their own reflections in the shining water, and the jagged peaks of the distant mountains glowed at morn and sunset like red-hot spear-heads, a boundary that none of her tribe had ever ventured to cross till the slave-hunter came that way and wrecked their happiness.

I have seen these poor Galla girls, fragile and pretty creatures enough, in the slave-market at Galabat, and I have often thought what dreadful memories must have accompanied them during the long marches across the desert, when they recalled the last view of their burning hamlet, with the father or brother, or perhaps even the mother, lying dead across the threshold.

But Osman cared little for these things, as he sat contentedly smoking his pipe on this spot, while the

new garden he tried to make himself outside the
walls of the suburb was being prepared, and chatted
with the swarthy Arab Sheiks over whom he was
presently to gain such influence.   However, I am
told that retribution is already overtaking him, for
he lives in such perpetual fear of being betrayed, that
he never sleeps twice in the same place, and has his
followers stripped before he allows them to approach
near, lest their clothes should conceal the assassin's
knife, while all his possessions at Suakin are in the
hands of the stranger, and his garden knows him no
more.

"How is it that he has gained such influence
with your people?" an officer asked of one of the
friendly Amarars; "you know that he is always
beaten if he tries to fight us, and he is your worst
enemy, because he seizes all your goods and converts
them to his own use on the pretence of making one
common stock."   "It is true," replied the Arab; "but
he tells a lie so beautifully that he wiles the very
hearts out of our breasts, and if any of our people
go to upbraid him for all they have lost, they stay to
praise him, for he persuades them against their own
senses, and makes them like wax in his hands when
once he gets speech of them."   Though the Soudan
Arabs are not a particularly untruthful race themselves, yet, like most Orientals, they have a profound
admiration for a man who can tell a lie with a
perfectly unmoved countenance, and who positively
declines to admit Mrs. Gamp's proposition that "facts
is stubborn things."   It is ever so; the man who can
calmly set facts aside as trivial, compared to his own
assertion, shows a superiority to circumstances that
soon attracts followers among the ignorant, and it is
to his consummate gift of lying that Osman mainly
owes his present power; nor did he ever fail to

celebrate each of our engagements with him as a victory.

But to return to the garden : When I was here before, I was much struck by a mimosa tree the delicate boughs of which were hung with hundreds of little globe-like nests, with round holes in the centre, from which innumerable birds of bright yellow plumage kept popping in and out filling the air with their joyous song ; but now, though it was nearly the same season of the year, not a nest was to be seen, and the yellow birds had departed. I had always associated this garden in my mind with little yellow birds, and had I described it to anybody I should have said, that is where you will hear yellow birds singing as they pop in and out of their little round nests. · It was therefore quite a disappointment to find them gone, almost as bad as having some cherished illusion of childhood ruthlessly swept into the records of the past.

On our way home we passed the camp of the second Battalion East Surrey Regiment, the band of which was discoursing sweet music as cheerily as if at a garden-party ; only, as there were no music-stands, a circle of soldiers stood in the centre with the music resting against their chests. One of the officers seeing us listening, came up with that genial hospitality which always distinguishes soldiers, and asked us to sit down and have a lime juice and seltzer with a large lump of ice in it ; this was nectar indeed, though we felt almost ashamed to accept a luxury which it seemed so hard to obtain in the desert ; but I verily believe no hot and thirsty way-farer ever passed the mess of this hospitable Regiment without being invited to tarry and refresh himself. Generous, indeed, is the man who will share his store of ice and soda water with the stranger in the desert.

We had just finished our simple dinner of stewed *boulli* beef and ship's biscuit, when an officer of marines, with drawn sword and greatcoat *en bandelier*, marched into the tent and asked what he was to do with forty men whom he had halted outside. " I have heard nothing about them," said P——— who was in command, " it must be a mistake." But the officer persisted that just as he was going to turn into his bed he had received an order to come to our camp at five minutes' notice, so it became evident that somebody thought we wanted additional protection, and the men were bivouacked ; the officer being, of course, invited to come in ; however, nothing would induce him to leave his men ; he had got his greatcoat, he said, and would be quite comfortable in a hole in the sand. I could not help admiring his resolution not to let anything tempt him from his post for a single moment, and nothing could have been finer than the hardy workmanlike appearance of the brave fellows he commanded, who, until the arrival of the Field Force, had hardly spent one night out of three in bed, and had displayed a cheerful devotion to duty during their long defence of Suakin, beyond all praise.

There was heavy firing in the night, the enemy having made an attempt to rush the Sikhs' camp, which they approached in detached parties, that were supposed to screen a stronger force behind, but the Sikhs turned sharply out and delivered some very effective volleys, which deterred them from coming on ; three dead bodies were brought in, notwithstanding the great rapidity with which the Arabs usually carry off their killed and wounded, so it was supposed that they had received a lesson, but this was a vain delusion, for the next night was to bring a still more serious attack.

CHAPTER III.

LIFE IN CAMP.

MARCH 11.—After a long conversation with Major —— of the Intelligence Branch, I rode down to the Ordnance store, to see about some camel saddles, and was struck by its isolated position, for it stood close to the seashore fully half a mile from any other camp, and was only partially surrounded by a laager of Maltese carts tilted on end. There was a jetty behind, on which goods were landed, and the *Dolphin* was so near, that by walking about a quarter of a mile along the shore, a man could hail her without shouting very loud. This near proximity to the guns of a vessel on which a vigilant watch was kept night and day, no doubt led to the belief that the store was quite safe ; as otherwise it would be hard to understand why so important a dépôt was protected by only a sergeant's guard of twenty-four men ; but it required no very astute military critic to perceive that it was practically impossible for the *Dolphin* to use her guns for its protection, as the camp beyond was in the direct line of fire. Indeed, I was much puzzled when riding home to understand the principles on which the camp had been planned,—its general disposition being as follows :—

The Guards Brigade, consisting of the Coldstreams,

Scots Guards, and Grenadiers, were encamped in rear
of West Redoubt, which was a small fort, our most
advanced post on the Suakin Berber road ; behind
them was the Berkshire Regiment, and to the left
of the Guards Brigade there was a great gap : then
came the camps of the Shropshire and East Surrey
Regiments, and then another gap, between them and
the Right Water Fort.   A line, therefore, drawn between the West Redoubt and the Right Water Fort,
would have represented our front, but there was no
continuity in the camps along it ; another line from
West Redoubt to the Ordnance store would have
represented our right flank, but here again there
was a great gap between the Ordnance store and
the nearest camp ; while a third line from the Water
Fort to the camp of the Indian Contingent S.W. of
the town, represented the left flank, which had also
a big gap in it facing South.   In rear of these our
advanced lines, were the Marines, Royal Horse Artillery, 19th Hussars, the Headquarter camp, and the
camp of the Army Hospital Corps, dotted promiscuously over the plain with considerable intervals
between them, intersected by shallow gullies down
which it was easy for the Arabs to creep unobserved
on a dark night.   In fact, the various camps were
scattered so far apart that an enemy could pass between them, and yet were sufficiently near together
to render it impossible for them to protect their
flanks without firing into each other.   True, there
was a line of pickets drawn round the whole camp,
stationed in little circular Redoubts, or "pepper
boxes," as they were called, but these were far apart,
and, as events proved, quite unable to prevent parties of the enemy from creeping in between them.

Musing on all these things, and hoping in time to
arrive at a comprehension of the plan pursued by the

ruling powers, I rode back to our camp only to find
that it had reduced itself into a few bales of canvass
on which the men were sitting disconsolately in the
sun waiting for camels. In fact, the order had come
for us to strike tents and move the camp to the
second Brigade, a nice piece of sand being assigned
us on the front line between the East Surrey Regiment
and the Right Water Fort. After baking in the sun
for about four hours, we were not sorry to see our
camels approaching, and prepared to load up, a task
that rather taxed the patience of our young soldiers,
as the camels, soon discovering that they were new
to the work, invariably got up before their loads had
been secured and pitched them all off again, while
Tommy Atkins made desperate efforts to imitate
the guttural " *Grrah* " with which the native drivers
induce them to kneel down.

Our new camping-ground commanded a beautiful
view, and was much more dry and healthy than the
last one, but it had the strategical objection that
not only was the front quite open to the mimosa
covered desert extending unbroken to the mountains,
but there was a wide gap between our left flank and
the Right Water Fort, down which ran a deep gully,
our position being so advanced that the guns of the
fort could not command the gully without firing into
us ; while a shelter trench, which the East Surrey
Regiment on our right had thrown up to protect *their*
left flank, was rendered useless for the same reason.
These peculiarities of our position must have struck
the General commanding the Brigade when he rode
up, for he inquired who had chosen it ; and the
C.R.E. presently appeared on the scene with a suggestion that we should have a nice little earthwork
run up with a redoubt at the corner, which he promised to send some Engineers to construct next

day ; meanwhile we were left to the unscientific
protection of that sweet little cherub who sits up
aloft, and it is to be hoped watches over Tommy
Atkins as well as poor Jack.

There is no twilight at Suakin, and it was dark
when, fairly weary with the work of pitching a new
camp, we turned in to dinner. " They are beginning
early to-night," said a friend, as he ladled out the
inevitable boulli beef from a big black saucepan, and
a few shots were heard along the front, but we were
getting used to this nightly serenade and soon sought
our beds, determined to snatch a few hours' sleep
while the night was still young. I had been suffering
from an attack of fever, owing to the rain-storm of
the other night, and had taken an opiate which made
me particularly drowsy, but at this time there was a
very peculiar custom in camp. The sentries at the
various posts would shout out to each other every
few minutes in lugubrious accents, " Number one,
All's well, Number two, *and* All's well, Number three,
etc.," accompanied now and then by the remark,
" Firing on the right," or " firing on the left," as if we
required to be informed of such a self-evident fact.
I do not know who originated this antiquated custom,
which reminded one of the cries with which the old
London watchmen made night hideous in the days
of our grandfathers, and naturally only served to
inform the enemy of the exact position of the sentries,
while it banished sleep from our eyes ; but an army
is very like a flock of sheep in a field, and so universally was it followed, that even the Staff officers
imagined at first that it must be some good and
necessary usage of war, nor was it till several days
had elapsed, that it struck some bright spirit it was
time this absurd practice should be put an end to.
In spite of my opiate, these mingled cries and the

firing kept me awake, and at last in despair I tried
a dose of sal volatile and chloric ether, which was
apparently the right remedy, for I presently fell into
a delicious warm sleep that bid fair to sweep away
all fever by the morning.

Not for long, however ; hardly five minutes appeared to have elapsed, before I was roused by a
hoarse cry of " Guard turn out," followed by a rush
of hurrying feet, and the bugles sounding the " fall
in," and " double," in rapid succession, all along the
line.   It was evident the pickets were coming in,
and that the enemy must be in force, so out we all
bundled from our beds, and, snatching up swords and
revolvers, ran to the rallying point near the horse
lines, where the men were rapidly assembling.   The
night was pitch dark, for the moon was in her last
quarter and had not yet risen, but we could see the
flashes of the rifles and hear shots all along the front,
while some Remington bullets came flying into the
camp from the desert with that peculiar sharp *whew*,
or whistle, which seems to say, " Where are you ? "
and has made many a brave man bow at their approach ;—I may remark in parenthesis, that, putting
all question of example aside, it is not of the slightest
use for any one to duck to a bullet, as sound travels
so slowly, that by the time the whistle is heard the
bullet itself is passed.

Soon the pickets came tumbling in, and as the
front was thus cleared, the firing became fast and
furious.   We could see the Sikhs, and the people at
the camel depôt in rear, also hotly engaged, and the
Guards firing volleys to our right, while down near
the Ordnance store, the *Dolphin's* guns fired five
shots into the open desert ; then the electric light
from her mast-head swept over the camp, throwing
out all the white tents and groups of figures standing

at their posts in bold relief, only to pass away again,
leaving the darkness profounder than before. So
we stood peering into the blackness of the night,
and waiting the attack, while the bullets kept cutting
up the sand between the tents. Presently three
heads appeared over the edge of the gully on our left,
and we at once recognized them as a patrol returning,
but before we had time to utter a caution, a sentry
—not one of our own men—knelt down and fired,
two more sentries at once followed suit, and the next
moment to our horror, we heard the main body,
who were standing about twenty yards behind us,
bring their rifles to the ready. " Ease springs, order
arms," we thundered, afraid that in their excitement
they might pour a volley into our backs, and the
next moment the sentries who had fired on the
patrol were recalled. " I hope I ain't been and
killed any one, sir," said one of them, a mere boy, as
he was put under arrest, and luckily for him he had
not, though the patrol had a narrow escape. Some
of the camps directly in our rear now appeared to
be engaged, for their bullets came whizzing into our
lines ; this was very unkind of them, as it placed us
between a cross fire of friends and foes, and exposed
us to the chance of being hit in the only region
where a soldier considers it inglorious to be wounded,
namely, his back.

While this general skirmish was going on all
round, the Ordnance store had been marked out for
a special attack, led by Abdul Assad, or Ahad,
" Abdul the Lion," Osman Digma's own standard-
bearer. This man, who was a very black negro of
gigantic strength and stature, had formerly been a
wharf porter at Suakin, and knew the locality well ;
the isolated position of the depôt from whence we
drew all our equipment had not escaped the notice

of our cunning adversaries, and accordingly they determined to wreck it.

Major St. G——, the officer in charge of the store, had gone to bed after posting the usual guards ; he always slept in a tent by himself, with a lighted candle on a writing-table near the head of his bed, on which also stood the portraits of his wife and children, placed so that he could get a last look at them before he went to sleep. I have seen him so a dozen times when I have been into his tent late at night, but this evening the candle, luckily for him, had gone out. The guard was sleeping in the guard tent, and the sentries were walking up and down on their beats, listening to the shots which could be occasionally heard along the front of the camp, a mile and a half away, but dreading little danger, for the Arabs had always shown themselves chary of approaching the guns of the ships, and though there was an unbroken expanse of desert on the North side of the store, they had never come that way before. But, when one of them saw a dark figure suddenly emerge from the shadow of the pier, he promptly challenged, "Halt, who goes there !" "Friend," replied a voice, probably that of Abdul Ahad, who may have picked up a few words of English when he laboured at the wharf ; and while the sentry, knowing that the coolie labourers some- times hung about the pier, hesitated what to do and tried to peer into the darkness, the gigantic black was upon him and cut him down with a blow of his two-handed sword ; another sentry who came to his assistance, shared the same fate, and with a bound some fifty Arabs, who had crept round the shore and sheltered under the shadow of the pier, rushed on the guard tent, hoping to surprise its occupants who were now, however, tumbling out to meet them.

One who slept on the deck of a ship that night, said that he could hear the sentry's last cry of "murder" ring right across the harbour, and that only five shots were fired after it, for then the Arabs had closed with the guard, and a silent but desperate struggle ensued between spear and bayonet. It is worthy of remark that the Arabs uttered no yells, and from their adopting the stratagem of answering the sentry in English, it is probable that they hoped to surprise and slay the small guard at the store without alarming the ships in the harbour, after which they would have fired the mass of valuable *materiel* collected in the enclosure, with a view to crippling our resources; the attacks on the other parts of the camp being simply intended to keep the remainder of the troops engaged. This was a proof, if any were needed, that it behoved us to exercise the greatest vigilance with an enemy so quick to detect and take advantage of any negligence on our part. But Abdul Ahad had not reckoned on English pluck, and though the enemy numbered fifty, and the guard in the tent only fifteen, though in that fierce struggle in the dark, three of our men were killed and nine wounded; the heroic Berkshire men—for they belonged to that splendid Regiment—would not give way, and finally the Arabs, finding they could not overpower them, ran round the camp, and entering it at another point, rushed through the store, stabbing at all they met in their course.

St. G——, who was aroused by the cries, jumped out of bed, and groped for his sword and revolver, which he was not able to find. At this moment he heard one of the Arabs entering the tent, and, not caring to meet him unarmed, bolted out of the other door, and scrambled under the curtains of the next tent, where his Quartermaster lived, narrowly escaping being shot by his own comrade, who at first took him for an Arab. They left the tent together, and St. G—— found his sword and revolver, and joining the remnants of his guard, proceeded to search the ground which presented a sad spectacle, the dead and injured men having been frightfully hacked about. The Arabs, it seems, after "running a muck" through the camp, made off, carrying their own dead and wounded with them, for their quick ears had detected the sound of a boat being lowered from the *Dolphin*, which at the same moment turned on her electric light. This gave them such a start, that they actually dropped the body of Abdul Ahad, their leader, who had been killed by a bayonet thrust, and thus fell into our hands. When Osman Digma heard of his loss, it is said he lamented bitterly, and offered to give a sum of money and stop all further night attacks if we would give up the body and not burn it, for it is one of the worst reproaches to an Oriental to be called "the son of a burnt father." We did not give up the body, but it was not burnt, and now lies buried in the desert sand not far from the spot where Abdul the Lion met his death.

The *Dolphin*, meanwhile, opened fire on the re-treating Arabs, large parties of whom were seen by the electric light hovering round the camp, and the next day the Mounted Infantry found some more bodies which had been dropped by the party that attacked the Ordnance store, as they hurried towards the mountains. The Shropshire Regiment, also lost a corporal killed and two men wounded, belonging to a patrol which was incautiously coming in with sloped arms, when some Arabs, who had concealed themselves under a bush, sprang on them from behind and wrenched the rifles out of their hands.

A sergeant of this Regiment had a rather narrow escape, for, as he was getting into a redoubt, an Arab, concealed in the ditch, caught him by the leg, as I have known rats catch young chickens through the chinks in the pavement of a fowl-house. The sergeant, however, kicked the Arab over and jumped into the redoubt, pulling the plank he had been crossing by after him; what became of the Arab history does not relate.

There were some casualties in the other camps, and many of the enemy were supposed to have been shot, the Guards alone capturing three dead bodies and six prisoners; but as a rule the Arabs managed to carry off their dead, and on one occasion charged the Sikhs' lines no less than four times to recover one of their slain. It was difficult, therefore, to calculate their losses.

About 4 A.M. the firing slackened, and it became evident the enemy were retiring. So we were able to turn in for a short sleep, though a few dropping shots continued to be fired till daylight.

March 12.—General Graham arrived to-day and assumed command; he has been suffering from an injury to his leg, and is still a little lame. I spent a quiet morning trying to shake off the fever, which was not improved by last night's exposure. If our camp below was damp and unhealthy, this one is subject to a plague of dust, for when the Hamsin blows hard, which it generally does once in three days, the whole of this part of the plain is covered with a dense cloud of whirling sand which penetrates everything—eyes, nose, ears, clothes, watches, and boots, mixing with the water one drinks, and the bread that one eats, till it grates like cinders between the teeth.

When we looked out of the tent this morning we

could hardly distinguish objects twenty yards off, in fact it was as bad as a London fog, only the fog was palpable and hit you in the face ; nor do I know anything more exquisitely painful than to have to ride against the wind during one of these storms. There was no use in closing the tent doors, for the sand still came in through every chink and crevice, covering everything with a thick coating of dust, no doubt plentifully laden with microbes, bacilli, etc.; the germs disseminated by the dead camels and other objectionable matter about the camp. As a protection against these sand-storms and the glare of the sun, our men were all provided with blue goggles and gauze veils, attired in which the British soldier presented a very grotesque appearance, but in my opinion both were utterly useless ; for the gauze veil soon becomes clogged with dust, and the wearer discovers that it is better to be half choked with sand than to be wholly asphyxiated for want of air ; while the goggles are directly injurious to the eye-sight, as the constant heat of a glass in this climate over the region of the eye renders it sensitive and relaxed, and much more liable to become inflamed than when exposed to the air ; it acts in fact like a forcing-glass over a flower-pot, while the fine dust gets round the goggles and sticks all the more to the moist eyelids. Neither in dust-storms or sun did I wear veil or goggles, and I found my eyes became all the stronger for the exposure, the only precaution that is of real value, being to wash them as frequently as possible in cold water.

A word about dead camels; some of the Transport officers told me that they were the bane of their lives. Whenever a camel died, it was ordered to be buried at once, but the desert sand will *not* bury ; it is not earth, and has no deodorizing properties, besides which it has a habit of shifting in a most remarkable manner, and a camel that has been buried two fathoms deep one day, will have all four legs exposed the next; then the General comes by with his handkerchief to his nose and storms, the Transport officer of the Brigade is sent for, and told to do his duty; he sets to work with a fatigue party and erects a regular Barrow over the offending animal, only to receive a curt notification next day that the General saw an eye or one of its ears peeping out, as he went his morning rounds; so he sets to work again, feeling like the Giant Tredeger twisting ropes of sand. The camel is an animal which, if long-suffering in life, makes itself peculiarly objectionable after death; in fact the memory of departed camels floating about a camp is the camel's worst revenge, for there is a subtlety in the way they haunt the air, even when a couple of miles off, which I have known to empty a mess tent to windward, in five minutes. Wisdom is of slow growth in camp, and at first dead camels were buried where they lay, then they were ordered to be dragged a mile beyond the Brigade to which they belonged; still they made their presence known, and it took about two months before the simple principle was acted on, that, as the wind blew at this season from the North, all dead camels should be dragged two miles South of the camp.

We hoped to get some sleep this night, but were hardly in bed before we had to jump out again and prepare for an enemy who could not be seen in the darkness, though his shots could be heard whistling among the tents. When the alarm was over, and the firing ceased, we turned in for a few moments, only to snatch up our swords and run out again as another death cry, another rattle of musketry, and another rush of feet, warned us that the Arabs were prowling once more round the camp, and seeking where they could creep in, to continue their work of midnight murder. The bullets of the Sikhs, in rear of us, still came into our lines when they fired volleys, and one actually fell between two of our men as they lay side by side on their faces peering into the desert, another injured a mule, and it was wonderful that further damage was not done. All night long the force was under arms, and it was no use going to bed.

So cunning and daring were the enemy that they actually succeeded in entering a guard tent—I think of the Shropshire Regiment—and kniving some of the men, though a sentry was outside. Crawling up on hands and knees they watched him. on his beat till his back was turned, and then slipped noiselessly into the tent where they stabbed, or "scuppered" as the men call it, several of the sleeping guard before they could spring to their feet ; the moment the alarm was given, they glided out into the darkness and vanished like spirits of evil. Naturally a feeling of uneasiness begins to pervade the camp, for no man knows when he lies down whether he will not wake up with a spear through him.

I remember when I was a boy reading thrilling stories about Red Indians, who used to creep snakelike through the grass and tomahawk our sentries, during the war with the French in America ; but here was the real thing going on daily, with a foe just as cunning and just as cruel as the biggest "Big Buffalo," or the most ruthless "Yellow Snake," of fiction. One night we were awakened from a short sleep by a shriek so piercing, so full of mortal terror and agony combined, that the horror of it literally seemed to freeze our blood, as with fingers instinctively closing round our revolvers we sat up to listen. In the middle of his sleep, perhaps while he was

dreaming that he was back again in the safe shelter
of his village home, with loving faces and green fields
about him, an English soldier had awakened to meet
his death agony. A dusky figure sprang through the
tent door and melted like a shadow into the outer
darkness, while the man inside lay writhing on the
the ground pinned to the earth by an Arab spear.
With fury in their eyes and clenched teeth his comrades dashed out in pursuit, and there was cracking
and flashing of rifles all along the line ; but it was
too late—the silent enemy, who had stolen on them
like a thief in the night, was gone.

The comparative impunity with which the Arabs
repeated these assassinations night after night, was
quite enough to make young soldiers feel a little
jumpy when going on sentry duty. Indeed, the
position of a sentry was not an enviable one, when
he went out for his two hours' spell of watch.
Behind him, lay the white ghostlike tents of the
camp, dimly visible in the quiet starlight, in which
lay his comrades, armed of course, but probably
snatching a few hours of much needed sleep, trusting
to his vigilance and devotion to protect their lives.
Before him stretched the desert, a vast expanse of
sand and gravel furrowed by old watercourses, the
result of sudden thunderstorms, and covered with
low scrubby bushes and long tufts of dry weedy
grass, which it was hard at night to distinguish from
a crouching human form, especially if there was any
breeze to stir them. He knew he must not destroy
his comrades' rest and alarm the whole camp, by
firing at mere creatures of his imagination, still less
must he fire at a patrol or officer passing along the
line, without due challenge ; yet there was no countersign by which he might ascertain that the approaching person was not betraying him to his death. The

simple word "friend," so easy to learn, was to stop
him from pulling the trigger, and he must wait till
the approaching figure was near enough for him to
distinguish its outline in the truly Egyptian darkness,
for there were no watch-fires along the front to help
him, and half a dozen enemies might be stealthily
approaching him from another direction, while his
attention was directed to this one.   But more often
he saw nothing at all; the low, scrubby bushes might
be teeming with crouching Arabs, who regularly left
the mountains at nightfall to harass the camp, but
unless he was fortunate enough to catch the sparkle
of their eyes gleaming like the eyes of wild beasts,
close to the ground—the only thing that *did* betray
them in the darkness—he probably saw no sign of
their approach, and though aware of the danger that
menaced him, could not tell when or how it would
reach him.   The nearly naked Hadendowas, with
bare feet and greased skins as dusky as the night,
crept and glided on their faces along every hollow
and gully, carefully taking advantage of each bush,
or tuft of reeds that could screen their approach,
and, if alarmed, lying perfectly still after casting the
sand with a rapid noiseless motion over their prostrate bodies, so that the keenest eye could hardly
detect them from a stone.   When they wished to
make a sign to each other, they imitated the cry of
one of the desert birds with marvellous fidelity, and
often has this low, plaintive cry been the signal for
their onslaught.   Sometimes it was a volley followed
by a rush with swords and spears, but more often a
dark figure would seem to rise out of the very ground
at the sentry's feet and stab him in the back ; or if
it was impossible to get sufficiently near to him
unperceived, they would wait till he moved away on
his beat, knowing well his exact position by the

crunching of his heavy ammunition boots on the
gravel, and wriggling past like serpents, slip among
the tents ; then would follow the death scream, the
rush of feet and fierce volleys poured in rapid succession into the night, after a few shadowy forms
disappearing in the darkness, content at having
achieved their work of murder and mutilation ; this
would be the signal for a general alarm along the
whole line, the Arabs farther out on the desert would
open fire with their Remingtons, bullets would come
whizzing into the camp in all directions, and the
force be kept on the alert until the long hours of
the night passed away, and the sun rose on another
day of incessant work at the wharfs and trenches, for
men who had enjoyed no sleep.

It may well be asked, how was it possible that
a force of nearly 11,000 men, could be constantly
deprived of sleep for nine nights in succession, from
the 7th to the 15th March, inclusive, by probably not more than 300 or 400 Arabs ?   It
was simply because it took all this time before the
authorities were prepared to carry out such a reform-
ation in the arrangement of the camp as would
enable one portion of the force to sleep in security,
while the other watched.   For, I need hardly say
that the success of these night attacks was mainly
owing to the scattered position of the various camps,
though the absence of the common precaution
of the countersign, and of any line of watch-fires
which would enable the outposts to see figures
passing between them, had also something to do
with it.   I have sometimes thought that for this
kind of warfare, a number of good watchdogs would
be useful.   As for the electric light thrown from the
ships, though picturesque, it was more like a toy
than anything else, for being projected from so far

in rear, it dazzled us when it fell on our lines, and
only served to show the enemy the exact position of
our camp and pickets. Had it been possible by
means of wires to establish this light at West
Redoubt, on the right of our front, or if that was
impossible, had West Redoubt, and the Right Water
Fort, been each provided with powerful limelights,
they might have been of some use to illuminate the
surface of the desert, while our own position remained
in darkness : but the electric light from the sea-coast
simply bothered us, and the men who worked it often
forgot that a very small motion of the machine at
the base would make a ray of light two miles long
traverse the arc of a circle with giant strides, so that
it frequently came to pass, that after we had been
peering earnestly through our night glasses at some
gully or row of bushes where we thought the enemy
lay, and our eyes were getting to know the darkness,
this will-o'-the-wisp-like light would rest on the spot
in the most tantalising manner for one second only,
and then jump away again, making the darkness
seem ten times profounder than before, and leaving
us blinded and baffled.

But what struck me as the strangest thing of
all was that, though many of the Staff had seen a
zareba before, it never occurred to any one that,
by clearing the desert of the thorn bushes in front
of our lines and making a hedge round them, all
possibility of the Arabs being able to creep in or rush
the sentries would have been put an end to ; for a
hedge of thorny mimosas, laid side by side with their
heads outwards, presents about the most difficult
barrier a naked man can have to cross. This plan
was partially adopted some two months later—truly,
as I remarked before, wisdom is a plant of slow
growth in camps !

March 13.—A morning of manifold duties.   In
the afternoon rode to Headquarters, to inquire about
the Engineers, who were to have made our nice
little earthwork and redoubt, but have never appeared
on the scene.   The C.R.E. was very courteous, and
almost blushed, if a Colonel on the Staff ever does
such a thing, but he could not help me, as he said
his men were all engaged elsewhere ; however, he
suggested we might get a fatigue party from the
Shropshire and East Surrey Regiments, and gave me
carte blanche to plan out the trench myself.   So to
the Shropshire and East Surrey I galloped ; but the
men of the one were all engaged at the wharfs, and
though the Colonel of the other promised me a hundred men, they never appeared, which came to the
same thing ; he, however, lent me a subaltern who
incautiously passed within his range of vision.   " Mr.
———," he called, " are you doing anything in particular ? "   Mr. ———, who at that moment was
smoking a cigarette with his hands in his pockets,
couldn't say that he was.   " Very well, then ; will
you go with this officer and assist him to plan out a
shelter trench ? "   So the unfortunate Mr. ——— found
himself doomed to spend his afternoon bending over
a tape line.   He was, however, good-natured and
intelligent, and we soon had the trench marked out
along our front ; for, being of what my friends call
" a meekly obstinate disposition," I was determined
not to let another night pass without having something for the men to shelter behind.   Therefore, at
four o'clock, as soon as their tea was over, I got together forty of our own people, and set them to work
with pick and shovel.   The sun was hot, and they
had been labouring hard all day at other work, but
they now turned to digging with an energy and
cheeriness eminently characteristic of the English

soldier when on service ; and so well did they work,
that in two hours we had our shelter trench in the
second stage. The men were delighted, for, slight
though the defence might be, it gave them a feeling
of security, and they felt that they would sleep more
soundly for knowing it was there ; our plan being to
let half the men bivouac out in the trench, while the
other half slept in the tents, and *vice versa,* so that
every man might at least get half a night's rest. As
darkness was now setting in, there was no time to
carry the trench round our flank, so I got a lot of
spare tent ropes and picketing pegs, and made a rope
entanglement along the side of the gully, strewing
the ground with broken bottles between the meshes
of the rope ; for this, I thought, would suffice to
check a rush, and make it very uncomfortable for
any Arab who might attempt to creep through.

The night as usual was one of constant alarms,
but we did not attempt to undress, and lay on our
beds booted and belted ready to turn out at a
moment's notice. We were again much troubled by
the bullets that were coming in from the rear. In
addition to the Sikhs, the 5th Lancers were now
encamped directly behind us, and poured their fire
into our camp in the wildest fashion. We could not
exactly run up an earthwork against our friends, but
G. P. made a zareba of boxes round the back of his
bed, under the shelter of which he slumbered
peacefully ; he said he was more afraid of his friends
than his foes.

March 14.—Was sent for from Headquarters by
Colonel ———, who proposed that I should organize a Water Train to be worked distinct from the
ordinary Commissariat and Transport service of the
Brigades, and the special object of which would be
to secure a supply of that most important of all

necessaries water, to the army when in the field, and to any stations established beyond the camp.

I was rather troubled at this proposal, for knowing the character of the country, the tendency that water has to decompose under so fierce a sun, the likelihood that convoys might be attacked and delayed, the naturally wasteful disposition of soldiers, who would never understand the value of the precious fluid till they were actually in want of it, and the dreadful consequences that might ensue, should the water supply of the force when in the field fail through any accident or negligence,—I felt that the officer who undertook to keep 10,000 men from being thirsty in the plains of the Soudan, would have a heavy weight of responsibility on his shoulders, and that his post would hardly be a sinecure. Indeed, I pointed out to Colonel —— that as my previous military experience had been purely Regimental, an officer trained to Transport work, would probably be better fitted for the duty ; he, however, replied that when I visited the Soudan as a private traveller I naturally had to provide my own water transport, and ought, therefore, to be possessed of just that practical knowledge of the country which was required ; so, of course, I promised to do my best and cantered home to write out a draft scheme for approval.

It was only when I set myself to this task that I realized the full difficulty of the work I had undertaken, and the careful organization that would be necessary to guard against unforeseen accidents. After the anxious work of the day, sleep would have been a boon at night ; but no such luck was in store for us, and foes in front, and friends behind, fired steadily into our camp till sunrise.

A newspaper correspondent, writing on the 15th, says, "Numbers of the enemy were crawling

about the camp on hands and knees. The firing
was more continuous and general than during any
previous night." This was literally the case, and for
many hours we stood watching behind our men, who
lay concealed by the shelter trench and occasionally
poured volleys into the low scrub on the desert before
us. The night was chilly, and so dark that we could
hardly see each other, but every now and then there
would be a slight ripple, as it were, just perceptible
along the dusky outline of a sand-bank some
hundred yards in front of our camp, the undulation
of dark bodies moving, and then the command would
be given in a whisper rising to a shout, "At one
hundred yards, Ready, Present, FIRE!" A
sheet of flame would leap from our lines for a
moment, to be swallowed up in darkness the
next, and the rattling noise of the discharge would
echo across the plain, answered, as it died away in
the distance, by the dropping fire of the Arab
sharp-shooters farther away ; whose bullets generally
skimmed over our heads and knocked up the sand
behind us, as though they had been fired by men
kneeling on the ground and shooting from the hip.
I believe this was how the Arabs did fire in the
dark, hoping that *Inshallah !* their bullets might drop
into the unbeliever's camp somewhere or other, which,
to do them justice, they generally did ; but notwithstanding the continued firing this night, there were no
casualties that I heard of, and we suffered most from
want of sleep. Next morning an old barrel in front
of our lines was found to have thirty-two shot holes
in it, which looked suspiciously as if our return fire
had principally been directed against this barrel,
probably it was, as it stood against the skyline, and
no doubt in the darkness made a very good Hadendowa to the excited imaginations of the men.

March 15, Sunday.—Church parade at 7 A.M. in
the lines of the 17th Regiment.   There was no Chaplain, so the Colonel began to read the service, but when
he had got half through, a young man with a beard,
dressed in khakee, appeared and took the book.   We
thought he was going to continue the service, but he
only uttered a short prayer and began to preach a
long sermon instead, at which we were all rather
disappointed, for there is nothing goes home to the
hearts of the men so much as the grand simple words
of our morning service, and it is easy to see in their
earnest faces how they appreciate hearing them, when
far from home and engaged on an undertaking of
danger ; but I fear they regard standing under a
tropical sun listening to a sermon as mere weariness
of spirit, unless the sermon be a very eloquent one,
and if I were Chaplain General, I would recommend
the army Chaplains not to cut the service short, in
order to preach a long sermon, but to reverse the
process and cut the sermon rigorously down, making
it very brief and to the point, so that the men might
carry it away in their hearts without feeling wearied
by it.

Service over, there was no more rest all day, and I
had to go into the question of the Water Train minutely
with the Director of Transport, who kept me hard
at work till nightfall.   The cavalry went out scouting,
but without any particular result.   It has been determined to prepare a surprise for the morrow and
send two parties of Cavalry quietly on to the plain
just before daybreak, in the hope of catching some of
the enemy as they return from harassing our camp.
The elaborate cunning of this operation looks rather
like trying to put salt on a bird's tail, and I fear the
Arabs, who managed to walk safely over mined
ground so recently, will not let themselves be caught

by a squadron or two of Hussars jangling on to the
plain under the idea that they are invisible :—nor
did they.

After dark firing commenced again ; this is the
eighth night we have been without sleep, and we
are getting so used to it that I suppose we shall
not know how to sleep when we get the chance.
The health of the force is still wonderfully good, but
the strain is great, and will tell presently on the
constitutions of many when the reaction comes after
the excitement is over.　To-morrow, however, the
camp is at last to be remodelled, and an order has
been given that the cartridges issued to the troops
at night are to have the bullets cut in four, so that
they may spread on the buckshot principle, instead
of flying about the camp.　This is not very com-
plimentary to the judgment of the army, but as one of
the Cavalry Regiments in rear, the troopers of which
are little more than boys, has playfully constructed
a redoubt, so placed that its fire *must* come into the
front line of the camp, it is perhaps just as well.

March 16.—To-day the laying of the Suakin
Berber railway commenced.　There was no silver
shovel and no first sod to turn with it, for Quarantine
Island is innocent of verdure, and the only green
visible must have been in the eyes of any sanguine
person who thought the railway was really intended
to reach the Nile ; but nevertheless this day may
yet become memorable in history, should the line
ever be completed, as in after time it may, and
Eastern Africa opened up to civilization through
its agency.　At present the inscription " Suakin
Berber Railway," which Messrs. Lucas and Aird,
have had painted in large white letters on all their
rolling stock, looks rather " sarterick," as Artemus
Ward used to say.

The camp was completely remodelled to-day
and its general disposition much improved.   The
various camps now form three sides of a parallelogram
with some approach to continuity, the left, or South
face, consisting of the Indian Contingent, with the
20th Hussars and 5th Lancers in rear of them, extends from Osman Digma's garden just outside the
suburb of the town, to a point between the two Water
Forts.   The front, or West face, extends from the
Right Water Fort to a point in rear of West Redoubt,
and consists of ourselves, the Surrey, Shropshire, and
Berkshire Regiments, and the Coldsteams, Scots, and
Grenadier Guards; while turning the angle, the North
face stretches back to the sea, and consists of the
Horse Artillery, Mounted Infantry, Royal Engineers,
Marine Artillery and Marines.   The Field Hospital
is at H. Redoubt, in the centre of this enclosure, and
the camp of the Headquarter Staff is soon to be
moved into the gap between us and the Right Water
Fort, when I am to join it and enter on my administrative duties.

Another long day, arranging details.   When I
reached home, I found a tall young man in plain
clothes sitting in our tent, who turned out to be the
correspondent of the *Daily Chronicle,* whom P——
had brought up to dine and sleep with us, as he was
anxious to witness a night attack ; he was the first of
the correspondents I had met, for none of them except
Reuter's agent lived at Headquarters, but he did
not gain his object of seeing an attack, as probably
owing to the new formation of the camp, there were
very few shots fired during the night, and no alarms.
In fact, when he awoke in the morning, he was quite
cross and disappointed; saying that he had heard so
much about the Arab attacks, that he had fully
expected to pass all night behind the trenches,

instead of which he had eaten a good dinner, drunk
half a bottle of champagne, and slept as comfortably
as if he was in a private house.   These are the lights
and shades of a soldier's life—had he been with us
the night before, he would have got no sleep at all.

Apropos of the dinner, it was true we now fed
fairly well, for we had come to the conclusion that it
would be time enough to eat boulli beef and ship's
biscuit, when the advance was made, and for the
present supplied ourselves plentifully with potted
meats, fish, and vegetables from Suakin, where one
or two grocery stores had been opened, at which the
prices, though high, were not exorbitant ; and it is a
curious fact that you could get an iced brandy and
soda at the little Red Sea port, for exactly the same
price you have to pay for it in a London hotel, and
for only twopence more than you give at a club.   I
do not pretend to solve this mystery, but it is certain
that the love of enterprise which induces sutlers to
send creature comforts in the wake of an army,
though it may be sordid in its origin, is a boon of
no mean value to the officers, and, if the sale of
liquor is properly regulated, to the men as well, who
will be all the better in their health for being able to
procure a change of diet.   At Suakin the supervision
of the drink shops must have been strictly carried
out, for I only remember seeing one European
soldier suffering from drink while I was there.   I
do not pretend to assert that, because I saw so few
drunkards, the force was, therefore, absolutely teetotal
in its principles ; I simply mention the fact as
showing there was a very creditable absence of
inebriety, notwithstanding the temptations of the
climate, and because a foreign critic has insinuated
that our soldiers on service are generally drunk.
Sir Gerald Graham's despatch to Lord Hartington,

written this day, well describes our position, and proves that he was fully aware of the defective arrangement of the camp, though he gives no reason for the long delay in putting matters right.

HEADQUARTERS, SUAKIN,
March 16, '85.

MY LORD—I have the honour to report that I arrived at Suakin on the 12th instant, and assumed command of the force there assembled.

I consider the camp to be somewhat too extended, which renders small night attacks easy to such an enemy as we have to deal with, and entails the provision of a large force for outpost and picket duties. I have already taken steps to reduce the front occupied, and am preparing to curtail it still further, in view of the relatively small force which will be left at Suakin when I advance.

The enemy, acting doubtless under specific instructions, attack the camp in small bodies every night, and have succeeded in killing or wounding some of our sentries. The firing which is carried on at night by our outposts, though possibly unnecessarily frequent, is completely under control. Although its effect upon the enemy is inconsiderable, it has proved sufficient to deter him from anything approaching to a serious attack. The camps are now nearly all defended by zarebas or entanglements, and the enemy's policy is, therefore, to endeavour to creep in at unguarded intervals, and never to attack defended posts.

Spies state that Tamai is held by about 7000 men, and that a force of from 1000 to 1200 is at Hasheen. Tokar is stated to be held in small force, and Handoub is probably also held by a weak detachment.

I have no news of the fall of Kassala; but bazaar rumours to this effect have lately been rife.

The work of organizing the transport is proceeding steadily, and the arrival of the *Romeo* to-day will enable the water transport arrangements of the force to be taken in hand.

The provision of storage tanks for use in the field is at present inadequate, since the canvas supplied for this purpose from the navy last year is not now available.

The 20th Hussars disembarked to-day; the Artillery,

the Mounted Infantry, and the Australian Contingent have not yet arrived, and the Horse Artillery battery is incomplete.

As soon as the force is complete, and the water transport and field storage arrangements are fully organized, I intend to move at once.—I have, etc.

GERALD GRAHAM.[1]

March 17.—A very hot day, the thermometer 105° in the tent. The Cavalry were out scouting in the morning, but did not engage the enemy. More work organizing the water transport. It is now arranged that I am to have a permanent staff to assist me, consisting of four officers, two warrant officers, and one sergeant. To these were afterwards added a corporal and ten privates, to superintend the locking of the water tins, while five hundred Bheisties and Dhoolies, with their officers, were lent me for fatigue parties, to fill and carry the tins to the place where the camels were laden.

The camels were to be furnished by the Director of Transport, as required, from the different Transport companies, in complete sections with their own officers and drivers ; one of my officers being always in administrative charge of the convoy. Though my own quarters were to be with the Headquarter Staff, I was to establish a depôt near No. 5 pier, where the condensing ships lay, at which the work of filling the vessels and preparing the convoys could be carried on night and day ; and as the storage of water in the field is usually an Engineer service, Major —— of the Engineers was appointed to take charge of the tanks and tins for containing the water, which he issued to me as required; but after we had worked together very harmoniously for some little time, he was transferred to another post, and most of his duties passed into my hands,

[1] Egypt, 13. Despatch No. 8.

by which I became responsible for several thousand
pounds worth of Government property, and the anxie-
ties of my stewardship were not a little increased.

My plan was, briefly, to have the water vessels
laid out in lines on an open space óf ground, with
sufficient interval between every two tins for a camel
to kneel down ; the camels were then brought down
at sunset after being watered, and picketed in rows
of fifty between their future loads, with their evening
meal before them. So that it was only necessary,
when the time came to start the convoy, to lift the
two water-tanks, lying on either side of each camel,
into the *saletahs*, or nets, attached to the saddle,
and make it stand up. By this means five hundred
camels could be loaded in a very short space of
time, and marched off in a compact column without
any confusion or delay. After some difficulty, I
succeeded in obtaining one native driver for every
two camels, so as to have them thoroughly under
control, and the maximum weight of water that I
allowed to be carried was well within the strength of
the weakest camel of the convoy, so as to obviate as
much as possible the chance of a breakdown. A
certain number of European privates were also
allotted to each section of camels, to see that the
native drivers did not steal the water ; and each
section of camels furnished by the various Transport
companies was accompanied by its proper proportion
of officers or warrant officers, while I myself, or my
representative, always went in administrative charge
of the whole convoy, and superintended the safe
arrival, storage, and issue of water in the field, and
the return of all empty vessels to the depôt ; where
another of my officers was constantly engaged having
them filled, and keeping an account of the water in
hand, required, expended, etc.

When I mention that the condensed water, which
was alone to be used, was pumped from the condensing ships into iron tanks, from which it had
again to be pumped into long wooden troughs, from
which it had to be drawn by means of numerous
taps that I got fitted to them, so that several barrels
could be filled at the same time ; that every tin or
barrel had to be washed before it was filled, and
locked and unlocked with a key by a European—
for we never could get the natives to shut a screw
properly ; that leather funnels had to be provided
for filling the tins, and taps and syphons for emptying
them ; that there were five different patterns of water
vessels of four separate sizes each, locking with three
kinds of keys, and some of them, as, for instance, the
ten and twelve and a half gallon barrels, so nearly
alike, that it was difficult to distinguish one from the
other, though the difference in weight was quite
enough to destroy the balance of a load, and cause a
breakdown ; that most of the work had to be carried
on at night, in order that the water might be as fresh
as possible, and the convoy in its place before the
troops assembled at dawn ; that orders were
frequently given for the advance of a large force at
the very last moment, and that there was much
difficulty in ascertaining the exact number of men,
horses, etc., that were going out,—it will be understood that very careful calculation and untiring
supervision were required to get this abominable
Water Train into working order, and my little staff
were fully employed.   But at the date I am writing
of, I had no staff or fatigue parties of any kind at
my disposal, and I was obliged to start the work
almost single-handed.   G. P., whose services I
borrowed, helped me most zealously until his health
broke down under the heavy strain, and I was also

much indebted to D——, a Yorkshire M.P., who has since held a very high post at the War Office, and was indefatigable at lending a helping hand wherever help was needed ; he was not a soldier, and then held no official position, but he loved the very hardships of war with a soldier's love, and never shall I forget the night before the advance to Tofrek, sitting on a damp stone beside him, into the small hours of the morning, while we tied with our own hands pieces of string to nearly a thousand greasy and oderiferous " mussacks," or goat-skins, with the hair on, which had to be filled before the convoy could start, and the strings of which had been forgotten, when they were purchased at the last moment by the Government for a pound a piece.

Not very long afterwards I had to sit on a Board which condemned these skins as unfit for use, and recommended that they should be speedily buried, as the doctors declared that they were contaminating the air. Of course I had nothing to do with the purchase of the " mussacks," and never saw them till the night they were to be filled, so I may safely venture an opinion that no one was to blame in the matter. It is true they cost over a thousand pounds, and being badly tanned, proved unfit for permanent use ; but at the time they were purchased they were the only skins in the market, a sufficiency of camel tins had not yet arrived from England, and it was absolutely necessary that the advancing force should have its water carried somehow. The mussacks answered their purpose for one day. And the blame, if any, rests with those who were responsible for the delay in forwarding camel tins from England. I have mentioned this little incident simply to show how easily blame may be wrongly applied if all the circumstances of a case are not understood ; but I anticipate.

The night of the 17th passed without any serious
alarm, and we only had to turn out once.   Half the
men still lay in the trenches all night, but P——— had
now constructed a strong redoubt of forage sacks at the
corner of my rope entanglement, and the men slept
with a feeling of security which was a great rest to them.

Many ingenious devices were now employed for
the protection of the camp ; of these the most important were the ordinary shelter trench and ditch,
parapets made of forage sacks, compressed hay, biscuit boxes, or firewood laid with the sharp ends of the
branches outwards, wire entanglements with broken
glass between, iron hay hoops scattered thickly on
the ground, etc. ; so that it became quite dangerous
to ride about the camp after dark, for fear of getting
one's horse's legs caught in some of these contrivances
for baffling an Arab rush.   But in a country like the
Soudan there is nothing so good as a mimosa hedge,
behind which, if rifle fire is expected, a shelter trench
can be constructed.

For ordinary warfare, I think it would be
useful to have a special quality of tough iron wire
made of a very small gauge, so as to be easily portable ; for with this and some rough wooden pegs, an
entanglement can be constructed in twenty minutes,
which will effectually prevent a night surprise, and
prove a great safeguard against a rush and sudden
panic.   It matters little how light the wire is, so
long as there is plenty of it and the entanglement is
wide enough ;[1] for it will be quite sufficient to throw
advancing men out of order, and keep them under
fire.   The gauge of wire used for this purpose in the
Soudan campaign was much too heavy, and consequently a sufficiency of it was rarely obtainable, while
it was stiff and troublesome to work.

[1] Gordon says, " Wire entanglements ought to be twenty yards in
depth."

CHAPTER IV.

OUR FIRST BATTLE.

MARCH 18.—Sir Gerald Graham sent for me this morning, and asked if I would undertake to put 13,000 gallons of water into the field at daybreak on the 20th inst. Said I would. A very busy day in consequence. Heavy dust-storms. As no officers have been appointed to me yet, asked that G. P. might be attached as galloper.

This was my first interview with the General. I entered his tent with the Director of Transport, and found him sitting at a writing - table, with several of the senior officers of his Staff, discussing the proposed advance. Broad-shouldered and tall, above the average height of even tall men, with iron-gray hair and strikingly handsome features, so far as looks went he was the *beau ideal* of a soldier, and wore his loose cotton dress, on the breast of which was the coveted ribbon of the Victoria Cross, with an easy grace which stamped him as a man used to fashionable society, and free from the pipe-clay stiffness of the camp. His voice was good, but his manner of speech slow, and he said very little at a time, while his eyes had a placid expression which reminded one somehow of the calm gaze of an ox—a placidity that never left him, I believe, even in the moment of danger ; indeed, dan-

ger was nothing to him—he enjoyed the whistle of a
bullet as other people like the scent of a flower, and
more than once exposed himself to the chance of
being shot, accompanying convoys, when there seemed
no necessity for the leader of the expedition to go
under fire. He looked you full in the face when
speaking, but his features rarely lit up, and were not
characterized by that bright alertness of expression
which distinguishes Lord Wolseley, neither did he
often offer a suggestion, simply saying, "I want to
do so and so, can it be done?" and apparently
caring little to inquire into detail. He was credited
with being deeply read in military lore, but it was
said that he did not even know all the officers of
the Headquarter Staff by name, and sometimes con-
fused one with the other. I never saw an instance
of this myself, but he certainly consorted little with
any but the officers on his own personal Staff, and
was so profoundly reticent, that the Heads of Departments were sometimes only informed of his
plans at a date when it was very difficult to execute
them properly; and, as orders were frequently changed
at the last moment, a sort of uneasy feeling prevailed
that no definite line of action had been decided on.
This was certainly unjust ; but reticence, though a
valuable quality in a commander, may be carried to
such a point that it will shake the confidence of his
troops. There is no doubt, however, that General
Graham could have been very popular indeed with
the force, had he cared to seek popularity, his fine
soldier-like appearance, and frank gentlemanly bearing, being sufficient alone, to predispose all men
in his favour. But it is a singular fact that tall
generals, as a rule, exert themselves less to win the
affection of their troops than short ones.

March 20.—Hurrah ! hurrah ! the order has

come; to-morrow there will be a general advance, and eyes are sparkling with delight as the news spreads that we are about to fight a battle; for the spies report that Osman Digma assuredly means to try conclusions with us, and new life seems imparted to every man, in glorious anticipation of the result. The fact is, that after eleven days of harassing work and nights of constant alarms, after losing so many of their comrades treacherously murdered, the men are simply mad to be up and doing.

This morning the Cavalry Brigade, G Battery B Brigade Royal Horse Artillery, and the Mounted Infantry, supported by the Indian Contingent, assembled in the front of West Redoubt, a gallant array, and marched out to execute a reconnaissance on Hasheen, a village about seven and a half miles distant, where the enemy are supposed to be in force. Their orders were to reconnoitre as far as the village and examine the wells there, but to avoid an engagement if possible, this being only, in musical parlance, a prelude to the real advance to-morrow.

The Indian Contingent marched about three miles beyond the camp and then halted, while the Cavalry, Mounted Infantry, and Artillery, pushed forward cautiously towards the hills, the Mounted Infantry on their active little horses, scouting on the front and flanks; a very pretty sight, as they boldly felt their way through the bush, and promptly seized on any point of vantage whence they could obtain a view of the country. The enemy's scouts were soon seen in small parties on the crests of the nearest hills, but fell back as the Cavalry advanced, and joined their main body at Hasheen; where considerable masses of them were at first seen, which presently retreated up the valley and disappeared

among the mountains, leaving only small parties of
about ten men each, mounted on camels, visible, who
were evidently acting as vedettes to the force in rear.
From the top of a large isolated hill, called Dihilbat,
in front, a few shots were fired, and a small party
of Hadendowas charged down on a patrol of the
20th Hussars, killing one private and wounding a
sergeant. Lieutenant Birch, of the Mounted Infantry,
having ascended a spur of this hill alone to get a
better view, was also attacked by five or six Arabs
lying in ambush, and had to defend himself as best he
could, which he did with great gallantry, receiving a
spear wound in the shoulder during the encounter ;
these were the only casualties. About 9.40 the
village of Hasheen was reached without further
opposition, and some thirty very rude huts of grass
and matting were found, which appeared to have
been recently cleared out, three Remington rifles
and a few cartridges were discovered, but nothing
else of value. There were only two wells, which
appeared to have been newly sunk, and contained
about seven feet of fairly good water, ten feet
below the surface of the plain.

At 10.15, the purpose of the reconnaissance having been accomplished, the Cavalry and Mounted
Infantry were ordered to retire under cover of the
Horse Artillery, who had been stationed on a low
hill whence they could command the plain, and by
12.30, every soul was back in camp again.

As a memento of the visit, a letter to Osman
Digma was left stuck on a cleft stick near the village
of Hasheen. It was an answer to the letter he had
sent into our camp on the 8th inst., and recapitulated
the history of the late Soudan wars from *our* point
of view, reminding Osman of his previous thrashings
and exhorting him to submit. Just as he had re-

minded us of the defeats of Hicks and Baker, and invited *us* to become Mohammedans. This system of staff letters, or letters fixed on a staff, is now the recognised means of postage in the Soudan, when we want to communicate with our enemies, but whether Osman was much impressed by the little game of brag, I do not know ; and I may mention here, that next day the letter was found trampled in the mud. Osman, they say, made merry at our expense when he heard that the reconnoitring force had retired, and said we were afraid, but he took the precaution to reinforce his garrison at Hasheen, with a thousand men from Tamai, during the night.

Meanwhile there was busy work in camp, preparing the water supply for the advance to-morrow. After receiving a few last instructions at Headquarters, I heliographed to G. P. to join me in the afternoon at No. 5 pier, off which the condensing ships lay, and galloped there as fast as my horse could lay legs to the ground. I could obtain no soldiers for fatigue work, and D—— therefore, kindly trotted off on a little white camel which he always rode, to ask Colonel Chermside, the Governor-General of the Red Sea Littoral, to lend me two companies of Egyptian soldiers, one to work by day and the other by night, drawing the water-tins from the Ordnance stores, filling them and laying them out ; they, however, did not turn up till 2.30, and then worked so badly, that matters had not much advanced by sunset, though G. P., D——, and myself, had toiled like niggers—or I should say white men, for these niggers would not toil at all—trying to instil some energy into the men. It was like making bricks without straw, getting these 13,000 gallons of water, which exclusive of the tins weighed 130,000 pounds, filled and carried to the loading ground, without a proper fatigue party, and it seemed absurd that when the authorities were so anxious about the water, they should refuse us men to do the work with; however, the work *had* to be done, and when it was dark, we signalled H.M.S. *Dolphin* to turn her electric light on the pier, and then set to work again, often moving the tanks and barrels with our own hands, as otherwise the task would never have been completed in time.

At midnight I got G. P. to turn into St. G———'s tent at the Ordnance store, for a couple of hours' rest, and the Director of Transport came down from the Headquarter camp and helped with all his might. At 2 A.M. G. P. relieved me, and I turned in until 4 A.M., when I was out again to see the camels loaded. We had eaten nothing since breakfast the previous day, save a small pot of tinned meat, which we devoured without bread, as they could give us none at the Ordnance store; but we had accomplished our task, and had the satisfaction of knowing that the men would not go waterless on their long march.

March 20.—By the first streak of dawn we were in the saddle, and had the large convoy of 500 camels laden with water fairly under way, marching in a compact column of companies of fifty camels abreast, towards the Western mountains.

It was two miles from the seashore to the point of rendezvous South of West Redoubt, and, by the time we reached it, the troops had already gone forward, and were only visible as a cloud of dust advancing slowly across the plain some miles before us, with the sun playing brightly on the glancing bayonets which flashed through it here and there.

The morning, like most mornings in this sunny region, was lovely; and the fresh breeze blowing

from the North, which had been cooled on the bosom
of the sea, proved most grateful to us after the long
and feverish work of the previous night.   In fact,
our spirits rose refreshed with the rising sun, and we
laughed and chatted gaily together, while our horses
seemed to share in our animation.   Among the dry,
scrubby grass, which grew in tussocks between the
stunted mimosa bushes dotting the plain, numbers
of tiny gray ring-doves with very long tails crept
cooing about, now fluttering up beneath our horses
feet, and again alighting a few yards farther on.
Pretty tame little soft-eyed birds, emblematic of
peace, and strangely at variance with the sanguinary
nature of the errand on which we were bent.   Frequently also, the clear tones of a lark carolling its
morning song in notes little different from those of
his English brother, and full of sweet home memories,
would strike the ear, but, strain our eyes and rick
our necks how we would, the bird itself was always
invisible ; and it was only when one of these little,
tuneful songsters flew up right under my horse's
nose, that I discovered that the larks of the Soudan
sing on the ground, and not soaring into the sky as
ours do.   Perhaps the enervating climate of the
country has made even them lazy, and they prefer
to warble at their ease.

We were now marching due West, across a broad
sandy plain dotted with mimosa trees, without guard
or escort of any kind, except the few men of the
Commissariat and Transport Corps, who accompanied
the camels ; while the white tents of our camp,
which had been left standing under charge of the
Shropshire Regiment and a few details, grew smaller
and smaller in the distance, till it looked little bigger
than a bed of mushrooms.

The whole of the remaining force was in front,

forming three sides of a vast square, with the rear open, and was composed as follows :—The Guards, in column of companies, on the right ; the second Brigade (East Surrey Regiment and Marines) in line of company columns of fours ; the Indian Brigade in column of companies on the left ; the Horse Artillery battery on the right of the line, and the 20th Hussars, 5th Lancers, 9th Bengal Cavalry, and Mounted Infantry scouting in front and on the flanks.

At 7.45, when nearing the lowest spurs of the mountains, the whole force halted for twenty minutes, to allow our convoy to overtake it, and the column of water camels entered the square, and closed up in rear of the front line. This had hardly been done when the first shots were heard (about 8 A.M.), some of the enemies scouts, who could clearly be seen clustered on the rocky crests of the hills in front, having opened fire on our advanced guard, as it approached ; but they soon fell back and retired up the Hasheen Valley to the big conical mountain called Dihilbat, which rose in isolated grandeur from the plain to a height of 828 feet above the sea-level. The crest of this gray rocky mass perfectly swarmed with the dark figures of the Arabs, as did also the summit of a little round hill to the right of it, appropriately named Beehive Hill, from its strange shape, and which screened the village and wells of Hasheen, situated directly in rear of it, from our view.

On the farther side of the plain, beyond these two isolated hills, the mountains of the Waratab range could be seen, a dark, volcanic chain of rugged peaks and spurs trending away N.E. towards Han-doub, and unbrightened by vegetation of any kind, though the nearly level plain below them was covered with a dense bush of thorny mimosa trees, six to eight feet high, the flat, spreading tops of which looked at a little distance like a brown carpet, for as yet they were not in leaf, though some of the prickly boughs were covered with little yellow balls of blossom, which gave forth a faint and not unpleasant fragrance.

At 8.5, the square advanced again, and twenty minutes later we reached some low foot hills, now abandoned by the enemy, between two of which Sir Gerald Graham had decided to form a zareba, which, he says in his despatch of the 14th April, "was required in order to protect my right flank in the impending advance on Tamai, to obtain a post of observation near the mountains, and to assist in overawing the tribes."

At the spot where we were halted, there were two hills of black, shingly rock on our right, one round and conical, 390 feet high, and the other an oblong ridge running N.W., some 200 yards long at the top, and 530 feet above the sea-level at its highest point. Some guns were quickly dragged up to the summits of these two hills, and the 17th and 24th companies of Royal Engineers, assisted by the Madras Sappers, set to work to build round them redoubts of loose stones and sandbags. Across the little valley between the hills, and connecting them together as it were, the East Surrey Regiment began to construct a zareba, or oblong enclosure of felled mimosa bushes, laid side by side with the heads outwards, which was to contain their future camp.

Meanwhile the transport camels were made to kneel down close under the shelter of a spur of the foremost hill, and the men of the Commissariat and Transport Corps were ordered to advance and lie down on the crest of a low shingly ridge of rock some hundred feet above the plain, and situated to the left and a little in advance of the two hills protecting the zareba. Here the General and his Staff took up their position, with a big telescope on a tripod, to watch the impending action.

No better point could have been chosen, for it commanded a magnificent view of the Hasheen valley at our feet, and the Dihilbat and Beehive Hills some 1700 yards directly in front of us, on and around which the enemy were now swarming in considerable force.

Having decided to clear these hills, Sir G. Graham ordered the infantry to advance in the following order:—Second Brigade in first line, Indian Contingent in support, Guards in reserve. The Horse Artillery to take up a position on Beehive Hill. Two or three Aides-de-Camps now detached themselves from the Staff and galloped off with the orders, and steadily, as if on parade, the troops began to advance through the thick mimosa scrub; which soon swallowed them up, though we could still see their bayonets glittering above it as they moved forward. The 20th Hussars and some of the Mounted Infantry, had previously been spread out like a fan in vedettes of two men each, to watch the left of the position where we were standing, for the scrub at this point was not very thick, and two squadrons of the 9th Bengal Cavalry patrolled on the left of the advancing troops, while, I think, two more squadrons of the same regiment and the 5th Lancers, protected their right. The remainder of the Mounted Infantry advanced towards Beehive Hill, the Horse Artillery being with the Guards' square.

The glittering array of these fine troops marching across the sunny plain, presented a very fine spectacle, and I found it somewhat difficult to realize that we were not watching a sham fight, as we stood quietly

resting beside our horses, looking on the busy scene
below, for as yet there had been no casualties, and
there was nothing to indicate that this was war in
grim earnest.

About 9 A.M., the Berkshire Regiment reached
the foot of Dihilbat Hill, which towered above their
heads like the wall of a house, while we could clearly
see the enemy clustering thick on its rocky cone.
But without firing a single shot, the Berkshire lads
began to swarm up the rugged sides of the mountain in attack formation, preserving a line that looked
perfectly wonderful in its unbroken regularity. They
were followed by two half Battalions of the Marines,
a little in rear, as supports.

The Guards Brigade was meanwhile formed in
square on the plain below, the Mounted Infantry
with the Horse Artillery and the Indian Contingent
swinging round to the right under a heavy fire from
the spurs of Dihilbat, to seize Beehive Hill, from
which the enemy slowly retreated before them.

The foremost spur of the Dihilbat mountain was
separated from the cone or summit by a deep ravine,
some half-way up, and it was not till they reached
the edge of this, that the gallant Berkshire paused
for a moment in their swift ascent and opened fire.
The rattle of the rifles now ran along the whole line,
echoing among the neighbouring mountains and
startling the gazelles on the plain, while we could
see the little figures of our comrades firing behind
the shelter of the rocks so clearly through our field-
glasses, that it seemed as if we could touch them.
A special correspondent thus describes the scene :
" After these good soldiers had quickly climbed
and lined the crest, sharp firing immediately commenced, very soon increasing to a rolling fire of
musketry which woke up a furious echo among the

surrounding hills.   Volley succeeded volley on both
sides, and bullets began to fall unpleasantly thick
around us, the sand puffing up in spirts between the
horses' legs."

In olden days, before rifles were invented, the
summit of a hill was no doubt a strong position,
simply because men who attacked with sword and
spear alone, would be more or less blown before they
reached the defenders at the top ; the Romans considered an isolated hill the best site for a camp,
but in the present day, it does not require the sad
experience of Majuba Hill to prove that, unless you
have command of the approaches, it is one of the
weakest positions that can possibly be selected ; for
the fire of the defenders has to diverge and be
scattered over a large radius, while that of the
attacking force is brought to focus on one point.

That the enemy felt the truth of this maxim
after receiving a few of our volleys, was evident from
the restless way they began to run about on the top
of the hill ; however, they were not going to yield
without a struggle, and opened a very brisk return
fire on the Berkshire, both from the top of the cone
and a point a little to the right of it.   The leading
half Battalion of Marines, in rear of the Berkshire,
was, therefore, advanced up the mountain in such a
way as to enfilade their position, seeing which, the
Arabs presently wavered, and then ran.

The Berkshire Regiment was not slow to seize
the advantage thus gained, and, giving a loud cheer,
crossed the ravine and scaled the steep rocky cone
with great spirit, never pausing to take breath, and
keeping their line almost unbroken till they were
close to the top ; when they detached one company
along a spur on the left, from which they were able
to open a heavy fire on the retreating Arabs, who

were now running down the back of the hill as fast
as they could, and moving through the bush South-
ward in the direction of Tamai.

Two squadrons of the 9th Bengal Cavalry who,
as I before mentioned, had kept on the left of the
advancing force, were now despatched to pursue
them, and ordered to dismount and fire volleys.
General Graham gives the following account of this
unlucky order in his despatch of the 21st March :—
"About 9.40 A.M. two squadrons of the 9th Bengal
Cavalry were detached by Colonel Ewart, commanding Cavalry Brigade, to pursue the enemy, who,
driven from the hill Dihilbat by the Berkshire
Regiment, were retiring South in the direction of
Tamai. Colonel Ewart ordered two squadrons to
dismount and fire volleys. These squadrons were
charged by the enemy in considerable strength, and
retired with loss on the square formed by the
Guards at the foot of the Dihilbat Hill." [1]

These unfortunate troopers, dismounted and at a
disadvantage among thick bush, suddenly found
their position reversed from that of pursuers into
pursued, and those who were fortunate enough to
mount their horses in time, simply rode for their
lives. An officer who was with them ran on foot a
great part of the way, having lost his charger, at a
pace he never believed himself capable of, closely
chivied by the Arabs, and was found later sitting
on a stone quite out of breath and in a very
excited condition after his race for life. There was
no possibility of charging in such dense cover, for
the thick thorny tops of the mimosa trees almost
touched each other, and the Arabs slipped snake-like
under the trees, hamstringing the horses as they

[1] On May 10, he requested that his report might be modified to
"Colonel Ewart ordered part of one of these squadrons to dismount
and fire volleys," etc.

passed, and ṣometimes even leaping on them from behind and stabbing the riders in the back.   Half a dozen riderless chargers clattering past the foot of the little hill where we were standing, was the first intimation we got of this accident.

A riderless horse! many artists have painted it, many poets have sung of it, and it is always a profoundly sad sight, even in time of peace.   More especially sad here, for we knew that the poor fellows who so recently filled those empty saddles had received no quarter from their relentless pursuers, and were now lying hacked and mangled where they fell, beyond all hope of succour.   The certainty that no quarter would be given by the enemy, was a very ghastly feature of this war.

The Arabs, however, were destined to meet with retribution; fiercely pursuing the flying Cavalry round the bottom of the Dihilbat Hill, they suddenly came full upon the square of the Guards Brigade drawn up in the plain below it, who had hitherto been standing idly listening to the bullets whistling over their heads, but seeing little of what was going on, owing to the thick nature of the bush.   To do our enemies justice they never hesitated for a moment, but raising a frantic yell flung themselves straight on the square with reckless gallantry, led by a youth on a white " *hygeen,*" or riding camel, who had become quite a celebrity in the camp at Suakin, for at every night attack, this youth on the white camel was always to be seen flitting ghostlike round our lines under the hottest fire, and bearing apparently a charmed life.

Steadily and methodically, as if on parade, the Guards levelled their rifles and poured volley after volley into the dark mass of rushing shouting Arabs, who fell before the fiery blast like corn under the

sickle ; the poor youth and his white camel being
among the first to bite the dust, the latter riddled
with bullets, though the youth himself, I believe, was
taken prisoner only slightly wounded. So effective
was the fire, that I was told none of the enemy
succeeded in getting within fifteen yards of the
square. As they broke away and scattered over
the plain, the 5th Lancers on the right and some of
the Bengal Cavalry, caught a portion of them in
more open ground, and seizing their opportunity,
charged through them twice with great effect.

It was in vain now that the Arabs tried their
usual tactics, of flinging themselves on their faces
and trying to hamstring the horses as they passed,
the long lances found them out relentlessly and
many of them were slain, but Troop Sergeant-Major
Nicholls, of the 5th Lancers, lost his life in one of
these charges. He was a gallant young soldier who
had only obtained his promotion the day before,
and looked little more than a boy, as he lay still in
the awful calmness of death beside his horse near
the hill where we were standing. The sword alone,
was found to be almost useless against Arabs armed
with spear and shield, and one officer who was
wounded, said that when he saw an Arab driving
his spear at him he tried to parry it, but found his
sword quite powerless to turn the fierce thrust of the
weighted spear, which entered his leg, nearly un-
horsing him by catching in the bushes as his charger
carried him away. Another force of the enemy, who
attempted to advance down the Hasheen Valley from
the N.W. threatening our right flank, were also
charged about 10.45 with success by the 5th Lancers
and 9th Bengal Cavalry, who turned back their
advanced parties and checked the movement.

Meanwhile the mounted infantry had succeeded

in driving the enemy from Beehive Hill, and the
Artillery placed their guns in position on a low spur
of it, from which they shelled any parties of the
enemy that they could see; the Indian Contingent
forming three sides of a square in the narrow valley
below, between Beehive Hill and Dihilbat, which was
now fully occupied by the Berkshire Regiment and
Marines.   The General, therefore, at this time, 9.40
A.M., may be said to have achieved his intention of
clearing these hills; but the Arabs were in no way
disheartened, and still hovered about in considerable
force to the rear and left of them, while some distance to the right, two other large parties could be
seen collected under the lower spurs of the Waratab
range, waiting a chance to attack.   One of these,
over a thousand strong, actually managed to slip
round on the right of our position and threaten the
rear; but they were fortunately discovered in time by
the gunners in one of the redoubts above the zareba,
who pounded them with shell, and dispersed them
before they could close upon us.

A rumour presently spread that a large number
of the enemy could be seen rapidly advancing from
the direction of Tamai, on our left, where there was
no adequate protection for the large convoy of transport animals; their only guard being two companies
of the East Surrey Regiment, which were barely sufficient to cover the whole flank when extended to
one pace apart.   It was probably for this reason that
the Indian Contingent was recalled at 12.45, from its
position between the two hills in front of us, and
ordered to form up on the more open ground to the
left of our position.   The Berkshire and Marines
covered this movement, and, descending the Dihilbat
Hill, formed square with the Indian Contingent as it
retired.

This change of position, checked the advance of the enemy from Tamai ; but no sooner did the Berkshire and Marines begin to go down one side of the Dihilbat Hill, than the Arabs, who had remained massed in considerable force under the shelter of its rearmost spurs, climbed up the other and reoccupied the summit, while detached parties of them hovered round our troops in the bush, evidently still full of fight. The Horse Artillery on the lower spur of Beehive Hill, were now taken into the square of the Guards Brigade, which, for some reason that I cannot understand, was still left in its original position among the thick bush after all the other troops had been withdrawn. I was told that some of the Cavalry were also taken with the guns into this square, but I can only give this story on hearsay. It is certain, however, that it was not till 1 P.M. that the Guards got their order to retire, and that after the withdrawal of the Indian Contingent and the Second Brigade, they were exposed to a hot fire from an enemy whom they could not see in the dense bush by which they were surrounded.

Several officers described to me the slow march back of this square, encumbered with guns, ambulance, etc., as a most trying experience. Bullets rained in on it from the bush, and all the troops could do was to halt every now and then and fire volleys blindly into the thick cover, in the hope of silencing their unseen foes. There was no excitement to enliven the men, and had the enemy been better marksmen they would probably have suffered seriously. As it was, they lost two officers killed, and twenty-two men wounded.[1] Poor Captain Dalison was shot through the heart by the first bullet that came into

---

[1] I have included Surgeon-Major Lane with the killed, as his wound was mortal.

the square, and Surgeon-Major Lane, a young army
doctor who had come out with us in the *Arab*, and
won everybody by his quiet gentle manner, was
mortally wounded by a shot that traversed his
lungs and injured the spine.   Poor fellow, he died
a day or two afterwards in the arms of the Chaplain
at Suakin.

It was sad to see an opening career cut short so
soon.   When he rode out to battle that sunny
morning on his spirited chestnut horse, he was full
of youth and health, and all the bright hopes for the
future that youth and health inspire ; yet the sun
had hardly crossed the meridian before all this had
passed away, and he knew that the sands of his short
life were already nearly spent, and that never more
would he mount horse again, or look on the loving
faces of kindred and the green fields of home.   This
sudden change from the fulness of life to the irrevoc-
able stillness of death, from the strong man in the
pride of youth and health, who chats with you so
gaily and confidently in the morning, to the helpless
cripple, for whom health is a thing of the past, and
youth perhaps means only lengthened years of misery,
is a thing which strikes and awes the imagination
more than anything else in war ; yet what grander
or more unselfish end could a man desire than that
of this young surgeon, giving up his life with all its
promise at the call of duty, when bent on the noble
work of succouring the wounded ?

I had never met Captain Dalison of the Scots
Guards, and this, I believe, was his first campaign ;
but when some time afterwards I rode with a former
brother officer of his, to look at the simple cross which
marked his grave in the little Cemetery by the seashore, my friend's voice was low and husky as he
simply said, " So that is all that remains of poor

Dalison !" and he rode for some time in silence with averted head, leaving me to judge how popular he must have been. His, too, was a young life too soon cut short, for he was only thirty-three.

"My mind," wrote one of our most thoughtful women-writers—George Eliot—" is in this anomalous condition, of hating war and loving its discipline, which has been an incalculable contribution to the sentiment of duty." And again, speaking of the men —"the devotion of the common soldier to his leader— the sign for him of hard duty—is the type of all higher devotedness, and is full of promise to other and better generations." Some such feeling of hatred for the horrors of war, and admiration of the qualities it brings out, must have struck every man who has seen a battle or a battlefield.

Let me turn from the sad side of the scene and relate a conversation which was overheard between two Guardsmen after the fight was over. During the retreat of the square, ——, their captain, had been constantly telling them to hold their heads up and not mind the bullets. " I don't think he ought to have spoke to us like that," said one to the other confidentially ; " 'cos why, he was a-ducking of his 'ed hisself all the time he was a-talking." But, trying though the fire was, these fine fellows behaved with the greatest steadiness throughout, and delivered their volleys with the precision of men practising in the barrack-yard.

On the return of the Guards' square, the General and his Staff left the low hill where they had been standing, and the Horse Artillery were planted on it, while the troops concentrated in the immediate neighbourhood of the zareba, which by this time was nearly completed. During the making of it, the East Surrey Regiment had frequently to stand to their

arms, being threatened by parties of the enemy
which succeeded in creeping round their flank, and
on these occasions, the Engineers and Madras Sappers quietly continued the work under cover of the
Linesmen.   They had also by two o'clock constructed
three small redoubts on the top of the long hill at
one end of the zareba, and a fourth on the conical
hill at the other, where a heliograph station was established to keep up communication with Suakin.

The enemy, meanwhile, reoccupied all their old
positions on the Dihilbat Hill, but the rattle of musketry had died down, and only an occasional shot
was heard from the guns mounted in the redoubts,
or the battery of Horse Artillery, whenever a party
of the Arabs showed themselves conspicuously.
There was, in fact, a lull after the storm.

It was now time for me to turn my attention to
the water transport, for the men had come in very
tired and thirsty after their long morning's work
under the hot sun, and were anxious to get their
dinners.   There were also about 6000 gallons of
water, equal to four days' supply, to be stored in the
zareba, for the future use of the East Surrey Regiment, part of which was poured into three large iron
storage tanks brought for the purpose, and the
remainder piled up in the camel tins.   There was
plenty of water ; but by the time everybody had
quenched their thirst, these arrangements been completed, and the empty tins collected and reloaded
on the camels, it was nearly half-past four o'clock,
and the remainder of the force had fallen in for the
march home.   G. P. had been working indefatigably
as my Aide, and we were only able to snatch a very
hasty mouthful ourselves, before we were obliged to
mount and come away.   The force moved off in
three sides of a square as before, the convoy, Field

Hospital, and Ambulance, in which our dead and wounded were carried, being placed in the middle, and the side of the square towards Suakin left open. The East Surrey Regiment, under Colonel Ralston, was left with four days' supplies to hold the zareba and the little redoubts above it, a position which the officers afterwards described as "dull and disgustingly safe."

We had fought our first battle, and according to General Graham's estimate killed at least 250 of the enemy, the strength of the force opposed to us being about 3000, but in such thick bush it was impossible to get an accurate idea of either their full strength or the amount of their losses.

"The conduct of the force was satisfactory in all respects," says the official despatch. "The Dihilbat Hill was carried by the Berkshire Regiment with the greatest spirit, and the behaviour of the Guards' square under a heavy fire from an unseen enemy was marked by extreme steadiness."

Certainly the assault of the Dihilbat Hill was the most picturesque incident of the fight, and the dashing yet orderly way in which the men, after a seven miles' march under a hot sun, scaled its steep and rocky sides in the face of a sharp fire, was the admiration of everybody who saw it.[1] Our own loss during the engagement was sufficiently serious, the number told me on good authority was twenty-two officers and men killed, and forty-three officers and men wounded, total sixty-five ; but it was difficult to obtain an exact account of the numbers, as the full returns were only sent in later by the different Regiments engaged, and the authorities were very reticent about letting them be known in camp.

[1] The 2d Brigade was under Sir J. M'Neill, who brought it out of action with the loss of only two of the Berkshire in assaulting Dihilbat.

It will be a matter of interest to the student of military history to inquire whether this sacrifice of human life was justified by the results obtained. If the object of the advance was simply to establish a defensive post to protect our right flank in the impending advance on Tamai, to secure a point of observation near the mountains, and to assist in overawing the tribes, as stated in the despatch I have before quoted, it would seem that this object might equally well have been obtained by halting the force at the first position we occupied immediately in the neighbourhood of the zareba, and repelling any attack the enemy might attempt to make during its construction ; which would have compelled our adversaries to expose themselves in the more open ground, where our guns and cavalry would have had a chance of inflicting a severe lesson on them.

If, on the other hand, it was thought that the enemy would not venture to attack in the open, and considered advisable to assault him on his own ground, with a view to " establishing a funk," as the Americans say, it appears clear that the troops should have been disposed in such a way that while one Brigade attacked the Dihilbat Hill in front, the other two Brigades should have passed round to the right and left of it and caught the enemy in rear, when he was retreating down the hill ; for it is only when a success is followed up, that the Arab mind accepts the idea of a defeat. It is, moreover, manifestly useless in thick cover to send one square in support of another ; an echelon of squares may answer in fairly open ground where men can see each other, but in the bush they are more likely than not to get in the way of each other's fire, besides which a square, formed four deep, ought to be able to take care of itself as a fighting unit.

By the tactics we adopted, which were the now somewhat obsolete ones followed by the King of France, who—

> " With twice ten thousand men,
> Marched up a hill and then marched down again,"—

the enemy cannot be said to have suffered any serious defeat. It is true they retired before our advance, but then they quietly waited behind the hill until we should leave it, knowing well that our men could not remain there without food or water, and as soon as they were gone, they reoccupied all their previous positions. This enabled Osman Digma to celebrate the battle of Hasheen as a victory, and to say with some show of reason that though we had attacked him, we had been obliged to retire and leave him in possession of the ground he originally occupied.

If he had been forced, if attack he did, to attack *us* at the zareba and been driven off, he could not have said this, and the loss of life entailed by the retreat through thick bush from Dihilbat Hill, would have been avoided.

The position of the zareba itself, though practically impregnable, was not, I think, calculated to produce any great moral effect on the enemy ; for they knew well that it was on a spot where there was no water obtainable, and that it also would soon have to be abandoned ; while it certainly proved of no real assistance to us during the advance on the 22d, when the next battle took place. In fact, the result of our operations at Hasheen, was that the Arabs, far from being discouraged, were rather inspired with fresh confidence, as was proved by the furious way they attacked us at Tofrek, two days later.

I believe that the formation of the zareba near Hasheen, though it may have had some slight

influence in checking night attacks, did no good, as
its evacuation a few days later, gave an appearance
of weakness to our movements, which was not
sufficiently compensated for by any object gained,
and was more likely to encourage the Arabs to
continue their resistance, than to demoralize them.
While I think that the advance on Dihilbat Hill,
could only have been justified from a strategic point
of view, had the force been so disposed as to intercept the retreat of the enemy and inflict a crushing
defeat on him.   Or secondly, had it been made with
the object of holding this hill and establishing a
zareba at its base, which would draw its supply of
water from the wells and impress the enemy with
the idea that we were prepared permanently to
occupy and dominate the Hasheen Valley.   To
achieve this second object, it would have been
necessary to make a clearing through nearly a
mile of bush to enable convoys to pass ; but if the
wells at Hasheen, the water of which is described in
General Graham's despatch of the 21st March, as
" reported to be good " by the reconnoitring force,
were sufficient to supply the requirements of a
Regiment holding the zareba, there is little doubt
that dry provisions to last the garrison a long time
could easily have been stored.   Of course, I am
only expressing my personal views ; but in support
of my opinion that the attack on and retreat from
Dihilbat Hill and the temporary occupation of a spot
like that selected for the zareba, was, to say the least,
impolitic, I may quote Lord Wolseley's own words
used on another occasion, " Every retrograde step
is regarded by uncivilized races as a sign of weakness
and fear."[1]

It may, no doubt, be fairly urged that the forma-

[1] Despatch of 1st March '85.

tion of a zareba near Hasheen, prevented Osman Digma from concentrating his forces there during our advance on Tamai, and threatening our flank and rear ; but the question, then, arises—Would it not have been to our advantage had he tried to do so ? For if we had first formed a zareba on the road to Tamai, and *then* attacked him at Hasheen, we should have commanded his principal line of retreat and perhaps inflicted a wholesome lesson on him. Whereas, by simply driving him from post to post before us, we enabled him to lure us farther and farther into a practically waterless region, and to gain every advantage the sterile nature of the country afforded him for his peculiar kind of warfare. In my next chapter I shall briefly review the whole plan of the campaign as far as I could ascertain it, in order that the future events may be properly understood, and shall leave it to my military readers to decide whether it was a good or a bad one.

The march home was uneventful ; some men fell out from sunstroke, for they had been twelve hours under a broiling sun and were naturally much exhausted. Even my horse, which I had been riding more or less constantly for the last fifteen hours, was so tired that he rolled over on his nose as we reached camp about 6.30, and seemed very loath to get up again ; but there is compensation for all things, and those who sit at home at ease cannot tell what a luxury it is to turn in for the night, after a day like that I have endeavoured to describe.

CHAPTER V.

WE MARCH TO TOFREK.

AT the time the advance on Hasheen took place, the reticence at Headquarters was so great, that a Colonel on the Staff told me he had been unable to discover anybody who understood the general idea of the operations, and that if Sir Gerald Graham had decided on a definite plan of action, he kept it strictly to himself. The special idea of a movement like that on Hasheen, had naturally to be communicated to those engaged; when it took place, but what would follow was involved in a delightful mist of uncertainty, though all sorts of camp "shaves" abounded, and it was a favourite amusement with some officers to begin the day by starting a story, the more improbable the better, with the usual question, "Have you heard so and so?" which gradually grew as it was repeated from mouth to mouth, till by evening it had assumed the proportions of quite a respectable fact, fit to be seriously discussed at Mess. In this way Osman Digma was two or three times killed, sometimes by poison, sometimes by the assassin's knife ; he was about to surrender unconditionally ; he was summoned to a conference with the Mahdi ; the friendly Arabs had agreed to capture him for ten thousand pounds. Our troops were to advance to Sinkat, and there go

into summer quarters ; an expedition was to be sent
to Tokar ; the Italians were going to send troops
from Massowah, to act with us ; an expedition was
to be despatched for the relief of Kassala, after which
the force was to summer at Es Sibil, on the Suakin
Berber road, which was believed to be a sort of
terrestrial paradise in the mountains, etc. etc.

To arrive, therefore, at a proper understanding of
the General's real views and intentions, it is necessary to refer to his own despatch of the 30th May,
in which he says—

"The Secretary of State for War directed me to
organize a Field Force, and to make such transport
arrangements as were possible, so as to secure first
the most pressing object of the campaign, viz. the
destruction of the power of Osman Digma.

"I was directed to arrange next for the military
occupation of the Hadendowa territory lying near
the Suakin Berber route, so as to enable the contractors to proceed with the railway which it was
proposed to construct from Suakin to Berber.   In
the Secretary of State's letter of the 27th February,
1885, my attention was again drawn to the necessity
for rapidly constructing this railway.   The direction
of the works was to be entirely under my orders ;
their details and execution being in the hands of the
contractors.

"It will thus be seen that there were two distinct phases of the campaign contemplated, after
organizing the force and its transport, viz. :—

"(1) The destruction of the power of Osman
Digma, and the clearance of the country for the
construction of the railway.

"(2) The construction of the railway, and the
location of the troops for its protection at points
where the summer heats could be best endured."

It is clear from these remarks, that the General considered the primary object of the campaign to be the destruction of Osman Digma's force of fighting men ; and that to achieve this end it would be necessary to march straight upon him wherever situate, and fight a decisive battle, so as to effectually break up his influence in the country. No doubt this course was almost forced on Sir Gerald Graham, by telegrams from home urging him to make haste and do something brilliant. At the end of February, Lord Wolseley, telegraphing to Lord Hartington, said, " It is important to crush Osman Digma, and restore peace to the country now under his influence, in order to push forward the railway, and by a *brilliant success* near Suakin, to make the Soudanese realize what they must expect when we move forward in the autumn." Not only had Lord Hartington in his instructions said that " the first and most pressing object of the campaign " was the destruction of the power of Osman Digma, but he had directed General Graham to attack all the positions which he occupied, and disperse the troops defending him. In fact, it was clear the Government were anxiously waiting for a " brilliant success near Suakin," which would strengthen their hands in Parliament ; while the newspapers at home did not fail to grumble at every day of delay in the commencement of active operations against the enemy. So the General found himself put under considerable pressure, the natural result of the expedition having been sent out too late in the season, for which *he* was not to blame,—those, who only adopted the Suakin route at the last moment, when forced to it by public opinion, being the really responsible persons. Whether the plan of seeking a brilliant and sanguinary success, instead of steadily pushing forward the railway, was a sound one, I shall presently inquire.

Whatever may be our opinion concerning the delay in re-organizing the camp, it cannot be said that, considering the difficulties of the country, General Graham wasted much time in preparing for an advance, when we remember that he only took eight days after landing at Suakin, to organize his transport, before marching on Hasheen. I have already quoted the reasons he gave for planting a zareba there, and stated my own opinion that the operation was not justified by the results obtained ; and I may further say that the existence of this zareba served to cripple our transport resources, by diverting a portion of the camels, water tins, etc., which were urgently required for the general advance, to its service, so long as it was maintained, besides necessitating the employment of a considerable force on escort duty with the convoys sent there.

However, having secured, what he describes in a telegram to Lord Wolseley, as "a strong position commanding the Hasheen Valley, and protecting my right flank and line of communication in the ensuing operations against Tamai," General Graham decided to march boldly on the latter place, where Osman Digma was reported by the spies, as stated in his despatch of the 16th March, to be established with his main body of seven thousand fighting men. The distance from Suakin, about fifteen miles as the crow flies, was too great for troops to march out and back in one day ; and it was therefore decided to establish two intermediate zarebas along the line of advance, one eight miles from Suakin, and the other four.

Allowing only an interval of one day after the battle of Hasheen, for necessary preparation and rest,

the troops were accordingly pushed forward again
into the enemy's country.   Here, also, the desire to
hurry matters made itself manifest, for it was decided
to send a convoy of about 1500 animals, carrying
a vast quantity of supplies for the advanced zareba,
in company with the troops, who, as they were now
entering a region which had never been properly
reconnoitred, ought, under ordinary circumstances, to
have been as little encumbered with baggage animals
as possible.   It turned out to be a case of more haste
less speed, and, owing to the impossibility of driving
the huge convoy beyond a certain pace, the idea of
two zarebas had finally to be abandoned, and one
only was established, six miles from the Left Water
Fort.

Events happened there, which rendered it impossible for the General to continue his advance on
Tamai, until the 2d April, eleven days later, when
he established a second zareba at Teselah Hill,
about seven miles beyond the first zareba, and the
following morning some of the troops pushed two
miles farther on and burnt the village of New Tamai,
which was found to be abandoned by the enemy ;
only a very small number of Arabs being seen in the
mountains, who retired as we advanced, after exchanging some shots at long range.

It was clear, therefore, that Osman Digma intended to elude our grasp, and that there were but
two courses left for us to pursue.   One was to
follow him up into the mountainous country towards
Tamanieb, on the vague chance of catching him
there,—a difficult operation, as the water supply
at Tamai would have required great development
before it could have been rendered adequate to the
requirements of the transport animals, which would
naturally have required to be watered there, before

advancing farther. And the other was to return, like a man who is going to be hanged, to the place from whence we came. After due consideration, the General decided on the latter course, and, on the 4th April our force returned quietly to Suakin, without achieving that brilliant victory which was so much desired.

The zareba at Hasheen had, meanwhile, been evacuated on the 25th March, another proof of how little value it was to protect our right flank, and as soon as the stores, which had been accumulated in vast quantities at the first zareba on the road to Tamai, could be brought back to Suakin ; that, also, was abandoned. On the 6th April, work on the railway, which had been stopped on the 22d March, was recommenced ; and then, for the first time, General Graham turned his serious attention to pushing it forward. The preliminary work done during the early days of March, had been simply to lay down sidings on Quarantine Island, and get the line across the causeway to the mainland ; two and a half miles being all that had been laid to a point in rear of West Redoubt, when the work was stopped.

Before criticizing the policy of these operations, it is only just to point out that, as, Osman Digma had accepted the hazard of a decisive battle the previous year, General Graham had some grounds for supposing that he might do so again, and, as I have already said, his hands were more or less tied by instructions from home, which he considered rendered it his duty to crush Osman Digma first, and to push on the railway afterwards. At the same time, it should not be forgotten, that they also called his attention more than once " to the necessity of rapidly constructing the railway."

The actual result was that, from the 5th March, when the ships were arriving at Suakin in quick succession, and Brigadier-General Hudson, commanding the Indian Contingent, reached that port with his Staff, to the 6th April, when work was recommenced on the railway, a period extending over a whole month, only two and a half miles of the permanent way were laid, and that within our own lines.

Now, though Osman Digma had accepted a battle the previous year, he was signally defeated on that occasion, and to those who understood the character of the man, it was a subject of great doubt whether he would so commit himself again. In fact, it was well known among the Arabs that he had completely changed his tactics, and the Intelligence Branch was no doubt informed of this fact. General Graham himself, says in his despatch of the 30th May, " I may be permitted to remove a somewhat confusing idea that Osman Digma is a great and warlike leader.   The facts, as ascertained, are that he himself never appears on or near the scene of conflict, but is content to urge on his men from some safe position or inaccessible fastness."

If the General knew this at the commencement of the campaign, it must have been all the more manifest how unlikely it was that any successful result could be achieved by an attempt to follow Osman into his own country, unless it was intended to hold permanently all the wells at Tamai, Tamanieb, Sinkat, etc. ; which was quite impossible, owing to the difficulty of keeping open communication with those places, and the limited number of our force.

To follow foes like the Arabs, who think it small hardship to go twenty-four hours without food or water, through long tracts of waterless bush, with a heavily-equipped English force, was to play into the hands of the enemy and leave too much to chance— the chance that Osman would consent to stand and give battle ; which is just what it was not his interest to do. For, by constantly retreating before us, harassing our camps and transport, and trying to lure us farther into the mountains, he could show his followers our weakest point, viz. :—the difficulty we experienced in moving from our base, while he secured to them ample pickings from the transport animals they were able to cut off, and thus kept alive their lust for fight and plunder.

The writer of a paper in the *United Service Gazette*,[1] who, I have good reason to believe, was well informed, says, alluding to the camp "shaves" I have before mentioned—"There was one rumour which showed remarkable tenacity of life, and at length came to be credited by all, from General to drummer-boy—viz. that Osman had resolved once more to hazard the issue of a battle and to assail the first force which should show itself beyond the entrenchments. This came at last to be believed by all—why, no one could tell. But at Head-quarters there was accumulating a secret store of trustworthy information of the very highest import-ance bearing on this subject. Thus—

"*February* 14.—Spies reported, 'if the English come out, the enemy will not wait as before, but attack them in their zareba.'

"*February* 22.—'The rebels all say they will attack the English in their enclosure.'

"*March* 4.—'If the troops encamp on their way either to Tamai or Handoub, they are to be suddenly attacked during the night.'

[1] 25th July 1885.

" *March* 5.—' If a zareba is formed on the way to either of Osman Digma's positions, he has given orders to have it attacked ; he will not make the mistake which caused his losses last year, of letting the British attack him.'

" *March* 6.—' On the day the English leave Suakin the enemy are to rush the camp suddenly, and are not to allow them to make a zareba.'

" *March* 12.—A woman repeated the above statement.

" *March* 13.—' Osman has given orders that if the army leave Suakin, his people are to attack it before it has time to unload or settle down.' "

Now this information, if carefully considered, does not, I think, justify the idea that Osman intended to hazard the issue of a regular pitched battle. He was not going to allow us to attack him, nor was he going to attack us when we were fully prepared to receive him ; it all points to the fact that he meant to surprise us when we were unprepared, by a sudden charge of some thousands of his fighting men, while we were busy making a zareba ; and, if the rush proved unsuccessful, it was presumable that his men would vanish again into the bush, as they had done at Hasheen, without making any determined stand, and continue their tactics of hovering round us and harassing our movements, while they declined to expose themselves to the chance of total defeat. In short, the information showed that the very greatest precautions should be taken against surprise, but held out little promise that Osman would allow us to force him to a decisive battle.

General Graham seems to have had his doubts on this point, for in his despatch of the 8th April, he says, speaking of the advance on Tamai : " I decided to advance on that place on the 2d inst., and attack Osman Digma in his chosen position, although it had been ascertained that there was some doubt that he would accept a battle, notwithstanding his proclamation and his endeavours to impose upon his followers by asserting the power of his arms."

Indeed, there is little doubt Osman's proclamation advising us not to venture beyond the walls of Suakin, was a mere blind, intended to draw us on in the hope of delaying the construction of the railway, which was the only thing he really had to fear; as, when it reached Tambouk, our advance guard would threaten his line of communications. Every day he could keep us from *that*, and induce us to wander after him through waterless bush, was so much time gained ; for he knew the summer heat would soon render work on the line practically impossible and decimate our troops, unless the railway had been pushed on to a healthy camping ground among the hills.

Under these circumstances, I venture to repeat an opinion which I expressed emphatically at the time, viz. :—that the better course to follow, would have been to confine our operations entirely to pushing forward the railway with inexorable determination and promptitude, leaving Osman to come out and attack us on our own ground, if he dared. The advantages this course offered were :—

(1) That if Osman hesitated to attack, he would lose influence with his followers every day he so hesitated, for they would attribute his inaction to fear, and accuse him of not being able to carry out his proclamation.

(2) That if he did venture to attack, instead of *our* being harassed by difficulties of transport, want

of water, etc., *he* would be subjected to these troubles, and obliged to operate at a considerable distance from his own base and principal source of supply, while our troops, covering the head of the line, would be able to bring up all their stores by rail.

(3) That the country through which the line ran, was practically devoid of thick bush and favourable to cavalry movements, being distinctly unfavourable to Osman's style of warfare ; that a chain of block-houses, mounted with guns every five miles along the line, would place a considerable area of the plain under artillery fire, and ensure prompt warning of the approach of any large force of the enemy ; while an armoured train could be kept always ready on a siding, to take reinforcements to a point that was menaced.

(4) That as soon as the line reached · Tambouk, we should command a road to Sinkat through the mountains, by which we could turn Osman's rear if he ventured to attack us, and cut off his retreat, the only way to inflict a crushing blow on such an enemy ; while the crests of the hills offered many fine positions for small redoubts commanding the line, which would be perfectly able to hold out till assistance reached them, if attacked.

(5) That every ten miles our force advanced from Suakin, it would be entering higher and healthier ground, where the summer heat would be less disastrous to the men's health ; while the Arabs, seeing that we always advanced and never turned back, could not fail to be impressed with a sense of our power, and would begin to believe in our determination to hold the country.

(6) That by always having the railway behind us as we advanced, the necessity for gigantic convoys, the adequate protection of which forms the principal

difficulty of campaigning in this country, would practically be done away with, and a series of small zarebas in the neighbourhood of the block-houses or redoubts, could easily be kept standing, for the reception of any convoys considered necessary to supplement the ordinary service of the line, or for sheltering friendly sections of the tribes when they came over to us.

I have before observed, work was not resumed on the railway till the 6th April—"From which date," says Captain Kunhardt, R.E., "the active rapid plate-laying may be said to have commenced;" and I find by reference to my diary, that on April 30, the line was already within half a mile of Otao. So that had we devoted the month of March to pushing on the railway, instead of wandering after Osman Digma, it is probable the line would have actually reached Otao by April 6, the date when we first began seriously to advance it from Suakin, after losing many valuable lives and a great number of transport animals in our abortive marches through the wilderness.

From Tambouk, the next wells, six miles beyond Otao, a road leads through the hills to Sinkat, only twenty-five miles distant, while there are many routes by which a light camel force stationed at this point might have cut off Osman's supplies. Telegraphing on the 25th April, General Graham says : " Strongly recommend crushing Osman before withdrawal. In a few days shall be in a position to move to Sinkat from Tambouk, with 500 camel corps and 1000 infantry." But it was then too late. Had the railway reached Otao in the first week of April, by the middle of the month it would have been at Tambouk, and reached Es Sibil some time in May, where a small but beautiful valley would have been found 2300 feet above the sea, the fresh herbage and

good water of which would have gone far to make
a healthy and pleasant camping ground for a portion
of the force left at Suakin, rendering it unnecessary
to abandon the line ; while Osman would either
have lost his prestige by failing to attack us before
he seized these points of vantage, or he would have
had to fight us on our own ground, in which case
we should probably have been able to give him
a severe lesson without serious loss to ourselves.

I have given this brief sketch of the policy we
did pursue, and that I think should have been pursued, in order that my readers, when I describe to
them subsequent events, may be able to form an
opinion for themselves.　But to return to my journal.

March 21.—The troops are having a day of rest
after their fight at Hasheen yesterday, but there
is no rest for officers on the water service ; like
Tennyson's *Brook*, it goes on for ever ; and as a
force is to move out to-morrow in the direction of
Tamai, I am ordered to have a convoy ready before
daylight with 11,500 gallons of water.　Captain T——,
who is acting as secretary to the Director of Transport, is very anxious to see a fight, and is to go as
my galloper ; he is senior to me in service, but
will drop his seniority, as he might not otherwise get
the chance of being present at an action ; fortunately
for me, my special duty enables me always to be at
the front.　S——, F——, and M'A—— are to
report themselves with 580 camels at sunset.　Of
course sending out this convoy means another night
of incessant toil.

I may here remark that it should not be supposed that we had no anticipation of being attacked
on the 22d, for not only was the rumour I have
before quoted current in the camp that Osman Digma
would attack us, but we fully counted on his doing

so. Writing home a pencil-note on the evening of
the 21st, while the men were working at the convoy.
I said, "At 2 A.M. we shall have 200 of the Guards
to load the camels and get away by daylight, and
probably engage the enemy during the day. I do
not mind telling you, as you will have heard all
about the fight long before this reaches you." Not
only did Captain T—— ask to accompany me in the
anticipation of seeing a fight, but the Director of
Transport told me when I selected the warrant and
non-commissioned officers who were to accompany
the convoy on this occasion, not to take those who
had wives and families unless they were anxious
for the duty, an unusual thing for him to do, and
which clearly showed he had some misgiving that
the service would be attended with more than
ordinary danger. All who were well-informed
thought that it was probable we should be attacked,
and it was only when the country appeared so un-
expectedly clear of the enemy, that a false sense of
security asserted itself.

After receiving instructions at Headquarters, I rode
to No. 5 pier, which I am beginning to loathe, and
set a fatigue party to work. When they had filled
and carried to the loading ground 449 barrels and
157 camel tins, I found the supply had run short, all
the rest being at Hasheen, so we set to filling a great
pile of mussacks (native goat-skins) which had just
been purchased at £1 each. They turned out to be
unprovided with thongs to secure them when full.
So went off to the Ordnance store with D——, who
in his usual cheery way is lending a helping hand,
to try and get some string.

It was now late at night, and everybody except
the sentries asleep, nor was it an easy operation to
get into the Ordnance camp in the dark ; for, since

their recent night attack, they had taken to balancing iron buckets on the wheels of the Maltese carts that enclosed it; and if any one attempted to move one of these carts to get inside the laager, the chances were he would bring half a dozen pails clattering about his ears, and a volley of bullets whizzing from the guard tent. There was a small hole, however, left in a wall of biscuit boxes, about the size of the trap the harlequin jumps through in a pantomime scene; and having groped my way to this, I achieved the undignified feat of diving through it head foremost, sword, spurs, and all. Landing on all fours at the other side in front of a sentry, who, until he could get a clear view of me, kept his bayonet uncompromisingly levelled at my stomach, I proceeded in search of St. G——, and woke him out of a sweet slumber. He, in turn, woke up a hard-sleeping, hard-snoring sergeant; and at last I got half a hank of stout twine, all that could be found, and returned in triumph to D——, with whom, as there was no one else to do it, I sat on a stone, under the pale electric light from the *Dolphin*, and performed the unsavoury task of attaching strings to some nine hundred as greasy and dusty goat-skins as the bazaars of Suakin could produce. As fast as we could prepare them, they were filled by the working party, the distended skins looking very like headless bodies when they were carried to the loading ground. At 1 A.M. the last mussack had been filled, and, after seeing that the picket and sentries were properly posted near the camels, I turned into St. G——'s tent for an hour of much needed sleep.

March 22, *Sunday.*—Up again at 2 A.M., and commenced loading the camels by electric light; the Guards' party did not appear, so set the native drivers to do the work. Shortly before sunrise, when the

task was nearly completed, we discovered the missing
fatigue party quietly bivouacking on the pier; it seems
they had passed the loading ground in the dark
without seeing us, but they made no sign when the
electric light was turned on, and Colonel ———, who
had come down with T———, to see us off, rather
jumped down the throat of the young officer in
charge, without taking the trouble to remove his
spurs, as they say.

We were under way before daybreak, and had
some difficulty in piloting the vast column of shadowy
camels across the rough and broken ground ; for the
moon was only just reaching her first quarter, and
everything looked weird and indistinct in the dark
hour before dawn, while a heavy white mist lay along
the seashore, clinging about us like a winding sheet,
and drenching our thin khakee jackets with. its
clammy moisture.

The rough sandy plain, covered with tussocks of
coarse grass, was intersected down here near the sea
by numberless channels, and dry holes full of gleaming crystallized salt, among which our horses alter-
nately shied and stumbled ; while there was a perfect
labyrinth of trenches, loose rails, and sleepers, the
unfinished work of the railway, which it took some
trouble to get the great mass of camels safely over.
At last a faint tinge of yellow showed itself above
the long gray line of the sea, which had hitherto been
merged in the sky, and the heavy bank of mist hanging over the plain began slowly to lift, and disclose
the dark outline of the town to our left, and the
orderly rows of tents on our right, with the dusky
form of a sentry pacing up and down on his post,
and the curling white smoke of the camp-fires, which
had been lighted to boil the men's coffee ; while here
and there, a pariah dog, or a jackal, stealing away

from his nocturnal rambles through the camp, might also be seen.

Passing the old Arab burying-ground, we entered the great khor or gully, behind the Water Forts where the principal wells are situate, and keeping to the left, formed up in close column on the broad gravelly plain beyond, with the Water Forts behind us and the head of our column turned towards Tamai, between which and the forts, lay an unbroken expanse of level bush-covered country, bounded in the distance by a great semicircle of low mountains, trending gradually down to the sea-coast on the East.

The troops had not yet arrived, and for a few moments we sat on our horses idly gazing at the always beautiful spectacle of the shadows of night flying before the awakening touch of the sun. But we had not long to wait ; a squadron of Lancers soon appeared, followed by the serried columns of the Infantry, marching with steady tramp across the sand. The Indian Contingent formed a hollow square into which we entered, and we were soon joined by another large column of camels carrying commissariat stores, carts with iron storage tanks, pack mules with ammunition, the Field Hospital's Ambulances, etc.; until the square was so full that it could contain no more. The whole convoy on this occasion was composed of about 1500 baggage animals, divided as follows:—580 camels with 11,500 gallons of water, 500 camels carrying supplies, and over 400 pack mules, draft horses, baggage camels, etc., of which no exact record exists. It will be easily understood that the 1080 camels forming the two first-mentioned convoys alone, formed a gigantic and unwieldy column, requiring a small army of native drivers to accompany them, while the pack mules displayed all that aptitude for kicking, biting, plunging, and creating confusion, which distinguishes those amiable animals when crowded or hustled in any way. However, so promptly was every order carried out, that by 6 A.M., before the sun had fairly risen, the whole mass of men and beasts were in motion and on their way towards Tamai.

The force advanced in echelon of Brigade squares, and was composed as follows :—One squadron 5th Lancers scouting in front ; the Naval Brigade, about thirty strong, with four Gardner guns ; a detachment of Royal Engineers, with Field Telegraph and party; one Battalion of the Berkshire Regiment, and one Battalion of the Royal Marine Light Infantry, in the leading square, with some spare ammunition and water carts in the centre. A company of the Madras Sappers, the 15th Sikhs, 28th Bombay Native Infantry, and the 17th Bengal Native Infantry, with the whole of the Transport, in the second square, which followed in the right rear of the first ; and one squadron of the 20th Hussars patrolling in rear, between the force and Suakin, to keep open the line of communication. This little army was under the command of Sir John M'Neill, assisted by General Hudson, commanding the Indian Contingent; and Sir Gerald Graham accompanied us for about two and a half miles of the way, when he left and returned to Suakin.

As we advanced, the telegraph waggon uncoiled its field wire, keeping us in direct communication with Headquarters, a communication which remained unbroken till 6.30 P.M. In his despatch of the 28th March, Sir Gerald Graham describes the object of the expedition in the following words : " My intention was to form a zareba about eight miles from Suakin, to act as an intermediate depôt for supplies and

water required for an advance in force on Tamai. I
further intended that the Indian Brigade on returning should leave one Battalion in an intermediate
zareba, about four miles from camp."

The direction of the march was a straight line,
nearly due S.W. to Tamai, and the force was under
the guidance of an officer of Engineers, who had
a year's experience of the country. I have been
informed that Sir John M'Neill did not choose his
direction, but marched to order. It was soon
apparent that something had displeased him, for I
could hear him expressing his disapprobation of the
arrangements pretty strongly, whenever I happened to
ride near him; and I afterwards learned that he had
no previous idea of the great size of the convoy he
was expected to take out, and that he considered
the small force of Cavalry at his disposal, a single
squadron in front, quite insufficient.

We had not proceeded far, before we plunged into
thick bush, the thorny mimosa trees, six to eight
feet high, often growing so close together that it was
difficult for even a single horseman to force his way
between their widespreading heads, while great
tangled masses of wild capers, and a sort of cactus-
like plant, all thorns and prickles, often blocked up
the way; making it very difficult for the front of the
square to keep its formation. The camels naturally
refused to face the thorn bushes and swerved aside
from them, but, so closely were they packed in the
square, that there was hardly room for them to
move, and the consequence was that they jostled
against each other; striking their loads together and
displacing them, or sometimes knocking them altogether off, in their attempts to rush through the
more open spaces between the trees.

To pack camels closely together in a small square,

where their loads cannot help coming in collision, to try to force them through thorn bushes, or to make them travel beyond a certain pace,—even to march them continuously under a hot sun,—is to ensure their breaking down ; and once a camel determines to strike work it is hopeless to urge it on; it prefers to die, and *does*, in the most unaccountable manner.   In the wide expanse of the Eastern desert, where the caravan may stretch for a mile or more in length, with plenty of room for each beast, as it plods steadily in single file across the plain, in the cool of the morning, or under the starlit sky at night, halting and resting each day till the heat is past, the camel is unsurpassed as a beast of burden, and, if not too heavily laden, I have known it accomplish marvellous feats of endurance.   Doctor Williams, in his *Life in the Soudan,* says : " Instead of employing blows or ill-treatment to increase their speed, the camel-drivers sing cheerful songs, and thus urge their animals to their best efforts."   In fact, the camel is a thorough Oriental in its dislike to anything like hurry ; packed tight in a British square, jostled and harassed, it is thoroughly out of place ; and, notwithstanding its vicious propensities, for this kind of work, the tough, wiry, ill-tempered little mule would prove the more valuable transport animal of the two.

The difficulty of sending so large a transport through such thick bush, without first clearing a road for it to traverse, soon became apparent, and the more heavily-laden supply camels were quickly involved in difficulties, losing their loads, breaking down, and straggling out of the rear of the square, so that constant halts had to be made to get them in again.   The water camels did not give quite so much trouble, first, because I had secured for them

a position at the head of the convoy, immediately
behind the leading face of the square, where they
could not be disarranged by any block in front, and
secondly, because they were lightly laden with only
two vessels each, and thirty of them were in reserve
to pick up fallen loads ; indeed, I am not aware that
we lost a single water barrel during the advance,
but the confusion at the rear of the convoy was considerable, and the Staff soon got very red in the face
in their efforts to hurry on camels, to which they
sang anything but cheerful songs, and which broke
down all the faster the more they were driven ; while
from the centre of the square rose a solid column of
dust nearly fifty feet high, as the mass of hot and
panting beasts swayed and surged, struggling through
the prickly bush as best they could, and kicking up
clouds of the loose shifting sand till our faces were
as brown as our khakee jackets.

Riding in my place behind the leading face of the
square, the view in front was bright and peaceful. The
wide plain, covered with mimosa trees, just low
enough for a horseman to see over their flat-spread-
ing tops, but so thick that he could not see under
or through them, appeared to quiver in the heated
atmosphere, the sun having now begun to assert its
power and treat us to what an eye-witness of the
subsequent fight has described as " a broiling red-hot
day." Far away in my West-country home the white
snow-flakes were beating in the faces of the good
people going to church ; but here in Africa the
deceptive glamour of the Mirage was visible over
the more distant landscape, and the trees seemed
floating above the plain with their inverted forms
reflected in broad sheets and streams of water.
Before us the mountains could be seen so distinctly
through the clear atmosphere that you might count

every rift and cranny on their rugged sides ten miles
away ; overhead was the blue unclouded sky, with
the fierce rays of the tropical sun burning almost
vertically on our helmets, and casting but a small
circle of shadow around us, while some seven miles
to the left the long burnished expanse of sea slept
tranquilly in the sultry heat, with our empty transports lying at the southern anchorage, about twenty
miles from Suakin, to which Osman Digma often
pointed as a certain sign that we meant speedily to
leave the country.   There is always much that is
exhilarating in the pomp and circumstance of war,
especially when there is the glorious chance of being
soon engaged in battle, and I felt little or no fatigue,
notwithstanding the almost continuous work of the
last forty-eight hours.   I had noticed at starting the
neat and alert look of the Naval Brigade with
the Gardner guns, and especially of poor Seymour,
so soon to meet his end, and I saw a bright smile
and a happy laugh on the faces of several who were
never to behold the sun set ; but we saw nothing of
the enemy.

Twice or thrice we heard the boom of the guns
above the zareba at Hasheen, and the *Dolphin* also
appeared to fire a shell or two.   I cannot exactly
say how many shots were heard, but there was
nothing approaching heavy firing, to indicate that
any large bodies of the Arabs were visible ; and,
as it was a matter of almost daily occurrence to
hear a few shells fired at stray groups of Osman
Digma's camel-men, whenever they appeared on the
plain, and the telegraph wire from Headquarters
brought us no news, these few shots gave us little
cause for anxiety.

It is true, that shortly after we had plunged into
the bush, the Cavalry scouts in front reported small

parties of the enemy as being seen retreating in the
direction of Tamai, but these were invisible to us in
the second square. Sir J. M'Neill, however, immediately sent an officer back to ask General Hudson
if he thought himself able to protect the transport;
and the reply was that he would do his best, but that
the convoy was unmanageable, the animals casting
their loads, the bush becoming closer and the squares
unable to see each other, though they were so near
together that they would be in danger from each
other's fire.

"In short," says the writer of the letter in the
United Service Gazette, before quoted, "the struggle
of the mere advance was so arduous and continuous
that General M'Neill became seriously apprehensive
lest, if attacked while moving, the greater part of
the Transport would be sacrificed; at 10 o'clock,
therefore, when summoned to the Indian square by
General Hudson, he was not unprepared to learn
from the latter that farther progress was impracticable. The state of matters was at that time deplorable, for, notwithstanding the utmost exertions
of the Indians, and the fact that already many men
had been detailed to act as drivers, the rear face of
the square was obliterated by the straggling multi-
tude; camels and loads were down in all directions,
and despair of retaining their formation was seizing
on all ranks."

General Hudson was in fact getting so disgusted
with the slow progress he was making, scarcely a
mile and a half an hour, and the failure of his
attempts at amateur camel-driving, which only made
confusion worse confounded, as the poor beasts broke
down more hopelessly the more they were hurried
by inexperienced hands, that he was for giving up
the attempt to proceed farther. General M'Neill,

however, wished still to advance a little longer, though he recognized the impracticability of carrying out the original design, and saw that, if we tried to penetrate eight miles into the bush, the Indian Contingent would only get home long after dark, a very dangerous proceeding with so large a convoy ; while in any case it would be out of their power to build a second zareba four miles from Suakin, on their return march.   Sir Gerald Graham, thus describes our position in his despatch : " Sir J. M'Neill's convoy, on its march through the dense scrub which lies between Suakin and the hills, experienced much difficulty.   The great mass of camels enclosed in the Indian Brigade square was continually getting into disorder, owing to the high prickly bushes through which it was obliged to force its way.

" Thus frequent halts were necessary in order to get the camels back into position, and restore the chain of defence with which it is necessary in such a country to surround the transport animals and non-combatants.

" It was soon apparent that the original plan could not be carried out in its entirety ; since, if the force advanced eight miles, there would not remain sufficient daylight to allow a zareba to be formed, and then for the Indian Brigade to return and form an intermediate zareba."

Sir J. M'Neill, therefore, considered that his best course would be to split the difference, and establish *one* zareba only, six miles from Suakin, which would still answer the practical purpose of an intermediate depôt between that place and Tamai.   Accordingly he desired General Hudson to continue the advance a little longer, and told the guiding officer, that he would carry on for half an hour, and after that halt

on the first ground he considered suitable.   To
which he replied, he would put him near thick bush
so as to get the zareba easily.

At 10.30, we emerged on a fairly open piece of
ground, which has been aptly described as "a horse-
shoe shaped clearing, of which the part corresponding
to the toe pointed to Tamai." I have been unable
to ascertain the exact width of this clearing, but
from the plan attached to Sir Gerald Graham's
despatch, it appears to have been from 300 to
400 yards across ; the bush, however, I believe, approached the site of the zareba much nearer on the
North and West sides than indicated on the plan.
The soil was gravel and sand, and there were thorn
bushes scattered over it, most of which were soon
cut down, while all around was a ring of thick bush
and scrub, sufficiently high to hide a horseman from
sight at a little distance.

The leading Brigade of Europeans, which first
arrived on the ground, and from which parties were
at once told off to begin cutting bush, was halted in
square, with the guns in the centre, at the end of the
clearing nearest Suakin, and a little to the left, they
being intended to form the reserve post or "citadel,"
as the General termed it.   The Indian Brigade,
which next marched on to the ground, advanced
farther forward and formed, roughly speaking, in
three sides of a large square, with the transport in
the centre, and the European square in rear of the
East, or open side.

General Graham thus describes the position,
"The force was formed up as follows :—The Indian
Brigade took up three sides of a square fronting
nearly E., S., and W.; the transport animals were in
the centre.   The Berkshire Regiment, Marines, and
the Royal Engineers and Madras Sappers, began at

once to cut brushwood." But in the plan accompanying the despatch, showing the position of the troops at 2.30 P.M., the three sides of the Indian square are represented as facing nearly N., S., and W., and I think that was the position they originally took up, and that the statement that one side faced E. is a misprint in the Parliamentary report. Meanwhile the Cavalry in front were halted, and formed an arc round the site of the zareba, about 800 yards from it. But one squadron, "and that a weak one," as General M'Neill remarked, was a mere handful in such widespreading bush, and totally inadequate to watch the country. Indeed, so much were they lost to view in the bush, that many officers present honestly believed that there were no vedettes more than 50 yards from the zareba, because they could not see them, which led to a false impression getting abroad ; but I have since, by careful inquiry, ascertained beyond a doubt that the vedettes were there, though, from the smallness of their number, they proved practically useless to give due notice of the enemy's approach. Besides the Cavalry vedettes, outposts, consisting of groups of four men each, were placed at 80 to 150 yards beyond the three sides of the Indian square. The Indians stood " easy," with bayonets fixed, the Europeans piled their arms, and those who were not working lay down beside them, being much exhausted by the heat, for so tedious had our progress through the bush been, that it had taken us four and a half hours to march only six miles. In all cases the cartridges were loose in the ball bags, and it is asserted, on good authority, that more than two-thirds of the whole force remained by their arms.

The barren clearing, which that morning had only been tenanted by a few desert larks and sand

grouse, and which that evening was destined to be a
human shambles, where the carrion crow and vulture
would revel in their ghastly meal, soon presented a
scene of busy animation.   Fatigue parties were out
in all directions cutting down bush to fence the
zareba, which the Engineers were engaged marking
out with their pegs and tape.   It was to consist of
three diamond-shaped enclosures, or zarebas, placed
corner to corner ; the farthest corner being in the
direction of Tamai, and the nearest in that of
Suakin.   At each of these two salients, a round
sand-bag redoubt was to be constructed with ditch
and parapet, about twelve feet in diameter, and
capable of holding two Gardner guns.   The zareba
was to be the usual hedge some four feet high,
composed of mimosa trees, with a two-foot ditch
behind.   Each side of the zareba nearest Suakin,
measured 75 yards, and it was intended to contain
the Royal Marines, with half the Naval Brigade and
two Gardner guns in the redoubt.   The next, or
central zareba, joining it at the S.W. angle, was
calculated to hold 2000 camels, and measured 120
yards square ; while the third, or farthest zareba,
the angle of which pointed to Tamai, measured only
65 yards, and was intended to hold the Berkshire
Regiment, with the two remaining Gardner guns and
the other half of the Naval Brigade.

It will thus be seen, that, when the Indians
returned, the design was to garrison the two end
zarebas only : which, from their position, would be
able to sweep with their fire all the sides of the
central zareba, intended for stores and camels.

CHAPTER VI.

THE FIGHT.

WE had hardly arrived on the ground before Sir J. M'Neill called me, and pointed out the spot in the central zareba where he wished the water stored, and asked me to superintend the placing and filling of some large iron tanks, which had been brought out on carts with considerable difficulty, owing to their great weight. He gave me a party of the Madras Sappers, under a European officer (I think it was poor Newman, afterwards killed), to do the work, and the placing of these tanks, and filling them from the nine hundred mussacks, naturally occupied a considerable time. At first I made the camels, when unladen, kneel· down on the farther side of the tanks, but still inside the proposed enclosure ; I, however, received an order to have them taken outside, and formed up in column facing Suakin, on an open piece of ground East of the central zareba, as the Engineers required the space inside kept as clear as possible for their work. The camels, therefore, filed out as soon as they had discharged their loads, and were made to kneel down in a massive column beyond the zareba, with their heads turned towards Suakin. They then had the European square in front, the lines of the zareba, protected by the 15th Sikhs and 28th Bombay N. I. on their left, and six companies of the 17th N. I. nearly in rear of them, while on their right or East side, was a belt of bush stretching away towards the seashore, about seven miles distant.

The first step Sir J. M'Neill naturally took on reaching the halting ground, was to telegraph to Headquarters by the field wire, stating his inability to complete his orders, and his intention to build the zareba where he then was. The answer was of a kind that caused no anxiety—" Go on if you can ; if not, zareba ;" and here may be mentioned a curious point in the history of this expedition. I have in the previous chapter quoted the information it is alleged was in the possession of the Intelligence Branch on the 13th March, and which clearly pointed to the fact, that on the first opportunity the enemy intended to surprise and rush our troops before they had time to form a zareba ; yet the well-informed writer who publishes that information, tells us that Sir J. M'Neill, " started on his dangerous mission with no other indication of the enemy's designs than the vague rumour above referred to,[1] and a cheery ' Look out for attack,' from the Chief of the Staff ; no other warning than that conveyed to him by his own soldierly instinct."

Now it is clear that the mere fact of a General being in an enemy's country, is in itself a warning to him to look out for attack ; at the same time any information, however slight, which can help him to gain an insight into the designs or position of the enemy, may be of vital importance in guiding his actions, and should undoubtedly be communicated to him. The writer referred to, however, goes on to say, " On the morning of the 22d, about half an

---

[1] Viz. " that Osman had resolved, once more, to hazard the issue of a battle."

hour after the force had entered the bush, it was
reported to the interpreter of the Intelligence
Department by a spy, that an attack by 5000 Arabs
was actually about to take place. Yet no whisper
of this vital news reached the Brigadier." I should
not have quoted the author of this letter at such
length, were it not that Sir J. M'Neill himself told
me that the incidents mentioned by him were strictly
correct, and that Mr. Brewster told him of the report
referred to in the presence of three other officers
of high rank. I am bound to say, however, that I
have ascertained on excellent authority, that the only
telegram that reached the Intelligence Department,
was one sent at 8.10 A.M., on the morning of the
22d March, to say that, according to the report of
a spy, 8000 Arabs were at Deberet, about one and
a half miles from the Surrey Regiment at Hasheen.

It seems to me of little moment at what hour the
telegram was despatched, or whether this telegram
was the correct version of the news alluded to by
the writer in the *United Service Gazette*, so long as
the fact remains that information of a large concentration of the enemy on our flank was received
before we halted, and never found its way to the
General in command. Deberet is about equidistant
with Tamai from Tofrek, and was much nearer to
the zareba at Hasheen than us, but it was on our
right flank, and if, as Sir Gerald Graham said in his
despatch, the object of the Hasheen zareba was " to
protect our right flank in the impending advance on
Tamai, to obtain a post of observation near the
mountains, and to assist in overawing the tribes,"
it is clear that we had little reason to expect danger
from this quarter, or at least, we might have expected
warning of it. When General Graham rode out
with a convoy to Tofrek on the 26th, the news that

Bendigo had won the Lincolnshire handicap was heliographed to the zareba, while the convoy was engaged with the enemy. But on the 22d, the purely strategical intelligence that a strong concentration of the enemy had taken place on our flank, was apparently not considered of any interest to us. Now, it did not require a very astute military mind to perceive that this concentration probably had an object. The secret intelligence, before quoted, showed that Osman did not intend to attack an already formed zareba, and its object must, therefore, have been either to attack us, or if not, to hold the troops at Hasheen in check while some other force did so. In view of this concentration, then, to continue pushing forward a force through thick bush hampered with a large and unmanageable convoy was a bold venture, while to urge it to " go on if you can," without a word of warning as to the position and probable intentions of the enemy, was like saying to the General, there is no information at Headquarters that need cause you special anxiety.

At 1 A.M. an officer of the 20th Hussars, Major Graves, arrived from Suakin, with orders " to communicate and return," but he also appears to have been entrusted with no message of warning ; had he been so, there would yet, perhaps, have been time to order up the squadron of Hussars from the rear, and push forward the Cavalry to feel for the foe, while the working parties could have been drawn in and the force disposed to resist attack. When afterwards I was lying ill on the *Ganges*, I heard it said, though I cannot vouch for its correctness, as at the time I was too ill to inquire into the matter, that at the very moment a message reached the vessel to say we had commenced building the zareba, with no enemy in view, the sailors at the masthead could see the whole plain around us swarming with camel-men. From the redoubts above the Hasheen zareba, I should think also, the approaching mass of Arabs might have been visible, and if so, a message helio-graphed to Suakin and telegraphed to us by the field wire, would have warned us of what we could not see down in the plain ; while heavy firing from their guns would have let us know that something was wrong, but no such message or warning arrived.

Already clouds of dusky spearmen were creeping up like snakes, and the plaintive cry of the desert lark, their signal note, could be heard rising from the bush all round, so admirably imitated that it was impossible to distinguish it from the tones of the real bird ; but we laughed and jested, as men will on the eve of a cataclysm, unconscious of the im-pending danger.   We had expected, in a general sort of way, that we should be attacked on our march out, but we had met with no opposition for over four hours, and had remained for as long again in peaceful possession of our clearing, without a vestige of the enemy being seen beyond the small parties I have before referred to ; it is not to be wondered at, therefore, if few of us on that hot Sunday afternoon had any thought of immediate peril.

Meanwhile, the work had been progressing steadily. The zareba nearest Suakin being nearly completed, half the Naval Brigade with two Gardner guns and the Marines, were ordered inside it ; and the latter began at once to dig their two-foot trench.   The farthest zareba towards Tamai, was also in a fair state of progress, and, after inspecting it, Sir J. M'Neill ordered half the Battalion of the Berkshire Regiment into it, who, piling their arms, sent out fatigue parties to cut bush to complete the hedge, while the other half

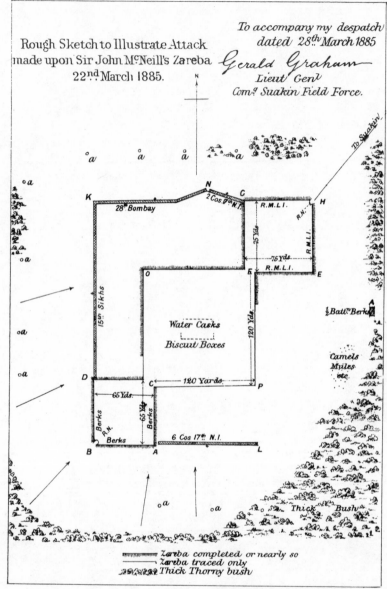

Rough Sketch to Illustrate Attack made upon Sir John McNeill's Zareba 22nd March 1885.

To accompany my despatch dated 28th March 1885

Gerald Graham
Lieut Genl
Comg Suakin Field Force.

To Suakin

28th Bombay

2 Cos 9th N.I.

R.M.L.I.   R.N.

R.M.L.I.

35 Yds.

75 Yds.   R.M.L.I.

15th Sikhs

Water Casks
Biscuit Boxes

120 Yds.

½ Battn Berks

Camels
Mules
etc.

65 Yds.

65 Yds.   Berks

Berks   R.N.

Berks

120 Yards

6 Cos 17th N.I.

Thick Bush

Zareba completed or nearly so
Zareba traced only
Thick Thorny bush

Vincent Brooks Day & Son lith.

of the Naval Brigade, under Lieutenant Seymour, set
to work to plant the two remaining Gardner guns
in the redoubt. The field telegraph waggon was
also removed into the Marines' zareba, and the
European square outside, was, therefore, reduced to
half a Battalion of the Berkshire Regiment, which
the General allowed to be served with food and
water, as the officer in command reported his men
to be much exhausted with their long and hot day's
work, for it must be remembered that they had been
nearly ten hours without food, the breakfast having
been served at 4 A.M. The hedge of the central
zareba was rather more than half completed, and, at
this time, most of the camels had been unloaded and
the water tanks filled, the empty mussacks and tins
reloaded ready for the return to Suakin, and the men
of the different regiments served with a ration of
water, etc. General Graham describes the disposition
of the force at 2.30 P.M. to have been as follows (see
plan) :—

" Half the Berkshire Regiment were S. of the
zareba ABCD, cutting brushwood ; their arms were
piled inside. The line AL was held by six
companies 17th N. I., their left being somewhat
en l'air; the line DK by the 15th Sikhs;
KN by the 28th Bombay N. I. ; NG by two
companies of the 17th N. I. Outposts aa . . .,
consisting of groups of four men each, were thrown
out from 80 to 120 yards to the front of the three
Indian Regiments. These three Regiments themselves were formed in two deep line. The other half
Battalion of the Berkshire Regiment were having
their dinners at about the point R, 250 yards to
the E. of the zareba. The Marines were inside the
North zareba EFGH, having just finished cutting
brushwood. The camels had been unloaded in the

central zareba and had begun to file out, in order to
be formed up outside, ready for the return march.
The squadron 5th Lancers formed a chain of Cossack
posts (each four men), at a distance of about 1000
yards from the force, the rest of the squadron being
held in support on some open ground about 500
yards to the S.W. of the zareba. A squadron of the
20th Hussars was patrolling the ground between
the zareba and Suakin."

About 2 o'clock, feeling a healthy hunger growing upon me, after twelve hours in the saddle—for I
had first mounted my horse at 2 A.M.—I called ———,
who had had his lunch, and asked him to take my
place for a short time, while I got something to eat ;
and then repaired to the shade of a friendly thorn
bush, beneath which some brother officers were drinking cocoa and discussing a potted tongue.

After rapidly swallowing a portion of these
luxuries, with a relish that would have made a
dyspeptic alderman's mouth water, I felt like a
giant refreshed, and returned to the tanks, where I
found ———, looking very hot, with his face all blistered
by the sun, and the bridge of his nose glowing like
a mountain peak at sunset. Indeed, it was like
being under a burning glass to stand in the open at
this hour, and the parched sand reflected up the
heat from below like firebrick. ——— reported all the
arrangements inside the zareba now completed, and
we rode out together to look at the camels beyond,
which struck me as being rather too scattered. This
was about 2.30 P.M., and a Staff officer, who was
passing, told me that the Indian Brigade would
march off at three o'clock, and that I had better get
my convoy formed up in rear of the Marines' zareba,
ready for the homeward journey. I therefore requested ———, and the other two officers in charge of

the camels, to get their beasts closed up in column
and move them to the place indicated, and, while
this order was being carried out, sat on my horse
watching the busy scene.

Nothing could have been more peaceful and
smiling. The sun shone brightly on the tranquil
sea, which looked like a great mirror in the East;
the nearly level expanse of bush all round, appeared
perfectly deserted and silent, save for the low plaintive note of the lark, which every now and then
came trilling softly through the balmy air. The
long chain of purple mountains slept in the distance,
with that look of calm repose so characteristic of
mountains, beneath the slopes of which countless
generations live and die while they remain immovable, unchanged, and which so impressed the ancient
Egyptians, that they vainly strove to imitate it in
their vast pyramids. In this clear atmosphere, even
a small body of men moving quickly, sends up a
column of fine dry dust that can be seen for many
miles, like a pillar of smoke floating above the trees,
and it seemed quite impossible that any large number
of human beings could be drawing near us without
betraying their approach. Our force was accompanied by two mounted "friendlies," sent to scout
for us, Mohammed Osherik, and Nuffer Mahmud,
both Fadlabs, but, supposing these men were faithful, even their trained senses gave no warning of
the coming danger. I was told that when they
came galloping back into the zareba at the first
alarm, an officer of the Berkshire Regiment, emptied
two chambers of his revolver at one of them, mistaking him for an enemy. And, as a friend of mine
afterwards remarked, his misses at the poor Fadlab
may be taken as one of the advantages of the
inattention to revolver practice in our army. These

Fadlabs were merry fellows, always grinning as if they saw something very funny in our elephantine attempts to reach Osman Digma, and they were exceedingly fond of tobacco, which some of the officers gave them, but they gave us no warning when most we needed it.

Already the last sands of not a few gallant lives were nearly sped, the sword of the destroying Angel hung poised over many an unconscious head.   At home in England, allowing for the difference of time, in peaceful church and stately minster, the voices of our kindred and countrymen were raised in prayer, saying : " O Almighty Lord God, King of all kings, and Governor of all things, that sittest in the throne judging right, we commend to Thy Fatherly goodness the men who, through perils of war, are serving this nation, beseeching Thee to take into Thine own hand both them and the cause wherein their Queen and country send them.   Be Thou their tower of strength where they are set in the midst of so many and great dangers.   Make all bold through death or life to put their trust in Thee, Who art the only Giver of all victory, and canst save by many or by few, through Jesus Christ our Lord."

And we may be sure that prayer did not remain unheard, though some knew it not at the time, may not even know it yet.   How little did those wives and mothers, and children and sisters, and sweethearts and friends, whose thoughts had flown from the snow-clad fields around to the sultry plains of the Soudan, when that prayer was raised, know of the danger that, even as the words trembled on their lips, hung over the heads of their beloved ones, like a black cloud in the sunny sky !   How little did we know it ourselves ?   Yet it was a danger that might

have ended in a disaster more ghastly than Isandl-
wanha, nothing less than the total destruction of a
force of over 5000 men. Surely the prayer was
answered, and there were few on that day who were
not " bold through death or life."

Around me was the busy hum of voices, hearty
English voices, laughing and chatting confidently, as
if they were at a picnic ; for the English soldier is
the same wherever he goes, and, though the work
had been hard and the day hot, the men who had
come off work were good-tempered and cheerful, as
they lay beside their piled arms, smoking their pipes
or drinking their coffee, for several camp-fires had
already been lighted, and exchanging rough chaff,
which, if not particularly new or witty, seemed to
have lost none of its power of amusing them by
being transplanted to the Soudan. The working
parties were mostly in their shirt sleeves, with their
braces hanging down behind, and Tommy Atkins
was busy cutting down trees in that methodical
manner peculiar to him when on fatigue duty, and
which gets through a good deal of work, though it
is somewhat amusing to watch ; for an English
soldier hardly ever labours alone, and, if a bucket
has to be carried twenty yards, two men go and
march it off, solemnly keeping in step one on
each side, as if it was a prisoner of war. So in
cutting down mimosa trees, one man throws a rope
over the tree and bends its head on one side,
another takes an axe and gives two or three chops
at the stem, two more stand on the right and left
waiting till the tree is down, and then all four set to
work to haul it to its place.

It is eight minutes to three o'clock ; the water camels
have been formed into a close column and are just
beginning to move ; I have turned my horse's head

towards the central zareba, intending to ride back and report to the General that everything is ready, when a strange, shrill, startled cry rises from the rear of the camels behind me, and I see some twenty or thirty of the native drivers running towards me as fast as they can.

I had not heard a single shot fired, and so little was I aware of any imminent danger, that I supposed the Somali and Indian drivers were fighting among themselves, as they sometimes did, and that these fellows were running to me to have their dispute settled ; I therefore turned round, and then, for the first time, the truth flashed across me, for a glance showed the dark forms and gleaming swords and spears of the Hadendowas behind, hacking and stabbing right and left as they charged. They appeared to be coming through the rear ranks of the camels from the direction of the sea-coast, but the head of the convoy was undisturbed, and almost simultaneously a great shout rose from the S.W. side of the zareba, and a few shots were fired. I frankly confess my first impulse was to ride straight into the zareba behind me, where I could see the troops already hastening to snatch up their arms ; but remembering that the officers at the head of the convoy, which was a very long one, might not be aware of what was happening in rear, and that, as the camels were some distance from the zareba, they and their unfortunate drivers, who were quite unarmed, might be cut off, I determined to try and warn them before it was too late, and galloped back to the head of the convoy, stopping for a moment beside each section, and calling to the non-commissioned officers in charge to get the drivers at once into the zareba, for alas ! I could not speak Hindustanee myself.

The shrill cry which had first attracted my atten-

tion soon changed into a frantic yell, the hoarse roar
of 5000 tongues, and the black swarm of Arabs
seemed rising up like the sands of the desert all
round us ; indeed, so numerous were they, that the
very stones might have been transformed by the
stroke of a magician's wand into swarthy warriors
armed with spear and sword.   To reach the head
of the convoy I had to ride away from the zareba,
and I had hardly given my last caution, before
the huge concourse of animals shivered, swayed, and
then burst into motion ; pouring down upon me
with irresistible force, like the waters of some mighty
dam when it bursts its banks.   Those who were
watching the plain from Suakin, said that at this
moment a gigantic column of dust suddenly rose
into the air, which they took for a charge of Cavalry,
then the whole of our little force appeared to burst
asunder, amid smoke and fire, like an exploding shell;
and the plain was instantly covered with riderless
horses, camels, and mules tearing towards Suakin in
mad terror.

It was through this chaotic mass of terrified
animals that I had now to force my way to regain
the zareba.   I saw the familiar faces of friends pass
by me like the vision of the damned in Dante's
Inferno, and even exchanged a word or two with
some ; but the next moment they were swept away
and far out of reach, divided by the roaring, plunging
rush of camels, riderless horses, carts without drivers,
pack mules chained three together, with loose ammunition boxes clattering behind them, all bolting in
mad panic towards Suakin.   The Arabs were running
among them, cutting and stabbing, nimble as cats,
but my chief anxiety was to save my legs from being
broken, or my horse thrown down by the sheer
weight of rushing beasts.   It was fortunate for me

that my heels were armed with sharp jack-spurs, and
that I was riding a powerful English mare, steady and
courageous, which obeyed my guiding hand with un-
questioning faith.   She had been chosen by C——,
the quartermaster who came out with us in the *Arab*,
an old Lancer, and a good judge of horse flesh ;
but, as he had not much riding to do, he exchanged
her to me in a weak moment, a circumstance which
he ever afterwards regretted so much that, to comfort him, I had promised that he should have her
back again, as soon as I could find another to suit
me.   But it was not to be, and her bones are now
bleaching near the scene of the fight.

By a vigorous use of knee, spur, and bridle, I at
last succeeded in shaking myself free of the stampede,
and saw the dark and welcome fence of the Marine
zareba, beyond which I had been swept, rising before
me.   I think everybody else on that side had got
in, and the Arabs were close behind.   I could see
the men's rifles levelled over the hedge, and the
thought struck me, if they fire a volley now, I shall
never get over ; but they waited till, with one last
dig of the spur, I had leaped in, and then the whole
face of the zareba burst into a crackling line of fire,
and for a moment the heavy smoke hid everything
outside from view.

" Steady, men, fill up the intervals, fire low," I was
calling to those nearest me, when a yell behind, warned
us that we were menaced in another direction.

For some reason the Marines, with a few of the
Transport corps and Indians, were all collected along
the two lower sides of the zareba, near the Gardner
guns, and the upper, or East side of the enclosure
was undefended.   According to one account, the
Marines had been swept away from this side of the
zareba by the stampede of the Transport animals, a

part of which had gone across it ; but I think it
more probable that the arms were piled near the
Gardner guns, and that the men who were digging
the trench, accordingly, first rallied on the sides
nearest to them.   However this may be, the Eastern
side of the zareba was not lined with men, and a
portion of the Arabs who had attacked the camels,
now dashed over the hedge with great intrepidity
into the very middle of the square.   The Marines
in the front rank still continued firing outwards
with much steadiness at the enemy, now swarming all round, but the rear rank faced about, and I
saw some of the men kneel down to shoot under
our horses' bellies, for most of the mounted officers
were between them and the Arabs who had entered
the zareba.   It was a trying moment, for the men
found themselves attacked both front and rear, and
by the way they clustered back to back, and the
strained expression of their faces, it was easy to see
that they felt their position to be critical.   Indeed,
any flinching might have led to a panic.   " Steady,
men, stand steady," rang out the quiet, reassuring
voices of the officers, who, drawing their revolvers,
fired down on the advancing Arabs, while the men
aimed under their horses, or between them, as
best they could.   For a moment the centre of the
zareba was full of smoke, but when it lifted not an
Arab was left standing, the foremost having reached
within about six yards of the rear side of the square,
and the rest turned and fled, leaving six of their
dead in the centre of the little enclosure.   The East
side was now immediately lined, and the firing all
round became fast and furious.

I copy textually from my journal :—So near
were the blacks, that we had hardly been in the
zareba a moment, when they came jumping over

the hedge at the other side and tried to rush across
brandishing their spears, while others swept round
outside, or fired into it from the bushes. The noise
and smoke were tremendous, and the men fought
back to back, huddled together at the two lower
corners of the square, firing both into the enclosure
and out of it. It is a terrible sight, the few mad
moments of a desperate fight, when man is striving
against his brother for dear life. Yet the joy of
battle that we read of does exist, and a strange
thrill of exultation stirs the hearts of those who,
sternly bidding defiance to death, stand, as it were,
on the brink of eternity, prepared to yield back life
to their Maker, and all that in this world we hold
most dear, without hesitation, or question, at the call
of duty.

All round the gray-green mimosa bushes swarm
with swiftly moving black figures, who seem to court
destruction, so recklessly do they rush on the hail of
bullets that now pours from the zareba, striking desperately with their spears and swords even after they
are mortally wounded, and hardly ever missing their
blow. Around the zareba a wreath of white smoke
hangs over the heads of all, broken here and there
by the yellow flashes of the rifles and the gleam of
the bayonets shining through it. The men, with
hard, stern faces, are clustered together in knots
firing desperately fast ; and the mounted officers,
revolver in hand, are trying to control their terrified
horses and steady their men's firing. Through the
whirling wreaths of smoke some dark figures, brandishing swords and spears, come running across the
square, only to totter and fall before they reach the
centre under the furious shower of bullets that are
whizzing in all directions. At my feet a dead
soldier, who has been shot beside me, lies pale and

motionless, a splash of blood across his young brow,
the intense stillness and tranquillity of his face contrasting strangely with the fierce action and turmoil
all round.   Presently no more black figures can be
seen inside the zareba, and the troops steady a little
and spread out properly to line the sides, so that
there are no gaps left through which the enemy can
rush.   But the last five minutes have been moments
of intense anxiety to the officers, who knew that but
for the steadiness of a few clusters of brave men,
who did not lose their heads in the moment of surprise, the whole affair might have been a terrible
disaster.

The firing still continues fast and furious from
the sides of the zareba, and our great anxiety is
to prevent our men from shooting any of their
comrades, some of whom have formed small rallying
squares where they were surprised, and are now
making their way back into the zareba.   But I
cannot any longer see what is going on beyond, for
just after the centre of the square had been cleared,
a shower of bullets from among the mimosa trees
outside flew past me, and my mare reared bolt
upright, shot through the head, and then rolled over,
with her off fore-leg also broken by another bullet
which struck her as she pawed the air ; so I have
come down, and as my orderly with my second
horse has bolted in the stampede, I have to be content to fight the rest of the battle on foot.

After about twenty minutes, the bugles sound the
" cease fire," and cheer on cheer rises from the men
as they see the ground clear before them, though
strewn with many a dusky form and whole sheaves
of camels which have fallen before our own fire.   A
great deal of independent firing still goes on, as
some of the enemy are seen moving among the

bushes, and there are one or two false alarms which
produce volleys ; but the fighting is now over, and
parties begin to go out to collect the wounded.

Thus I wrote shortly after the fight, which is my
only excuse for dwelling so long on mere personal
impressions. I must now turn to what I afterwards
learned had happened in other parts of the zareba.

It appears that just before the attack, Generals
M'Neill and Hudson had met in consultation close
to the northern angle of the Berkshire, or more advanced zareba ; and Sir J. M'Neill cheerily told his
colleague that he hoped to release his Brigade and the
Transport at three o'clock, as the two defensive works
at either end of the central zareba were now nearly
complete. While the two Generals were still talking
and congratulating themselves that the work had
progressed so well, a Lancer galloped up to report
" the enemy collecting in front ;" on which, according to a writer in the *Pictorial World*, who describes
himself as " an eye-witness," Sir J. M'Neill at once
turned to his friend and said, " Hudson, you had
better see that your men look out ;" the next minute
another vedette rode hastily in, and reported that
the enemy were " advancing rapidly." On which
General M'Neill shouted " Stand to arms !" an
order which was promptly obeyed ; but before the
men could gain their places, the Cavalry vedettes
came dashing in, closely pursued by the Arabs.

Sir Gerald Graham says:—" Shortly after 2.30
three messages were sent in from the 5th Lancer
outposts ;" but I do not think the third ever reached
Sir J. M'Neill, and I happened to hear its fate. The
Lancer who brought it, having jumped his horse
over the west side of the large zareba, cantered up
to an officer who was standing there and said,
" Can you tell me, sir, where I shall find Capt.

Jones?"   The officer replied, "Who is Capt. Jones?"
And the man answered, "He is the captain of my
picket, and I want to report the enemy coming on
in force."   "Oh," said the officer, who, like most
of us, had not the slightest idea that the enemy
could be very near, "then you had better go out
there," pointing due South; "there are some of the
Staff officers, and I think General M'Neill also; you
should report at once to him."   The man trotted off
to obey, and tried to jump his horse out of the
zareba, but it refused the fence; the few moments
when warning might have been of value slipped
by, and he was still trying to make his horse face
the hedge, when the enemy were upon us.

The main rush apparently came from the direction
of Tamai, and was poured straight on the salient
angle of the Berkshire zareba; but there is little
room for doubt that the Arab army advanced in the
usual formation adopted by nearly all savage tribes
in Africa, which will be familiar to officers who have
fought against the Zulus, viz. a half-moon, the horns
of which are intended to close round in rear of the
force menaced, until it is completely encircled.   This,
in my opinion, was proved by the fact that I found
the enemy running through the convoy of camels on
the left, before I heard any firing in front; and
is confirmed by the reports of the *Times* and
Telegraph correspondents, who both happened to
be near that side, and the first of whom says:
" Suddenly, and without more than a hurried warning,
the enemy burst from the thick bush and dashed
headlong, without firing a shot, at the water transport," and the second,—" Suddenly, from in front of
me, there went up a sharp, amazed, and painful cry.
I looked up.   The whole mass of camels was swaying to and fro."   If we couple this with the evidence

that a large portion of the convoy was driven
inwards towards the zareba, and, indeed, across it,
I think there can be little doubt that the Arabs
designed their attack to strike our front and flanks
very nearly at the same time. I could not, of
course, see what happened on the other side of the
zareba, but, from the sound of their fire, the 15th
Sikhs apparently found themselves quickly engaged:
and very soon swarms of the enemy closed all round,
completing the circle. There is, however, no doubt
that the greatest weight of the charge fell direct on
the angle of the Berkshire zareba, where, unfortunately, the Gardner guns in the redoubt were not
yet ready to be brought into action, while many of
the Berkshire men forming its garrison were outside
in the bush cutting trees. I am told that the
Brigade Major saw the Arabs rushing through the
17th Native Infantry on the transport, and this is
no doubt correct, for, when they had driven that
regiment back, they poured on the rear of the
transport and completed its demoralization.

I should have hesitated to refer to the unsteadiness
of the 17th Native Infantry, were it not that it forms
an important link in the chain of evidence, and
undoubtedly contributed to the great loss of transport
animals and followers. But, as it is only fair to give
both versions of a story when there are two, I will
begin by quoting the report of the correspondent of
the *Daily Chronicle,* who says :—" The 17th Loyal
Poorbeahs fought splendidly from beginning to end.
They were as hard pressed as the Marines in the
early stages of the fight, and although they suffered
some loss before they gained a position to repel all
attacks, no troops could have behaved more gallantly
under exceptionally trying circumstances." Unfortunately this correspondent is sometimes more

picturesque than accurate, and describes the alarm
as occurring "just at two o'clock," instead of at
eight minutes to three, which shows, either that his
watch was wrong, or that he had not acquired
that habit so essential to correspondents and Staff
officers, of noting the exact time that anything unusual occurs. The correspondent of the *Telegraph*
says :—" The 17th was at a great disadvantage,
being first overrun by Cavalry rushing in, and then
overwhelmed by a torrent of stampeded animals.
They found it impossible to reform, in spite of the
efforts made by both Native and European officers."
But he does not explain how they came to be overwhelmed by stampeded animals, when they were
drawn up between the rear of those animals and the
enemy ; besides, as he was carried away by the
stampede, he could not himself see what happened.
The letter of a distinguished officer now before me,
says :—" The 17th bolted before the enemy reached
them ; " and adds, " Hudson reports, had 17th stood,
hardly a camel would have been lost." That may
perhaps be a somewhat sanguine view to take, but
there is not the slightest doubt that if the 17th
had remained firm on the ground where they were
originally placed, and fired volleys steadily into the
advancing Arabs, it would have materially altered
the results of the day.

Instead of doing this, they appear, when the
Cavalry vedettes came galloping in upon them,
closely followed by the enemy, to have discharged
one wild volley and then broken and streamed, or
at least part of them, into the Berkshire zareba,
where General M'Neill in person gallantly attempted
to rally them, though without success, for they
could not be prevailed on to stand, and, after firing
another volley, retreated as the Arabs advanced

into the central zareba, where a portion of them
were at last rallied and induced to line the fence,
the remainder breaking and following the stampede towards Suakin, only to be ruthlessly cut
down by the enemy when overtaken. I myself saw
those in the central zareba firing in a very wild
fashion, some of their bullets coming into the
Marines' square where I was standing, and others
apparently being fired into the air. However, since
Prince Hohenlöhe has laid it down as a maxim
that even the phlegmatic German infantry may be
considered to have attained a certain degree of
proficiency if they can be induced to put their
rifles to the shoulder when firing in the face of an
enemy; some allowance must be made for the excitement produced by such a sudden attack; and it
is quite possible that the vedettes first galloping
through them, disorganized their ranks. For, as
Lord Wolseley has said in his *Soldier's Pocket-book*,
" the very noise of the horses galloping has a terrify-
ing effect, that frequently goes home to the heart of
Infantry." It is also possible that, as their left flank
was what General Graham calls " somewhat *en l'air*,"
they may have imagined that their rear was turned,
if on looking over their shoulders they saw the Arabs
attacking the flank of the transport animals. I do
not mention these points as any justification of their
conduct, but simply as perhaps explaining it; and,
if they had stood steady, all would have been well,
for they had both the Marines' zareba and the half
Battalion of the Berkshire, to protect their rear.
Their gallant commander, Major Beverhoudt, lost
his life while unsuccessfully striving to rally his
men, though both the Native and European officers
did all in their power to check the panic.

It is pleasant to turn from this painful incident

to the excellent behaviour of the other Native Regiments, the 15th Sikhs and the 28th Bombay N.I., who stood their ground most gallantly, pouring volley after volley into the enemy without any sign of unsteadiness. The action of one Native officer commanding the flank company of Sikhs, was specially worthy of praise, for he saved the lives of two of the Berkshire men, who had been employed outside on the left of his company, by flinging himself between them and the pursuing Arabs, three of whom he cut down with his sword. The Madras Sappers were also perfectly steady wherever engaged.

The men of the Naval Brigade in the redoubt towards Tamai, suffered severely, for, on the retreat of the 17th from the Berkshire zareba, they were left nearly alone with their useless Gardners to bear the full brunt of the Arab charge ; but they would not desert their guns, and poor Seymour and five of his men were slain, while bravely defending them from the enemy, who actually planted a white standard worked with red letters on the redoubt. After this, no less than 112 of the enemy poured into the zareba, but *not one of them left it alive*, for the Berkshire men who had been out cutting bush, now dashed boldly into the enclosure after the Arabs, in many cases with empty hands, and snatching up their rifles from the pile, engaged the enemy hand to hand with the bayonet. Before long 112 dead Hadendowas were lying in this small enclosure 65 yards square, and the Berkshire men had triumphantly relined its sides and commenced sweeping the surrounding country with their fire. This, to my mind, was the most notable achievement of a day which was conspicuous for the many acts of personal gallantry that were performed.

The other half Battalion of the Berkshire Regiment, which, as I have before said, was being served with food and water on the open ground about 250 yards east of the zareba, at the first alarm formed a rallying square round its officers, and, notwithstanding that a large portion of the stampeded transport rushed down on it, remained so firm and poured such a steady fire on the Arabs, who repeatedly charged it, that it did not lose a single man ; though over 200 of the enemy were afterwards found dead round the spot where the square had stood.   One man alone was wounded by a spear, which a dying Arab managed to hurl at him with desperate tenacity ere he fell.   This was another proof, if any were needed, that even a small body of men are practically safe against the fiercest Arab charge when armed with breechloaders, so long as they have ammunition and fire steadily.   When the first heat of the onslaught was over, this little square retired slowly on the Marines' zareba, the men sticking their helmets on their bayonets to prevent the troops inside from mistaking them for the enemy, as they approached through the dense clouds of smoke which hung heavily all round.   I was in the zareba at the time, and there was some little difficulty in restraining the men's fire ; but somebody, whether intentionally or in error I do not know, called out, "It is reinforcements coming;" this was repeated from mouth to mouth and had an immediate effect, for the men stopped firing and began to cheer.

I have already told how the Marines cleared their zareba when it was broken into from my own observations, and it now only remains for me to describe the action of the squadron of 20th Hussars, who, it will be remembered, were instructed to patrol between the zareba and Suakin.

It appears that they marched out at 10 A.M., and on their way saw small parties of the enemy to their front, between Suakin and the zareba, but these parties retired without fighting, and the squadron reached the zareba at 1 o'clock. At 1.30 the officer in command, having communicated with Sir J. M'Neill, commenced his return march, and had gone about two miles, when he was met by a squadron of the 9th Bengal Cavalry. Just then, the roar of our firing was heard, and the two squadrons forming together, hastened back towards the zareba. When they were within about a mile of it, they met a great number of the baggage animals, together with many camp-followers, some Native Infantry, and a few English soldiers, in full flight for Suakin; closely pursued by the Arabs, who were cutting them down and killing numbers without resistance. Half the Cavalry were then dismounted and some volleys fired, which checked the pursuit : mounting again, they pushed forward, occasionally repeating the same tactics, so as to drive the Arabs before them ; and about this time they appear to have been joined by a squadron of the 5th Lancers.

A large number of the enemy, meanwhile, finding their pursuit checked, tried to creep round by the sea-coast and turn the flank of the Cavalry, in order to continue it. An officer was, therefore, sent with a troop of the Bengal Lancers to intercept this movement, and was fortunate enough to come across about twenty fugitives and wounded of our side, whom he escorted safely to Suakin. As soon as the flank had been cleared, the remaining Cavalry, numbering some 180 lances and sabres, pushed forward, forcing the Arabs back on the zareba ; where they were enfiladed by our fire, and soon began to disperse towards the sea. The Cavalry then formed a cordon round the remaining baggage animals outside the zareba, while we went out to bring them in. Several of our wounded and some of the fugitives had taken refuge behind the Cavalry as they advanced, and were thus able to regain the zareba, while others made good their escape to Suakin.

I left off the extract from my journal when my horse was killed, which happened a few minutes after I had gained the zareba, and when the Arabs who had entered it were either all slain or put to flight. I will now try to describe the scene inside the enclosure.

There was still plenty to do, for the men were firing much too fast, and their tendency to cluster together had to be corrected and the intervals filled up. Details from various regiments, who had run hastily in, were all mixed together ; and officers like myself, who had no men of their own, busied themselves attempting to discipline the fire of those who seemed most to need it, and warning them not to shoot whenever a straggling party of their comrades made its way up to the zareba, for many little knots of men working in the bush had found themselves cut off during the first rush of the enemy, and had to stand back to back defending themselves as best they could, till an opportunity occurred for them to regain their companions. It was essentially a soldier's battle, for there was naturally no manœuvring, and the men had simply to stand and fight where they were, while all the officers could do was to encourage them. I found time to light a pipe during the scrimmage, not because I particularly wanted it, but because it was as good a thing to do as anything else, for inside a British square one cannot be always waving a sword like the officers in the illustrated papers, and perhaps—for so small are the motives that influence our actions—because I had somewhere read in the *Soldier's Pocket-book*, of a Staff officer who sat cheerily smiling and puffing a cigar while round shot were rolling like polo balls between his horse's legs, and a shrapnel shell carried off his wig and eyebrows as it passed. This is perhaps not quite a correct version of the story, but it is somewhat like it.

Under the shelter of the telegraph waggon, the doctors were already busy succouring the wounded, while the telegraph people sat calmly wiring to Headquarters the intelligence, which by this time must have been clearly apparent, that we were now engaged with the enemy.[1] I saw the *Times* correspondent, who then was a stranger to me, rapidly scribbling his notes, as he stood with the bridle of his horse over one arm, and the artist of the *Graphic*, also making thumb-nail sketches of the different corners of the zareba on his block, while the turmoil was raging all round. Outside, the heavy rolling smoke made the moving figures look dim and fantastic, like shadows seen through a thick fog, but, whenever the smoke lifted for a moment, we could descry large masses of the enemy hovering and circling round, searching for a weak place to rush in at ; while every now and then small groups of Arabs, sometimes only a single man, would run out from the rest at a sort of jog-trot, and boldly approach the levelled line of rifles, brandishing sword or spear in the air with an exaggerated affectation of defiance, which would have been absurd, had it not been pathetic, and apparently quite content to make one cut or thrust at an unbeliever before falling riddled with bullets.

---

[1] This, I believe, is the first time the telegraph has been carried into the actual shooting line of a fighting force.

These were the fanatics, the backbone of Osman Digma's army, the men who led the van in the desperate charges of his wild followers, and who joyfully sought death at our hands, as a certain passport to that Paradise where the true Moslem believes he will repose for ever under the shade of green trees, by sweet-smelling flowers and bubbling water,—a truly tempting prospect to the sons of the arid desert. Where he will enjoy that greatest of luxuries to the Oriental mind, perpetual idleness. Where he will not even have to move from his bed of roses to eat of luscious fruits that will bend down to meet his hand, and he may drink without breaking the law of that pure wine—

> "Which the Houris that dwell in the regions above
> Fondly press to lips of the Heroes they love."

Where the air will be ever fragrant with a thousand delicious perfumes, gliding insensibly from one to another, and the power of enjoyment will never fade, for, when he is borne from the field of battle by Angelic arms, he will be gifted with a perpetual youth. Where the notes of the birds will be as the sweetest cadence of the Bulbul among the rose-trees at twilight, and his slightest want will be ministered to by bevies of beauteous maidens, whose charms shall never fade or cloy, who shall be all different, and yet each a perfect

> "Queen rose of the garden of girls"

in herself, and even gifted with the power of changing her age and type of beauty at the will of her lover, so that should he desire to see her at fifteen, she shall at once become "a simple maiden in her flower," while would he look on the more developed charms of five-and-twenty, in an instant his desire shall be granted A Paradise, in short, where his existence will be one long, blissful, slumberous, sensuous admixture of fragrant scents, pleasant sounds, sweet smiles, beauteous sights, cooling drinks, and perfect rest.

Mad dreams these of an Oriental mind, of the earth earthly, but well calculated to fire the imaginations of the half-starved children of the burning Soudan, and contrasting favourably with the foul stenches, putrid water, and general filth and squalor of Suakin. A writer, to whom I am indebted for some information on this subject, has recently published the text of one of the Mahdi's proclamations, copied from an Arab paper, which throws strong light on the motives that induced these poor Arabs to act in the murderous and suicidal manner I have described. " Do you not know," it says, " that killing one infidel is more agreeable to God than offering prayers for a thousand months? Do you not know that not only from Mecca, the mother of cities, but also from every field of battle, a path leads to Paradise? Oh! ye faithful, I assure you that if you die in the morning fighting against the infidels, you will, even ere it is noon, be with the Prophet in Paradise. Silken robes of green will clothe you, and golden bracelets adorn you. You will repose by the banks of cool rivers, sipping refreshing drinks, while sixty ever-youthful Houris, bright as the moon, will smile upon you!"

Truly men impressed with the belief that their miserable lot would be thus transformed if they died in the act of killing us, were not foes to be despised, for no ordinary rules of warfare could be applied to them; they neither asked nor gave quarter, they knew not when they were beaten, and rather preferred to die than not.

But now the heavy rifle fire had done its ghastly

work, the fanatics had been thinned off, and the weaker vessels, who as usual formed the majority, and were not quite ready to exchange even such small pleasures as their life here might afford them, for the glorious prospects held out by the Mahdi, " drew off," to quote the words of a correspondent, "sullenly firing all the time, vanishing into the bush from which they had so spectrally emerged." The *Times* correspondent says, " As I write the fire is growing desultory, and the enemy seems checked, but bullets at long range are still flying over our heads." I mention this because there was some doubt as to whether the enemy had fired on us during the attack, and a general idea prevailed that most of our men who received bullet wounds, were shot by their own comrades ; this mistake arose from the fact that the roar and volume of our own fire completely drowned the scattered firing of the enemy ; but I saw their riflemen keeping up a very brisk fusilade on the zareba from among the mimosa trees, and, long after the fighting was over, when men were discussing the events of the struggle, and parties were being sent out to collect the wounded, one of these sharpshooters still continued firing on the square from behind some bushes about 400 yards away. His bullets flew overhead, but came nearer each time he fired, and I called the attention of one or two officers to the fact that he was slowly but surely finding his range. They all said that a volley ought to be fired into the bushes to silence him, but, perhaps for fear of creating an alarm, it was not done, and getting tired of hearing the continual whistle of his shot over my head, I moved to another part of the square. Shortly afterwards he *did* find his range, and mortally wounded a young officer in the neck ; then, of course, a volley was fired, the bushes became silent, and the persevering rifleman troubled us no more.

There is no doubt that some of our men were wounded by Snider bullets, but I do not know that there were any Martini-Henry wounds, and I think the percentage of men shot by their own comrades was very much smaller than at first supposed, and not above what might be reasonably expected in a fight where many isolated groups were outside the zareba, in positions where those inside could not possibly see them. The doctors who dressed the wounds afterwards confirmed this opinion. The half Battalion of the Berkshire, which escaped without losing a man, though so near the zareba, was fortunately in a slight hollow, so that the fire of the other troops went over it. I must mention, to the credit of the 15th Sikhs, that they did not deliver their fire at the approaching Arabs, till the front of their line was quite clear of the working parties and vedettes. The number of camels that were killed was an unavoidable incident, as so many of the enemy were among and behind them, that it was impossible to avoid shooting the beasts to check the charge of the Arabs, who would otherwise have run in among us, and broken our formation, under cover of the Transport.

At ten minutes past three, that is just eighteen minutes after the first shot was fired, the bugles sounded the "cease fire," and we began to have time to look about us, though of course there were still occasional dropping shots, and even volleys; but the struggle was now over, and we had the satisfaction of knowing that we had beaten off our stubborn adversaries, though no man could tell how soon the fight might begin again.

I quote from my journal :—It is wonderful how

many boys and old men there are among the bodies
lying thick outside the zareba ; they all wear the
Mahdi's uniform—a white dress, with square checks
of red or black sewn on it, and they have shaved
their heads, which gives them a very different appearance to that they had when I was last in this
country.   It shows what great influence the Mahdi
must have exercised to induce the people to completely change the fashion of wearing their hair, in
which they formerly took much pride, spending both
time and money in covering it with fat and butter,
combing it, frizzing it, and sometimes bleaching it
to a reddish tint with quicklime.   Now they only
wear little round caps of straw, ornamented
with diamond-shaped squares of cloth like their
tunics.   Many of our people go out to collect
swords, spears, etc., and two flags are brought in,
but I cannot myself strip the dead, and am content
with picking up a spear that has been thrown into
the zareba at my feet.   Our wounded, lying all over
the place, are a harrowing sight, but hardly a groan
is to be heard, and they bear their sufferings so
quietly that no one would know the amount of
human agony around us, who did not see the awful
wounds that the spears and swords of our foes have
inflicted.

There is much to do, shooting camels that are
wounded and bringing those that have escaped,
strengthening our zareba and making an earthwork round it, with wire stretched along the hedge
to check a rush from outside.   The wounded have
to be succoured and the scattered dead laid in rows,
with their faces decently covered ; food and water
have to be served to the living.   I cannot now
linger over this scene ; it is too painful, too horrible,
to draw a picture of.   ——— is missing, but we trust

he has escaped with those who rode into Suakin
when the stampede took place, as his body cannot be
found.   A message has been flashed from Suakin
that the Guards are marching out to relieve us, but
we do not want them now, and can hold our own.

NOTE.—The plan of the zareba accompanying this
chapter is a reduced facsimile of that Sir Gerald Graham
forwarded with his despatch of the 28th March, which was
made shortly after the battle.   The following are the only
points, so far as I am aware, that are not quite accurate
in it :—

The bush approached nearer the zareba on the N. and
W.   The line of the 17th Native Infantry was not exactly
parallel with the S. face of the Berkshire zareba, but sloped
from it, facing S.S.E. ; the convoy occupied a much larger
space in rear of this line than is indicated by the dots, and
the direction of attack is not sufficiently indicated on the E.
side.   There was also a gap on the N. side of the central
square at the angle F. through which the portion of the
convoy that was driven across the zareba escaped.

CHAPTER VII.

COUNTING THE COST.

I SAW young Charteris, Sir J. M'Neill's A.D.C., brought in, and heard that he had been attacked by several Arabs, and wounded in the wrist by a little boy of ten, who I believe severed an artery with his spear. He looked very pale as he lay in a dhoolie talking to D——, who was kneeling beside him, but did not appear to suffer much. A little to the left a poor fellow lay dying, his face livid, and his dim eyes taking a last look at the world he was about to leave, as he turned towards the doctor bending over him with kindly sympathy.

If our own wounded knew how to bear their fate with silent fortitude, so also did those of the enemy, and hardly a groan was to be heard from the ghastly heaps of bodies, over a thousand in number, lying round the zareba. These desert warriors die hard, and it was reported by the parties sent out to bring in the wounded, that they crept bleeding on all fours with their spears in their teeth to attack them, and even hobbled on broken legs towards them. I fear this led to some of the enemy's wounded being shot in cold blood, but I shall have to allude to this later, so will only give an anecdote here, to illustrate the mistaken impression that prevailed among the men. I noticed a wounded Arab in the Marines' zareba,

who had been shot through the foot and made a
prisoner. He was an oldish man with grizzled hair,
and now lay with his hands tied behind him in the
burning sun, writhing with pain and thirst. My own
flask contained whisky and water, which I knew in
his fanatical Moslem mind he would consider it a cruel
insult for me to offer him in his helpless condition;
so I asked Capt. T—— to give him a drink of pure
water from his bottle ; but before he could do so, a
man who was standing by said, " It is no good, sir,
offering these here Arabs water ; they won't take it
from us, they will only waste it." " Well, just try and
see," I said, and thus encouraged, the fellow put his flask
to the parched lips of the Arab, who, lifting his eyes to
heaven, drank down its contents with evident gratitude.
The man looked astonished ; like many of his kind
he had taken it for granted that it was no use trying
to help a wounded Arab, because in a few cases they
had refused aid, or returned it with ingratitude.

The total loss of the enemy on this occasion was
very heavy, over 1000 dead bodies being actually
counted, while many more were afterwards found in
the outlying bush, so there is little doubt they lost
fully 1500 killed. When we remember that they
carried away most of their wounded, and during the
night even managed to bury some of their dead, it
may be imagined how terribly severe their punishment
must have been. Our own loss was quite heavy enough.
The *Times* of the 30th March says:—"Including sailors,
but exclusive of native Transport drivers and followers,
the casualties are now set down as 276." The figures
given me in camp afterwards by an officer who pro-
fessed to know, were as follows :—7 officers killed, 5
wounded, 66 men killed, 120 wounded, 125 missing ;
total, 323. This is exclusive of native drivers, of whom
I found 179 killed or missing from the water convoy

alone, when I called the roll the morning after the engagement; though some of these men no doubt got safe back into Suakin and rejoined their Companies. The camels killed, on official testimony, were 720, which out of 1080 represents exactly two-thirds of the whole number. I cannot say whether the grand total of 323 officers and men killed, wounded, and missing, tallies with the official record, as I have not seen it; but I saw a record which was being prepared of the total loss of men during the campaign from, I think, the 1st March to the 14th May, which I remember was as follows:—British troops killed, wounded, and missing, 236; native troops killed, wounded, and missing, 338, total, 574. If we deduct 65 for the casualties at Hasheen, and 323 for those at the zareba, it leaves 186 for the losses at other minor engagements, which would be about the correct proportion, so I do not think the figures I have stated can be far wrong. What the total loss in native drivers, camp-followers, etc., was, it is very difficult to estimate; but it must have been severe, as these poor creatures nearly all bolted, and were cut down in detail by the Arabs, the way between the zareba and Suakin being afterwards found strewn with their bodies. I think it is to be regretted that the drivers brought from India were not armed with swords and bucklers, with the use of which probably most of them would have been familiar, as it might have enabled them to defend themselves. A few of the Somali drivers, it is true, were given old obsolete sword-bayonets; a weapon which, without the rifle belonging to it, was quite useless against a Hadendowa armed with spear and shield. Of course there were plenty of stories going about of narrow escapes. One officer was said to have been struck down and to have received on his clothes and accoutrements no less than six spear stabs and one bullet, all harmless, and to have finally escaped with a slight wound in the neck. Another was declared to have owed his safety from a spear thrust, to some links of chain mail which his wife had persuaded him to let her sew in the breast of his jacket, and, as soon as this incident was published in the English papers, the wives of many of the married officers wrote out begging their husbands to wear chain armour, and the father of a friend of mine actually did send out a shirt of mail, which of course he never wore. I was told that an officer, finding himself cut off and surrounded on all sides, thought his last moment had come ; but, unlike Mrs. Dombey, determined to "make an effort," and ran wildly at the nearest group of Arabs, brandishing his sword round his head ; which warlike demonstration to his utter astonishment and great relief, caused them all to bolt before him.

There was many a young aspirant for the V.C. eagerly watching for the chance to dash out and bring in a wounded man ; but there were few such opportunities, for the men either regained the zareba, or clustered together and fought back to back. Several officers lost their lives fighting side by side with their men, but I did not hear a single instance of any being deserted by their comrades, though there were many of one man saving the life of another by a timely shot or bayonet thrust. General Graham says in his despatch : " I may mention Major von Beverhoudt, of the 17th Native Infantry, and Captain Romilly and Lieutenant Newman, of the Royal Engineers, as instances of officers who lost their lives in the brave effort to check the enemy's fierce onslaught ; while Lieutenant Seymour, R.N., with his gun detachment, also met his death at the post of duty."

As an example of the furious nature of the blows the Arabs dealt with their swords, I must describe the condition in which the rifle of a man of the Commissariat and Transport Corps was found after his death. He had evidently been carried away from the zareba by the stampede, and attacked by an Arab, armed with one of those long, straight, two-edged swords with cross handles, copied from the old Crusader pattern, the blades of which are now, or at least were before the war, manufactured at Solinghen, and shipped in great numbers to the Soudan; where the Arab hunters use them for hamstringing the elephant and rhinoceros, and even for attacking the lion in his lair. To guard himself against the blow of this formidable weapon, the soldier raised his rifle to the head parry, and the first stroke of the sword, cleaving the sling, had cut the wood down clean and smooth as if it had been taken off by a spokeshave, until it was checked by the trigger guard; again the sword flashed in the sunlight, and again the poor fellow—who, I suppose, had not got his bayonet fixed—raised his rifle in the regulation parry to protect his head; but this time the sword struck with such fearful force that it actually bit a quarter of an inch into the iron barrel of the rifle, and probably dashed it out of the soldier's hand, for he was killed.

Many of the camp-followers had their heads almost severed from the neck by a single blow of these long swords; but a few escaped by falling down and feigning death as the Arabs passed over them, while others crept into the lowest and thickest thorn or kittar bushes they could find, which was perhaps the best thing they could do, and lay still till darkness set in. One of these last attracted the attention of a Hadendowa, who turned him over

with his spear, but as he never winced when its
point touched him, the Arab thought he was dead,
and passed on. I heard a rather amusing story of
the way an officer commanding a company of the
Commissariat and Transport Corps was extricated
from the stampede by his sergeant-major, for whom
he afterwards obtained promotion. On hearing the
alarm, Captain P—— was endeavouring to form his
company in the central zareba, but was overwhelmed
and carried bodily out of it by the rush of stampeded
animals tearing across. His sergeant-major was a
type of the old school, a little man with a tremendous
deep bass voice, which seemed to come out of the
bowels of the earth from a fathom or two below the
place where he stood, and gifted with a power of
slow but scathing sarcasm, which on occasion could
make an erring recruit shake in his shoes. He
stuck close to his captain during the stampede, and,
when he found himself completely hemmed in and
borne away by the crowd of terrified beasts and
camp-followers, merely remarked, in deep sepulchral
tones, " We shall be in Suakin presently at this rate,
sir. I think it is time for me to make a little clearing." Then he lugged out his sabre and began
calmly prodding with it at the rear facings of men
and beasts indiscriminately, accompanying each prod
with a *basso profundo* growl, " Just make a little room
there, will you, heu !" and with each " heu !" the point
of his weapon conveyed what may be termed a stern
admonition to all concerned. Indeed, so effectual was
this argument, that all felt its point even if they could
not see it ; and in an incredibly short space of time
he had cleared a road for himself and his captain
to struggle out of the ruck, and gain the Marines'
zareba, where they presently collected their Company
together, and helped to defend one of its sides.

As it was known that officers had ridden out to look on at the battle of Hasheen, who were not detailed for duty, a strict order was issued to the military police to " run in " all amateurs who might in future display a taste for being shot at without orders ; but D——, on account of his many services, had a sort of roving commission to go where he liked, and on this occasion was sitting beside his favourite camel some distance from the zareba when the attack took place, and he appears to have actually trotted back into the square in company with the charging Arabs, who, strange to say, took little notice of him, though I believe he fired several shots at them with his revolver. Perhaps they only looked at the camel, and thought he was one of their Sheiks. The Colonel of the Berkshire Regiment was attacked by three Hadendowas, all of whom he shot with his revolver ; while his brother, the *Times* correspondent, had the unpleasant experience of being pulled off his horse by one of the ropes linking the camels together, which added so much to the confusion of the stampede ; but this adventure is best related in his own words. " It was only by a miracle that I escaped with my life in the desperate fighting which took place yesterday during the first surprise. I was carried away for a moment by the panic rush of struggling animals, and was pulled from my saddle by the rope which was attached to a string of camels. The Arab spearmen were close behind, but I regained my saddle and leaped the zareba. Had my horse refused, I should not now be able to chronicle this battle, the most desperate and the most critical of any that have been fought in this neighbourhood."

The fate of poor Richardson, of the 5th Lancers, was very sad. The story I heard was that he had

ridden into the Headquarter camp with two or three
troopers to report, and was ordered to go back
again, after which nothing was ever positively learned
of his fate, though his saddle and silver whistle were
found.

Presently, the short tropical twilight warns us that
it will soon be night. The bodies of our fallen
enemies have been dragged outside the zareba, the
wounded tended, the defences strengthened, the
watches posted, and the hour has come when, with
smoke-blackened faces and weary limbs, officers and
men can sit down on the blood-stained sand and
talk over the events of the day, discuss the victory
we have won, and count the cost. But nearly half
the men remain standing behind the fence with
fixed bayonets, while their comrades repose close
by with their rifles ready to their hands. No man
takes off boot or belt, for we know not how soon
we may have to be again up and fighting for our
lives. Biscuit boxes and meat tins, however, are
opened, coffee is made, and frank hospitality exchanged between those who have anything to give.
As I pass a group of Marine officers I hear the
popping of corks, and involuntarily my eyes follow
the direction of the pleasant sound ; instantly one
of them steps forward and proffers a foaming mug
of brown stout, with a kindly invitation to stop and
drink. Not nectar brewed from honey culled by
the bees that feed upon the flower-starred slopes of
Mount Hymettus, could have been more sweet and
grateful to my parched palate than that long, deep
draught of strength-inspiring porter, after such a day
as we had just gone through ! I fear I could only
repay the kindness very inadequately with a crust
of dry bread from my saddle-bags ; but as my
entertainers had no bread to eat with their cheese,

and I happened to have some to spare, we parted mutually content. I found afterwards some brother officers who had got a tin of boulli beef open, which, with some of the regulation biscuit—hard enough to serve for macadamizing a road—and a little coffee, made a very substantial supper. We did not feed quite so voraciously as Homer's heroes, but we had earned a good working appetite by the exertions of the day, which, I am ashamed to say, even the shocking spectacle of the carnage all round could not deprive us of. Then pipes were lit, and we prepared to rest our weary bones with our swords and revolvers beside us, so that we could spring up at a moment's notice fully armed.

" Let them give thanks whom the Lord hath redeemed and delivered from the hand of the enemy," are the words of the beautiful and very appropriate Psalm for this day, and many a bronzed soldier stood apart for a few moments, quietly and undemonstratively after the manner of Englishmen, thanking his Maker silently in his heart, for that in His great mercy, He had vouchsafed to deliver him this day from " darkness and the shadow of death." Then men who were not required to watch laid themselves down, and fell fast asleep in a moment from sheer exhaustion.

My greatcoat and blanket were on one of the stampeded camels, and now probably form part of the wardrobe of some Hadendowa Sheik ; but a bâtman brought me ——'s blanket, which had not been lost, and as he spread it out, remarked, with the matter-of-fact common sense characteristic of the British soldier, that if had —— escaped, he would no doubt be very glad for me to use his rug, and that if he was dead, he would not require it until he was buried. Poor fellow, I had searched for him in vain, and it was

dreadful to think I might have to write and tell his
people that he had been cut off while endeavouring
to carry out my last order.   I knew him first as a
boy fresh from Eton, and though I had not seen
him for some years, his grandfather and mine were
old friends, and it had been a real pleasure to me to
meet him again.   Now perhaps he was lying pale
and motionless under the silent watch of the stars,
never to speak a word of friendship more, and only
a few short hours ago I was laughing at his sunburned nose.   What lights and shades there are in
a soldier's life—it is comedy and tragedy hand in
hand !   But notwithstanding these harassing thoughts,
I could not shake off the feeling of intense drowsi-
ness that soon began to oppress me with irresistible
force.   After eighteen hours of constant work and
mental strain nature asserted herself, and a hundred-
pound weight seemed to be pressing on my eyelids.
With one last glance, therefore, at the dark figures
of the guard with their comrades lying still and
silent behind, I turned over and fell into a profound
sleep.   Not for long, however; a sudden cry, two or
three shots, and in a moment we were all on our
feet lining the sides of the zareba, while a perfect
torrent of flame poured from it in every direction,
sweeping the dark shadowy bush beyond with a
hailstorm of bullets.   It was only a mule breaking
loose that had caused the alarm, and the bugles at
once sounded the " cease fire."   But the rattle of the
rifles had been sufficient to scatter all my drowsi-
ness, and when I sought my blanket again, it was
with no inclination to close my eyes.   Indeed, the
half-hour of profound sleep I had enjoyed seemed
to have satisfied the imperious cravings of nature
and I was now quite fit and ready to watch all
night, if need be.

It was past ten, and the sky, which before had been overcast, was now clear ˙and the moon had risen. Deep stillness reigned all round. The *Times* correspondent mentions that he heard a wounded Arab near the Berkshire zareba, calling on the name of Allah, and answered at interval by a comrade farther out in the bush; but in the Marines' zareba, where I lay, there was hardly a sound to indicate the presence of the wounded, or to warn a foe prowling outside that nearly a thousand armed men were lying watchful behind the hedge. If any of the enemy *did* attempt to creep near us, they must have been astonished and dismayed at the suddenness with which our lines had burst into a blaze of fire, sweeping the bush mercilessly for 500 yards all round, and then as suddenly became still again. It is quite possible this incident may have had a beneficial effect, and deterred the enemy from attempting a second attack, for just before sunset, the Hasheen zareba had heliographed to say that a strong party of Arabs mounted on camels were proceeding in our direction, but they did not molest us, and the long hours wore away tranquilly ; the monotony of the watch being only broken by the silent changing of the men on guard, and the bright gleam of the electric light from the *Dolphin* lying at anchor in the creek nearly seven miles away, which searched the plain between Suakin and us from time to time. Occasionally the low signal cry of some party of the enemy creeping among the bush in search of their dead, or the snort of a horse, or the scraping of a fusee as a pipe was lit, would break the silence for a moment, but that was all, and the living lay almost as still as the dead around them.

About 4 A.M. two figures appeared picking their way among the prostrate forms; Sir J. M'Neill, with

one of his Staff, was going his rounds. He ordered
the guard to stand on the top of the bank which
had been raised behind the hedge, so as to be
able to see clearly over it, for the dark hour
before dawn was now approaching, favourable, as
every soldier knows, for a surprise, and when vigilance
should be redoubled ; just because it is the time that
men are apt to think their watch is nearly over,
and are least on the alert.   The long flickering line
of bayonets gleaming faintly against the dark back-
ground of the sky had a very weird effect, and made
the zarebas look like the strange outline of some
phosphorescent fish as seen on the sea at midnight.

Slowly, very slowly, the darkness begins to lift ;
the change at first is hardly perceptible, only the
outlines of forms that before were merged in one
indistinguishable mass, now become more clearly
visible ; while, like a curtain that is gently drawn,
the dark shadows of the night seem to roll back
from the sky, then a faint yellow streak of light
glimmers like a newly-lighted candle in the East, the
stars begin to fade, grow pale, and vanish altogether,
as the glorious sun leaping out of the sea appears to
rush up into the vault of heaven, and floods the
whole landscape with its cheery radiance.   Another
day has begun, and we spring to our feet and shake
ourselves, to find clothes and blankets drenched
with heavy drops of sparkling dew——the tears that
a compassionate sky has dropped in the silence of
the night over the dead and living alike.

March 23.——We had gained a victory——a victory
the full importance of which was only discovered
later, when it was found that Osman Digma's power
had for the time been completely shattered and
broken.   Sir M. Hicks Beach, when proposing the

vote of thanks after the campaign, truly remarked,
" It is not too much to say that the power of Osman
Digma had been absolutely crushed," and the real
break-up of Osman's influence dated from this battle,
which was fought and won under conditions the
most unfavourable, and which, according to the ordinary chances of war, should have ended in a disaster
that might have given a serious blow to the military
prestige of Great Britain.　We had, therefore, much
to congratulate ourselves upon, much to be deeply
thankful for.　But no amount of success can take
away from the profound sadness that characterizes
the day after a battle.　It is then the returns have
to be collected of dead, wounded, and missing, and
men begin to realize for the first time, after the
strain and tension of the fight is passed, that many
a comrade whose pleasant voice and happy smile
helped to brighten their lives and lighten the hours
of toil only the day before, has passed from among
them, leaving a gap in the ranks which, though the
survivors close up shoulder to shoulder to conceal it,
will never be filled again.

The enemy's dead are lying in many places
round the zareba thick as sheaves of corn cut by the
reaper, and bearing testimony to the mad fury of
their onslaught.　Most of them have been furnished
with the Mahdi's uniform, and they evidently formed
the flower of Osman Digma's army; but there are old
men and children, and even women among them.　It
is true they would have shown us no mercy had they
prevailed, but it is none the less sad to think how
many a village must have been nearly depopulated
in that brief twenty minutes of desperate fighting.
Still the sun shines brightly on all this hideous
scene, the birds sing, the sea sparkles merrily in the
distance.　Mother nature smiles on the work of her

wilful children ; they are powerless to ruffle her
serene brow.   She acknowledges no such thing as
death, for hers is the work of constant renewal, and
she only sees a change of form where nothing is lost.
Already a faint and sickly odour pervades the air.
The General is ordering the dead camels to be cut
open, and offering the short sword-bayonet he wears
instead of a sabre, for the purpose.   In a few more
years the camels and corpses will be dust, and the
tall desert grass, the kittar bushes, and mimosa
trees, growing all the greener from the enriched
soil; new generations of men will be born to take the
place of the old, and so the world will go on.   And
what of the comrades we have lost ? need we pity
them ? as La Motte Fouqué has said—

> " A moment—and thou sink'st to rest !
> To wake perhaps an angel blest
> In the bright presence of thy Lord !"

It is not those who have gone, but those who are
left behind, who most deserve our sympathy.   But
there is little time to moralize.   Pertinacious, though
defeated, the enemy are still prowling about the
bush threatening the burial parties sent out to dig
graves, and twice before 9 A.M. the men have had
to stand to their arms, though the attack does not
come.

Perhaps the doctors are the most hard worked
of all, for their patients are many, and, as yet, there
is no proper accommodation for them.   There is
only one tent, and in that the most serious cases are
put, while temporary shelters are rigged up with
blankets and spears to protect the others from the
already scorching rays of the sun.

At 11.30 the gleam of bayonets is seen above
the trees.   The Guards, accompanied by General
Graham, are advancing to our relief with a fresh

convoy of stores. Then cheer upon cheer rings through the air as the Household Brigade marches up, steady as if in St. James's Park, and halts in square on the left flank of the Marines' zareba. Very welcome to me are the tidings they bring that —— is safe. It seems he was carried away *nolens volens* with the stampeded cattle, and by the time he was able to extricate himself, the troops in the zareba had opened fire all round, rendering it impossible for him to get back. He, therefore, did the only thing practicable under the circumstances, and joined the Cavalry patrolling in rear, in their gallant efforts to save fugitives from being cut off by the enemy.

There was one alarm after the Guards arrived, and the men stood to their arms ; but it only lasted for a minute or two, and I heard no cause assigned for it. The Cavalry and Mounted Infantry went out into the bush and scouted, but did not come into collision with the enemy.

I heard one of the doctors attached to the Head-quarter Staff, as he rode in with the Guards Brigade and shook hands with his colleague at the zareba, say, "Well, how are the wounded?" "Oh, it's terrible!" replied the other, who appeared quite worn out, and was shortly afterwards invalided home, "they are all over the place." "Oh, well," said the first medico, cheerily, "remember I am fresh and you are not ; just tell me what you want done, and we'll get to work at once." The Generals meanwhile held a consultation, and it was decided to send back the Indians and reinforce the zareba with two Battalions of the Guards Brigade, while the third Battalion was to return to Suakin with the Indians. The new convoy of 700 camels had brought out fresh supplies of water and provisions, which were now quickly unloaded ; and I was

ordered to take the remnant of my late convoy
back with them to Suakin.

At 2 P.M. everything was ready, and the
Indians and Grenadier Guards moved off, forming a
large square, enclosing the camels and the dhoolies
with the wounded.   The Grenadier Guards formed
the rear face of the square, the post of honour, where
attack might be expected, and the Cavalry and
Mounted Infantry scouted all round.   We met with
no adventures on the homeward march, but it was a
shocking spectacle to see the number of dead bodies
strewing the route to within two miles of Suakin.
They were mostly native followers who had joined
the stampede, but there were also some Indian soldiers and Europeans among them ; while dead
camels, bales of compressed hay, biscuit boxes, and
empty water tins were scattered about promiscuously.
These, when practicable, were picked up ; but the
Staff were in a desperate hurry to get the baggage
animals along, and I heard the Transport officer in
charge declare that some of them took to amateur
camel-driving, and began thumping his beasts in the
vain delusion that they could be driven like donkeys.

I had borrowed a horse from a mounted sergeant,
whom I put on a camel, and when we neared Suakin,
rode on ahead of the square with Major B———, my
coadjutor on the water duty.   People used to chaff
this gallant Sapper on the way he curled his mous-
taches, but I noticed that he was none the less cool
and collected during what a friend of mine calls the
" hurrush " of the previous day, and I am not sure
that he did not give them an extra twirl before he
prepared to receive the Arab charge.   We soon
reached the wells outside the Left Water Fort, and
stopped to water our tired horses, which seemed,
poor beasts, as if they could never drink enough.

Then, as I rode up from the well, G. P. caught sight
of me, and came running down to shake hands. He
said he had an awful time of it for the last twenty-
four hours, as the fugitives flying from the zareba
brought in news that we had all been cut to pieces,
and reported, in the most circumstantial manner,
that they had seen P. C. F. and myself all killed.
So he had been sitting alone in his deserted
tent thinking how he should write the news home
when our bodies were brought in. Of course, he did
not believe all that he heard, but when he saw the
plain covered with riderless horses and wounded
men streaming towards Suakin, he naturally thought
we must have had a bad time of it. All the more
that Staff officers were galloping about saying that
the enemy were advancing in force, and the camp
was to be held to the last moment. He told me
one man came in with the back of his head nearly
chopped off, and sat down in front of him groaning
with his face between his hands ; and altogether the
last twenty-four hours had been like a frightful
nightmare.

I got a fresh horse, and galloped to the Headquarter camp to report. There, also, I found that I
was supposed to have been killed, for the first words
the S. C. O. said, when he caught sight of me, were,
" Halloo ! here's the dead man come to life again ! "
This made me very uneasy, lest the news should
have gone home. They were all very kind and
cordial, but I did not stop, and galloped on to the
Ordnance stores to see St. G———, to whom, as he
was near Suakin, I had heliographed a message
from the zareba, asking him to telegraph home to
say I was all right. When I entered his tent he
looked at me as if I was a ghost. His own officer,
E———, had been killed, and he fully believed I had

shared the same fate, till I suddenly walked in and
took him by surprise.   I learned that the heliograph
had never reached him, so rode on to Suakin to
send my message, and did not get back to the
camp till dark.   The kindly order afterwards issued,
which enabled officers to send home a telegram
after an engagement free of cost, was not then in
force.

There are few battles the experiences of which
are not useful to the military student, and there are
one or two points connected with that of the 22d,
worthy of remark.   A great deal has already been
said about bayonets bending and becoming unservice-
able, and there is no doubt that the steel used
for them should be of the finest quality.   In our
little wars against savage nations the bayonet is
brought into much more frequent action than it
would probably be during a European campaign ;
and our soldiers in the Soudan had to depend on
this arm alone at many a critical moment, as, for
instance, when they cleared the enemy out of the
Berkshire zareba.   It is therefore manifest that our
troops should be armed with a weapon on which
they can rely with confidence.   But, besides the
necessary improvement in the material, there is a
point to which I have not hitherto seen attention
drawn, and that is the shape of the bayonet.   Those
who have never witnessed a mortal struggle like that
of the 22d, can have little idea of the tremendous
force with which bayonet thrusts are delivered in
the moment of excitement, especially when a foe is
rushing on them with the impetuosity displayed by
the Hadendowas ; and it was a notorious fact that
in not a few cases soldiers plunged their bayonets
right over the bend at the shank into the bodies
of their adversaries, and were unable to withdraw

them in time to save themselves from being cut down by others of the enemy hurrying up behind. I heard of a case where a man actually had to drag the body of an Arab he had bayoneted for several yards after him along the ground, closely pursued by the enemy, before he could disengage his weapon to defend himself; and several lives were lost in this way. The conical shape of the bayonet naturally tends to expand the wound as it is driven home, and once the bend enters the body, it becomes fixed as if it were a harpoon. This is a ghastly matter to write about, but, as in savage warfare it may mean life or death to a soldier, it is worth consideration. I think that the time has come when a new form of bayonet should be adopted, somewhat on the pattern of the present sword-bayonet, but lighter, with a cross hilt to prevent its being driven too far, and a sharp cutting edge, so that it can be used as a knife on occasion.

I have already related how I saw Sir J. M'Neill at one time proposing to lend his own sword-bayonet for cutting open dead camels, as no proper knives could be found to perform an operation absolutely necessary in this climate, to prevent the bodies becoming distended with gas, and to enable the sun to dry them up; and there are many other occasions during a campaign, on which soldiers would find a bayonet of the *couteau de chasse* pattern more useful than a purely thrusting weapon. The principal disadvantage of the present sword-bayonet is its weight, which renders it too heavy to be used on the long rifle, and there are only two alternatives. One, to invent a shorter and lighter weapon, which would not have this objection; and the other, to arm the line with short rifles, such as are now used by Rifle Battalions. This would be a sweeping reform, but I believe it would not be a bad one, as the short rifle and sword-bayonet are more handy, and require a simpler drill than the longer weapon, while the shooting of the short rifle is, I believe, good enough for all practical purposes. If it is not, it is clearly absurd that our special Rifle Battalions, representing as they do twelve regiments, should be armed with the inferior weapon. In an earlier part of this book I have advanced an opinion that these Battalions should consist of picked marksmen, and if the superior shooting of the long rifle is a proved fact, it is certain the Rifle Battalions ought to be armed with it. I believe the short rifle was first adopted for these Battalions, because it was found more suitable for skirmishing drill ; but every regiment in the service is now called on to practice the same attack formation as the Rifle Regiments, and if the short rifle is best for this, all Line Regiments should be armed with it alike, and the long rifle only retained for the Household Brigade and a few Battalions of picked marksmen.

With regard to ammunition, I am very glad that there is now a likelihood that solid drawn cartridges will be used in the future. The pattern of cartridge sent to the Soudan was certainly not strong enough to bear the wear and tear of a campaign, and I noticed that even before they had become knocked out of shape by shaking about in the ball bag, they frequently fitted somewhat stiffly into the rifle and required a very forcible pressure of the thumb to drive them home before the breech could be closed. There is little doubt that the magazine rifle will be the weapon of the future, for it is now beginning to be understood that it will not lead to a greater waste of ammunition than the ordinary breech-loading system, and the possession of such a weapon will give greater confidence to the men, affording, as it does, facilities for pouring an almost uninterrupted stream of fire on an enemy at close quarters. It is not unlikely that in future wars the result of many an engagement may depend on the power of one side or the other to keep up a concentrated stream of fire for a few minutes consecutively. Sir Frederick Roberts has recently said, " It is very satisfactory to find that an improved rifle is about to be issued, and not only, I am glad to say, to the British, but to the Indian Army, for it has always seemed to me unfair that we should call upon our Native soldiers to fight alongside their British comrades, while we arm them with an inferior weapon." This unfairness might have recoiled on our heads in a most unpleasant fashion at Tofrek, for after the first two rushes of the enemy, I heard officers inquiring very anxiously where the Martini-Henry ammunition had got to, as some of the reserve store of the European troops was found to consist of Snider cartridges, while the Indians on the other hand had been given the Martini-Henry cases, which were equally useless to them. The consequences that might have followed this accidental mixing of the two kinds of ammunition when the mules were unloaded, may well be imagined, had the enemy rushed in again before the error could be rectified. Let there be, therefore, a uniform pattern of ammunition throughout the service, and I trust that before long the new rifle will be fitted with a magazine and an improved sword-bayonet.

With regard to the alleged jamming of the Gardner guns at the zareba, mentioned in the papers, and alluded to by Lord Bury in the House, on the 26th March, Sir Gerald Graham's despatch of the 28th March makes no mention of it, and simply says : " The Gardner guns were being placed in position at the time and could not be got into action, so that their detachments who stood their ground gallantly, suffered severely." The guns near which I was standing in the Marines' zareba were got into action after a short delay, and I do not remember hearing that they had jammed, though I have since been told they did, and it is clearly a matter of importance that the cartridges for these guns should be of a uniform pattern with those used for rifles, to obviate all chance of their becoming mixed. Lord Morley's reply to Lord Bury, that "the five-barrelled Gardner was not sent out for the use of the troops, except those from the ships, the military weapon having only two barrels," would hardly be a valid excuse in the future ; for now that the supplementing of military expeditions with naval detachments has become a recognized practice, the Admiralty and the War Office should strive to obtain complete uniformity in the ammunition for the small arms of both services.

It cannot be too constantly borne in mind by every one who has to do with an army in the field, from the Secretary of State for War at home, to the smallest bugler who has to sound a call, that though a battle may last for hours, there is generally some one five minutes in the day when the scale is turned for victory or defeat. That, according to the experience of all military history, the greatest issues have frequently depended on the action of one side or the other during some such brief space of time, and the most careful attention, therefore, to the smallest detail that can prevent an accident at a critical moment, is of vital importance to the welfare of an army.

No doubt, had the force which advanced on the 22d been accompanied by a captive balloon, we

should have known all about the enemy's movements, but I presume the balloon was not yet
ready ; a balloon, moreover, is liable to accidents,
and in a country of vast plains like the Soudan, I
would suggest that a waggon might be provided,
fitted with a light folding scaffold of bamboo, strong
enough to support the weight of one man at a
height, say, of twenty-five feet above the waggon.
A scaffold of this description, which could be erected
and taken down in a few minutes, is not difficult to
construct, and it would be of great value for military
purposes as a signal-station and watch-tower.

I can give an illustration of this :—It appears
that the reason the enemy left us so long unmolested, was that they knew we were to march
eight miles, and were expecting us two miles farther
on.   When they found we had halted only six miles
from Suakin, they had to creep over the intervening
distance without exciting our suspicion.   But, had
we possessed an elevated point of observation, they
could hardly have succeeded in this, for the mimosa
bush does not conceal the plain when you get a
bird's-eye view of it, as the intervals between the
trees are clearly seen.

I will conclude these remarks with a few notes
on the circumstances of the battle.   Was it a complete surprise ? is a question that has been frequently
asked me.   If a surprise in military parlance may
be defined as an attack coming, either from an un-
expected direction, or delivered before the troops
attacked have had time to prepare to resist it, then,
in the latter sense, it certainly was a complete surprise, for, not only were the majority of officers and
men quite ignorant that there was any force of the
enemy in their immediate vicinity, but they found
themselves actually engaged before they had time

to fall into their places to resist attack. Sir Gerald
Graham, in his despatch of the 28th March, alluding
to the severe loss of officers, says that it "was due
to the fact that in the confusion arising from the
sudden attack, individual attempts were gallantly
made to collect isolated bodies of men to stem the
determined rush of the enemy." Thus even official
testimony confirms the theory of a surprise. Now
there is a military axiom which has been a good
deal quoted with reference to this fight, viz. that
a General may be defeated, but should never be
surprised. Just as it might be said that a ship may
founder, but should never run ashore. Nevertheless,
when one of our war vessels does so, if the officer in
command can prove that the accident was due to a
defect in his compasses, or his engines, or his charts,—
in short, causes beyond his own control,—he is held
blameless, and acquitted with all honour. I need
hardly say I have neither the wish nor the power to
constitute myself a judge in the present case : I shall
simply direct my readers' attention to one or two
points connected with it, which may help them to
form an opinion for themselves.

When we examined the composition of the force
ordered to march out on the 22d March, we find that
only one squadron of Cavalry was detailed to scout
in front of no less than five Battalions of Infantry
and other details, marching in two squares, the
second of which enclosed a very large and valuable
convoy. Sir J. M'Neill, there is evidence to show, was
much dissatisfied with this arrangement, but did not
actually apply for more Cavalry ; and here a question arises. Should a General, if he finds that he
has not sufficient Cavalry to scout efficiently, follow
the example of Oliver Twist, and ask for more ?
If I were in such a position I confess I should do

so, considering the safety of my force as a matter of paramount importance; and if the Chief did not like my asking, I would "just stand the wigging," as a gallant Colonel of the 60th, now on the Staff, used to say when he followed the dictates of his common sense.   At the same time it is manifest that it would be exceedingly inconvenient and detrimental to the discipline of the service, if junior officers were habitually to constitute themselves judges of what ought or ought not to be the composition of the force with which they were entrusted ; and a General may be perfectly justified in considering that he is displaying a more soldier-like spirit if he raises no question about the force given him, and simply does the best he can with it.

The next thing to consider is the route adopted. Not long ago one of our most distinguished officers mentioned to me that Baker Pasha told him there was a route to the left of that we followed which was comparatively free from bush, and, as one of his old zarebas was situated three miles to the left of ours, and about a mile and a half nearer Tamai, he ought to know.   But here again Sir J. M'Neill was not a free agent, and marched to order, halting on a spot chosen by the guiding officer as a fit site for the zareba.   It may be asked should a General, if his military instinct tells him that a halting ground is in a dangerous situation, consent to remain there ?   I think not, and he is certainly entirely responsible for the position he takes up.   But in the present case there appeared to be little option, or rather a choice of two evils, for the bush we had struggled through had already been so thick, and that before and around us appeared so interminable, that it seemed probable we might not find another clearing of the same extent, unless we

marched considerably farther, and to do that, would
have entailed delaying the return of the Indians and
convoy till after dark.

It has been asked in one of the newspapers, why
were not a few shells thrown into the bush to search
for the presence of an enemy?   And no doubt
nothing could be more efficacious in a country
like the Soudan, where any force of men rapidly
dispersing before an exploding shell would be certain
to send up a column of dust that would betray their
presence.   But, as we had no Artillery with us, it
is evident this plan could not be carried out.

Of the wisdom of halting, instead of attempting
to push farther, considering the difficulties in which
the Transport was involved, and the danger of delaying its return through such a country till nightfall,
there can be little doubt ; indeed, it is probable that
our halting when we did, saved us from much more
serious disaster.

It, therefore, only remains to consider the disposition of the troops when a halt was made.   Here the
question of the information in the hands of the General
arises.   Perhaps, if he had been possessed of the
special information gained by the Intelligence Branch,
before quoted, and particularly of the warning that
8000 men were concentrated on our flank, it would
have been his duty either to abandon the undertaking, or, on reaching the clearing, to hobble his convoy
inside the Indian square, and allow no man to stir
from his post until the Cavalry, supported by a fighting square of the Europeans, had pushed forward
into the bush and ascertained the exact position of
the foe.   But it has been truly said, " to expect an
attack is one thing, to be assured of an attack in
force is quite another ;" and without this specific
information, and in view of the fact that we had

advanced entirely unopposed, and that only small
parties of the enemy had been seen, who all retired
at once in the direction of Tamai, he could hardly be
expected to do more than make such general provisions for defence as the nature of the ground permitted.   The number of troops under his command
was not sufficient to entirely enclose the convoy, and
carry on the work of unloading it and building three
zarebas at the same time.   He, therefore, formed the
Indians, as before described, in three sides of a
square, facing the mountains, from which direction
attack might naturally be most expected, while he
kept his force of Europeans in reserve, a little to the
rear of the open side facing the seashore.   Pickets
and Cavalry vedettes were also posted as far out as
the thickness of the bush would permit.   I do not
know why a portion of the Cavalry was "held in
support on some open ground about 500 yards
to the S.W. of the zareba," as General Graham
avers, and it appears to me that in a place like this,
where Cavalry could hardly act on the offensive, it
would have been better had the whole squadron been
employed on vedette duty, for which alone their
numbers were far from sufficient.   But the portion
held in reserve must have been very small.

These general dispositions having been made,
the work of building the zarebas and unloading the
convoy had to be proceeded with *at once*, for time
was a matter of the utmost importance.   Any one
who likes to try how long it takes to empty a nine
gallon cask through the bung hole, will be able to
form an idea of the time required to empty 900
mussacks alone.   Besides these, there were 600
other vessels to be emptied or stored, Commissariat
supplies had to be unloaded and piled, the zareba
planned, the bush cut down and dragged to its

place, the redoubts for the Gardners built, the men
served with food and water, etc.   It is, therefore,
clear that a considerable number of men were
necessarily employed on work which could not be
entirely carried on inside a square.   The area,
where this work went on was, however, protected by
the Indian Battalions, though it was unavoidable
that parties cutting bush should occasionally work
in front of their lines, to obtain materials for the
zarebas ; whether these workmen could have been
protected by strong covering parties, I leave it for
others to decide.   But it must be remembered that a
certain number of men had to be held in reserve to
guard the guns and ammunition.   The camels, after
being unloaded, were taken to the only available
piece of open ground in rear of the Indian troops.
No doubt, their position was a weak one, as one
flank of the column was exposed to the bush, but
the 17th Native Infantry covered the rear of it,
while the European square protected its front ; and,
had there been any notice of impending attack, it
would not have taken long to move the whole
column within the lines of the zareba, and sweep
the clearing all round with rifle fire.

Even when the work was progressing most busily,
nobody was far away from his place, and I believe
that had five minutes' clear notice been given of the
approach of the enemy, the whole force could have
been disposed to resist attack without much loss.
That such notice was not given, I consider, was
wholly due to the smallness of the Cavalry force,
and, perhaps, because after a long and trying march
under a hot sun, and being left for four hours
unmolested, the men may have ceased to keep a
very vigilant look-out.   Even when they were
surprised, if every trooper had discharged his carbine

before he turned round and galloped back, I think there would yet have been time for all the men to run to their places, and stand to arms ; I know this is contrary to Cavalry traditions, but I would strongly urge that Cavalry scouting in thick bush, should be instructed *always* to give the first notice that the enemy is approaching by firing their carbines, even before they send a report, for it is a signal that the commonest soldier can understand, and will prepare him at once for action, whereas the sight of several horsemen galloping madly about, only bewilders him.

Sir Gerald Graham, in his telegram of the 23d March, says, " The Cavalry, 5th Lancers, did their best to give information, but the ground being covered with bush, it was impossible to see any distance," and it is far from my wish to cast any aspersion on this gallant Regiment, which behaved very well during the campaign.   I would only point out that if, as Sir Gerald Graham says in his despatch of the 28th March, " the squadron 5th Lancers formed a chain of Cossack posts (each four men) at a distance of about 1000 yards from the force," which there is no reason to doubt they did, and every man had discharged his carbine while the enemy were still at that distance from us, there would have been time to get the convoy, which was quite ready to move, closed into the central zareba, so that the half Battalion of the Berkshire could have protected its flank with their fire, and for the working parties in the bush to run in and stand to arms. The breaking of the 17th Native Infantry was an incident that could not possibly be foreseen by the General, and left the convoy isolated and at the mercy of the Arabs, while our men in self-defence had to fire on it to prevent the enemy breaking through them under cover of the moving mass.

These are briefly the principal difficulties and disadvantages with which the General had to contend, and it should be remembered that, though surprised, we were victorious ; which, after all, is better than being not surprised, but beaten, according to the regular usages of war.   There is not the slightest doubt that it was mainly owing to the bulldog courage and steadiness of the rank and file in a moment of great danger that the victory was due. But the General in command had an impossible task to perform with an inadequate force, and, according to the writer of the letter in the *United Service Gazette* of the 25th July, with imperfect information.   It would, therefore, appear that Sir Gerald Graham was only doing justice to the Commander of the Expedition, when he expressed the opinion in his telegram of the 23d March, " That M'Neill did everything possible under the circumstances."

The lessons taught by this fight are simple enough.   When a force has to advance into thick bush to build a zareba in the face of the enemy, it is dangerous to hamper it with the charge of a large convoy.   The work of clearing a road through the bush for future convoys, building a zareba, and perhaps fighting a battle, will be quite as much as can be done in one day ; and the convoy accompanying the force should be reduced to the narrowest possible limits.   This is more especially the case when the force is near its base, and convoys can be readily despatched to it once a road has been cleared.

It is advisable to provide a force advancing into such a country with a strong detachment of Cavalry or Mounted Infantry, to thoroughly search the ground ahead of it, and also that it should be accompanied by at least a couple of guns to shell the bush where the presence of an enemy is suspected. The General in command should be furnished with every scrap of information that may help to guide him in discovering the probable movements of the enemy, and it is better not to tell him to "Go on if you can," without due warning, if there is information at hand that a large force is concentrated on his flank.

I think every military man will agree that few things can press harder on a gallant soldier than to find himself condemned by public opinion for errors he did not commit, when he has honestly and faithfully endeavoured to fulfil his duty, and even obtained a brilliant victory under most unfavourable conditions. Of course I am only stating a personal opinion, but I believe that if any error was committed, it lay in the despatching a force so constituted, through such a country, in the face of the information that had been obtained of Osman Digma's probable intentions.

CHAPTER VIII.

THE ADVANCE ON TAMAI.

MARCH 24.—How delicious is a day of complete rest! Not that there is any pause in the duties of the Water Transport, and a convoy is going out to-morrow at daybreak, but G. P. has kindly undertaken to superintend the work this night, and I have been given leave to do what I please. Delightful thought, after so many sleepless nights and burning days! My spurs hang idle on the tent hooks; I may stand with my hands in my pockets and whistle without a care for a whole day if I choose. If I were in England, I would lie on my back on the grass and idly watch the fleecy clouds chasing each other through the blue depths of the sky—that is, if March in England were half as warm as it is here; but at Suakin there are no fleecy clouds and no grass, and, as I sit in my deck chair, with that pleasant languor over all my limbs, that is born of past hard work, I am content to watch the little white town in the offing through one of the four doors of the tent, left open to catch every breath of air that steals across the glaring plain.

Suakin, or Sowārgin, as the natives pronounce it, literally *Sàwa Gin*, "Together" (with the) "Genii": my mind wanders off to the old tradition which affirms that the people of this place derive their origin from seven virgins who dwelt on the coral island. How did these maidens come there? That is a tale that has been lost in the mists of antiquity. Perhaps those daring Greek mariners whom we are told sailed through the pillars of Hercules along the coast of Africa, with the sun rising each morning on their left hand, till at last, after many tempests and perils, though they had never lost sight of the coast, they were astonished one day to find it rising on their right; made their way into the Red Sea, and, enervated by the soft warmth of the climate, tarried to listen to the songs of the Syrens whom tradition tells us dwelt of old in the pink grottos beneath its coral islands, and during the bright tropical moonlit nights would rise to the surface, and sit combing their jetty locks and watching the reflection of their unearthly loveliness in the mirror of its pellucid waters.

Perhaps the stout ship which had borne many a sturdy buffet from rude Boreas was wrecked at last, and the sinking mariners found themselves encircled in the Sea Nymphs' cold embrace, and gazed upon by eyes that shone like stars in brilliancy, though their glance meant death. But these Greek heroes were a type of mortal the tawny Mermaids of the Red Sea had never seen before; they had nothing in common with the swart ill-favoured sons of Africa who usually fished in these waters. Their skins were fair as Parian marble, their bearing noble, their muscles moulded in the just proportions of athletes who had won many a golden wreath at the gymnic contests, their heads and beards a wild profusion of hyacinthine locks, framing faces beautiful in their pure classical outlines as the Sun-God's image. What wonder, then, if the Mermaids relented from their cruel design, and, instead of drowning these sons of Hellas, bore them gently to the

coral island and tended them with womanly devotion, laying at their feet all the riches of the deep.
Rare pearls and corals, and amber and gold from
the sunken fleets of Ophir ; while the facile Greeks
resigned themselves unquestioningly to a happy
dreamy idyllic life with their amphibious brides, now
gamboling with them in the sparkling waters of the
bay, now reposing in the balmy twilight beneath the
waving palm trees that bent over the fresh waters
of the great river, which it is certain at one time
emptied itself here into the sea, and cut the long
channel between the coral reefs through which ships
now enter.

Then might the Syrens' song be heard, accompanied by the Pandean pipes ; but even in those
halcyon days Greeks were treacherous and fickle,
and, when the mariners had amassed much treasure
from the depths of the Red Sea, they longed to behold once again the slopes of snow-capped Orbelus,
and, having secretly repaired their vessel, sailed away
one night, leaving the hapless Mermaids, now bur-
dened with the cares of maternity, to weep on the
shore like " mournful Œnone wandering forlorn."
Then was the song of the Syrens so sad and mournful, that tears rose unbidden to the eyes of the rough
fishermen when they chanced to hear it wafted across
the sea ; and the Bulbul, which till then had been
a blithesome bird, singing glad hymns of praise like
all the feathered kind, almost broke its heart as it
listened and copied the sad lament of the abandoned
Sea Nymphs, which it repeats to this day in the stillness of the summer night.

I have said that the women of Suakin are not
now beautiful, but it was not always so ; and seven
young maidens, stately as palm trees, supple as
willows, blending the graceful beauty of the Greek

with all the passionate mysterious charm of the
Egyptian Cleopatra, grew up to early womanhood
upon the island.   One beauty alone those who,
according to Arab traditions, are descended from
these damsels, retain even yet, and that is the most
lovely and perfect teeth it is possible to look upon.
Doctor Josiah Williams says, in a nasty scientific
way, that it is because the people of the Eastern
Soudan feed principally on *Sorgrum vulgare,* or
" dhurra," which contains one and a half per cent
more gluten than our wheat.   But I believe that
these bright quarrelets of dazzling teeth are an in-
heritance from those seven fair and stately maidens
who dwelt upon the coral island, watched over by
the Sea Nymphs of the Bahr-el-Ahmar.

At that time there were no inhabitants on
the mainland, which, then as now, was cut off
from the mighty Nile by a burning tract of desert
stretching between the river and the mountains ;
and we may be sure that no man ever put his
foot upon the island, for the Sea Nymphs, rendered
remorseless by their past experience of the fickle
ways of sailors, took care to drown every soul who
attempted to approach it.   The fishermen from the
Arabian coast told strange stories of the seven beautiful fair-skinned maidens, who were occasionally
seen from afar off on summer evenings, propel-
ling their swift canoes with dexterous hand
through the winding channels of the coral reefs ;
but the boldest never adventured near the island,
round the rocky sides of which the waves leaped so
angrily at their approach ; and the maidens lived
until they had attained their seventeenth year, a
strange isolated life, their wants being all supplied
by invisible hands ; for the poor Sea Nymphs in their
short love dream had learned enough of the feelings

of mortals to know, that even their own offspring
would shrink from them with horror, if they discovered that their occupation was to lure mariners
to their death ; and, though they often watched the
maidens as they slept and laid beside them rich
garments and jewels from many a lost vessel, they
never, after the first years of childhood were passed,
revealed themselves to their waking eyes.

So the young girls knew nothing of their origin,
and, though their hearts were full of vague indefinite
longings and aspirations, they were happy in that
their wants were all supplied, and they had no experience of any other life.   The milk of the cocoa-nut, the
fruit of the banana, date-palm, and pomegranate,
furnished their simple daily food, and were gathered
without labour from the various trees which at that
time bordered the great river, flowing like a silver
path across the plain from the dark range of the
Waratab Mountains in the distance.   Their companions were the tiny gazelles that came down at
sunset to drink of its waters, and the bright plumaged
birds that warbled in the groves with notes not
merrier or more musical than the maiden's own
laughing voices.   So they grew into the full perfection
of earthly beauty and were beloved by "the Sons of
the Stars," gazing tenderly down on them through the
silent watches of the night.

One evening, as the girls sat on the shore of their
island listening to the gentle sighing of the wind,
which, laden with sweet scents, swept softly over the
curling waves that flashed with pale phosphorescent
light as they rose and fell beating against the long
line of reef with rhythmic cadence, seven falling stars
suddenly shot out of the dark vault of the heavens
above, trailing behind them so brilliant a stream of
light that the maidens instinctively hid their eyes

with their hands.   When they opened them again, what was their astonishment to behold seven tall and handsome youths coming towards them from the opposite side of the island.   They had never held converse with a man, and they knew no fear of any living thing, but they could not help a secret thrill of alarm at the sudden apparition of these strangers, who seemed to have sprung out of the ground at their feet.   The young men, however, prostrated themselves with every sign of reverence, and, kissing the hem of their garments, said they were travellers and craved hospitality for the night ; but before the girls could form a suitable reply, an ominous roar rose from the sea, and in a moment huge waves came rolling up the shore of the island as if about to engulph it in their seething waters.

Indeed, the Syrens, ever watchful over their offspring, had beheld with rage and consternation the sudden appearance of the strangers.   No ship for seventeen years had neared that fatal island without being wrecked, and every man on board ruthlessly dragged to the bottom by the revengeful Nymphs. They had seen no boat approach, and yet here were seven young men actually standing safe and sound upon the shore talking to their daughters, and no doubt using those insidious flatteries which the Syrens had such good reason to remember had once been poured into their ears by the honeyed tongues of their faithless Grecian lovers.   To say that their feelings were outraged, hardly describes their condition ; they were mad with what Homer calls " a heart devouring rage," and they determined to get rid of these daring detrimentals at once and for ever, by raising such a tempest at sea as should sweep them off the face of the island ; and if they were once engulphed in the rising waters, and thus placed in their power, the Syrens knew very well what to do with them ; the sharks, the barracouters, and man-eating crabs should feed on their worthless carcasses in the dark caves at the bottom of the sea, and their beloved children be saved from the wiles of deceitful man.

But these seven youths were Genii, sons of the Hyades, who had assumed human form for love of the island maids, and, when they saw the waters thus rising, they summoned from the sky such a terrible storm of thunder, rain, and wind, that the waves were beaten down by the falling torrent, or rolled back impotent upon themselves by the fierce force of the blast. Indeed, so furious was the struggle of elements, that the old Sea King who lived at the bottom of the Red Sea came up to find out what was the matter.

Now when the Genii beheld him, they laughed in his face, and cried, " Oh, Sea King, verily thou sleepest sound that thou permittest thy Syrens to marry the sailors they should drown." Then the King was wroth, and his very beard curled with anger, as he replied, " Surely if they have done this thing they know the doom." At these words the poor Syrens trembled with fear, for they knew that, for every hair on the head of a sailor whom they spared, they would be condemned to pass a hundred years in the lowest depths of the sea in company with the slimy monsters that dwell below, and, when they thought of the luxuriant locks of their Grecian lovers, their hearts sank within them. No more on moonlight nights would they be able to sit decking their hair with pearls beside the sparkling waves and singing their wild sweet song ; no more would they be able to watch with fierce jealousy over those children in whom they secretly loved to see repeated again the beauteous features of their departed Greeks, even though the memory was fraught with pain. For thousands of years they would be condemned to dwell in semi-darkness at the bottom of the ocean, listening to the interminable nautical stories of the old King.   But the doom had been pronounced, and there was no appeal.

So the storm abated and the sun rose, and when the maidens, who had fainted with terror at the fury of the tempest, opened their eyes, they found the seven youths bending over them with tender care ; and in time they grew to love them, and for a brief six months another happy idyll was enacted on the coral island.

But Arab traditions tell us that these strange unions between mortals and the Genii, were ever fated to be disastrous to the denizens of this globe, and at length the hour arrived when the Genii were forced to return to the elements, from which for a short span of time the power of love had enabled them to separate.   They too, like the Sea Nymphs, had to pay the penalty of seeking to taste the sweets of earthly affection, and were condemned to sleep a thousand years for every day they had enjoyed in mortal form ; very sadly, therefore, did they gaze on the unconscious forms of their young and beautiful brides on the fatal night that was to separate them for ever. . . .

When the daughters of the Syrens arose in the morning, they found seven meteoric stones lying beside them, which bore some faint resemblance to the human shape ; but their husbands had vanished never to return.

The spell had departed from the island when the Syrens ceased to keep watch over it, and one day, a fisherman was driven into the Bay by stress of

weather and landed safely : he returned to tell his
wondering companions that he had found seven
young mothers nursing their offspring on this lonely
spot where never man had been known to tread,
and also that the Bay was a safe shelter and full of
fish ; which abound in it even to the present day.
Presently, others of his hardy and simple tribe went
there, and because of the story the women told them,
they called the place *Sàwa Gin,* "Together with the
Genii," and in time a colony was founded.   But the
once beautiful coral island gradually sank under
Ottoman rule into a nest of slave-traders.   The
population became degraded ; the river, as though its
pure waters shrank from mixing with such pollution,
fled from its sandy bed and sought the free companionship of the clouds, though the course it once
traversed may still be clearly traced across the plain,
and—

"I never heard a fellow snore as you have been
doing," said P——, later in the afternoon, as I
opened my eyes.   "Colonel —— has been here, but
he would not let me wake you, and G. P. is just
going down to the water depôt."   Did I dream this
dream then, or have I dreamed it later ?   It matters
not, I had at least enjoyed a good sleep.

While walking through the Headquarter· camp,
now moved up close to the Right Water Fort, I heard
that the S.C.O. had broken his collar bone ; I found
him sitting in a chair with his arm in a sling, but
apparently caring little about the accident, except
that it interfered with his work.   He told me his
horse had put its foot in a hole as he was galloping
past the hospital at H. Redoubt, and turned a complete
somersault, shooting him over its head ; but, notwithstanding the pain of the broken bone, he had walked
two miles through a hot sun to get back to Head-

quarters, fearing he might be detained at the hospital. When the doctors up here saw him, they wanted to send him at once on board the *Ganges ;* a measure against which he protested loudly, and, catching sight of the Chief of the Staff passing the tent, he called him to come to his assistance. The C. of S. soon settled the matter, saying, the doctors might go to Berber if they liked, but that his Senior Commissariat officer was much too valuable a man to be invalided, and it was therefore arranged that he should stay up here.

At first they insisted on putting him in the Right Water Fort, lest the camp should be rushed by the enemy, and I went to see if a snug corner could be fitted up for him ; but when I reported that, as the fort could only be reached by ascending a ladder, and twenty people slept in one small room, it was hardly a suitable place, and suggested that, though Colonel ——'s arm was disabled, he still had the use of his legs should the enemy trouble us, they consented to let me have a tent pitched for him in a nice breezy position, where he will get well all the quicker for the fresh air.

They say that Faggiah, one of the most celebrated of Osman's chiefs, was killed on Sunday, and that Osman himself watched the fight from a safe distance. He was on foot, for he never trusts his precious person on horse or camel. A convoy was despatched to the zareba at Hasheen this morning, under escort of the Shropshire, but returned without being attacked, though they reported the bush apparently swarming with the enemy. Indeed, the Arabs evince little sign of depression, notwithstanding their recent losses. Another convoy of dry Commissariat stores was despatched to the Tofrek zareba, escorted by the 15th Sikhs and some Cavalry.

When it got half-way out, it was met by the Coldstream Guards and Marines from the zareba, who
took over the convoy. A correspondent says these
had marched but a short distance back towards the
zareba, "when they were suddenly attacked by large
bodies of the enemy in the bush. The Lancers at
once deployed, and in a most gallant style dashed
into the bush, shooting down the Arabs with their
carbines, while the Guards and Marines threw themselves into square and poured volley after volley
into the enemy." The firing was renewed two
or three times before the column regained the
zareba, and the Sikhs halted when they heard the
volleys, expecting also to be attacked, and did not
continue their homeward march till they ascertained
that the Guards and Marines had safely regained
Tofrek.

At 7 P.M. two hundred camel-men and a large
force of foot were signalled as coming from the
direction of Hasheen, and crossing the plain from
N. to S. between the zareba and our camp.

March 25.—About 6 A.M. poor G. P. returned
from his night's work at No. 5 pier, looking very
tired and nearly bent double. He said that he had
strained his back lifting some of the water tins, as
no fatigue party had been furnished him ; he would
not have his back rubbed, and lay down on his bed
quite exhausted. I wish, instead of lifting the tins,
he had sent word to Headquarters that, as there
was no fatigue party, there could be no work. That
would have made them "sit up." Yet how could
he stop work knowing that his comrades would be
depending on his exertions for their water supply
to-day ? He was no better as the morning advanced,
so the doctors came and looked at him, and said
they thought he must have caught a chill ; I notice

that is what they generally do say when they cannot quite tell what is the matter.

The useless zareba at Hasheen was evacuated to-day,—a very good thing, considering how heavily it has taxed the men and convoys to keep it supplied. The men stationed there, though quite safe, have been practically imprisoned, being unable either to leave their zareba, or stop the enemy from passing along the foot of the hills to threaten the flank of our advance on Tamai. A convoy of camels went out under escort to bring in the stores, and the zareba was burned.

This day was memorable from the fact that the water convoy despatched to Tofrek was accompanied by the captive war balloon, which made its first journey very successfully. It was brought up to the Right Water Fort yesterday evening, and filled during the night from the tubes of compressed gas brought from Chatham. It only weighs 90 lbs., and contains 7000 cubic feet of gas ; its diameter is 23 feet, and it is made of gold-beaters' skin, the basket being large enough to hold one man conveniently. When inflated it is attached by a fine wire rope to a waggon, and on this occasion was sent up 200 feet, communication being maintained by means of notes attached to a string, which was let down and pulled up as required. Lieutenant M'Kenzie, R.E., a light weight, was in the car, and said he saw the enemy's camel posts near Hasheen, another party was re-treating towards Tamai, while a third was engaged capturing some of the stampeded camels near the seashore. The surface of the plain was clearly visible from this height, the mimosa bush appearing much more scattered than it does from below. The balloon remained up nine hours, and reached the zareba without adventure ; it was afterwards hauled down,

packed in its basket, and returned on the waggon
to Suakin with the escort. I afterwards heard a
story that when Osman was asked what the balloon
meant, he promptly replied that it was the Prophet's
coffin suspended between earth and sky over our
heads, and was a sure sign of victory to the Moslems.
This was rather sharp of him.

I went down in the course of the day to No. 5
pier and had another long spell at the water, as
every effort is now being made to store the Tofrek
zareba for the advance on Tamai. Worked all night,
and did not get back till 7 A.M.

March 26.—When I saw the troops marching
off with the convoy, the fresh dewy air and bright
sunlight, as usual, acted like a tonic, and I wished I
could go with them, but I had given the care of the
convoy over to another officer, so it was impossible.

The escort consisted of the 20th Hussars, the
Grenadier Guards, East Surrey Regiment, Shropshire
Regiment, 28th Bombay Native Infantry, and the
Sikhs, and moved off in the eternal square formation,
General Graham riding with it. When the square
had got about half-way to the zareba, the enemy
appeared in the bush, approaching to within three
or four hundred yards of it and opening fire, though
nearly all their shot flew high. The troops replied
with volleys, which drove the Arabs back, and continued the march ; but they had not gone far before
a small party of fanatics made a desperate charge at
the Grenadiers, who formed the front of the square.
These replied with a volley at close quarters, which
killed nineteen of the Arabs, among whom were
found four boys and a woman. If there were novel
writers among the Hadendowas, what romances they
could make about these African Joans of Arc and
youthful heroes, fighting with such desperate bravery

in their country's cause! After the repulse of this
forlorn hope, the enemy still continued to hover
round for some time, but they could not face the
steady volleys from the square, and when some guns,
which appear to have moved out from the zareba,
threw a few shells among them, they retired; their
total loss being estimated at over a hundred, while
ours was only three men wounded, and not a camel
lost. When the column returned a few hours afterwards, the enemy had already buried some of their
dead.

The *Times* of 30th March, alluding to this
incident, says: "How welcome the arrival of the
convoy was at the zareba may be imagined when
we mention that, owing to the fact that a large
number of camels broke away from the convoy on
Tuesday, the occupants of the post had been
receiving only a pint of water a day;" and also,
"We learn that the water in the zareba is not
accumulating to any appreciable extent, being con-
sumed almost as fast as it arrives. We are not
surprised that such should be the case, if the blunder
of sending empty barrels committed the other day
has been repeated." Accurate though the. *Times*
is, as a rule, these lines were written under a complete
misapprehension of facts, arising from an incorrect
telegram which the correspondent of another paper
sent home about this time, though he afterwards
published a correction of it. But the idea of empty
water barrels, men on a pint a day, etc., at once
seized hold of the public mind, and the story got
into all the papers; allusion was made to it in
Punch, and a question even asked in Parliament,
to which the authorities, as usual, replied that they
had "no information;" so everybody believed that
such a thing had happened, and probably nobody

took the trouble to read the paragraph contradicting
the tale, which was sent home by the correspondent
who had been its originator as soon as he learned
the truth. When I heard of all this, though my
seniors in camp of course knew that no such thing
as a convoy of empty water vessels had ever gone
out, I took it somewhat to heart, both because I
happened to be the officer who had organized the
water train, and was responsible for the supply to
the troops in the field, and because I had been
working day and night to prevent the possibility
of such an accident. I trust, therefore, I may be
forgiven for making what they call in the House "a
personal explanation," and saying, first, that Quartermaster Cassel, the officer placed in charge of the
distribution of water at the zareba, assured me in
the most positive manner that he never received any
order to give the men only a pint a day. The supply
he served out to each regiment and company being
never less than a quart per man, so that if they got
less it must have been a purely Regimental arrangement ; secondly, that the amount of water served
could not have been affected by the breaking away
of some of the camels on Tuesday, because the
Tuesday convoy was not a water convoy, and consisted entirely of dry Commissariat supplies, for
General Graham having brought out water to the
zareba on Monday, in addition to the large supply
already stored there on Sunday, no water convoy at
all was detailed to go to the zareba on that day,
the next one being ordered for Wednesday morning.
The convoy of Commissariat stores on Tuesday was,
however, accompanied by some large wrought-iron
storage tanks, to hold 400 gallons each, which were
sent out on carts in order that they might be ready
to be filled on the morrow, and no doubt if some

curious individual struck one of these, he found it empty. But, as I have already mentioned, these tanks were so heavy that it was with difficulty the waggons laden with a single empty one each, could be got along through the deep sand, and, naturally, it would have been impossible to convey a full one to the zareba, considering that the weight of 400 gallons of water alone is 4000 lbs. Yet that is how the story probably originated, unless somebody went among the return camels waiting to bring empty tins back to Suakin, and mistook them for the convoy just arrived. In any case, the official records clearly prove that in not a single instance did a convoy take out less water than was ordered, and generally 25 per cent more was carried to guard against leakage, waste, and the act of Her Majesty's enemies.

There was one way, however, in which the troops at the zareba suffered that was beyond our control, and it was from the number of dead bodies of men, camels and mules, decaying all round them, which could not be all buried, and so contaminated the air that the water in the storage tanks quickly putrified ; while, if it was attempted to keep water shut up in the smaller vessels, the great heat of the sun soon caused it to become so unpleasant that it was hardly drinkable. As soon as the effect of the tainted air on the water was reported, every precaution was taken and fresh convoys despatched daily ; but the attempt to store a large supply of water in the zareba was most heart-breaking work, as it almost invariably went bad in two or three days.

A woman from the enemy's ranks, who was suffering from thirst, gave herself up ·to-day ; but was very reticent. I afterwards learned that under kind treatment she gave some information, to the effect that 900 Amarars deserted from Osman Digma on the 25th, and that the Arabs the convoy came across this day, were part of 5000 men Osman had sent to punish them.   She said Osman Digma had 20,000 men at Tamai divided into four corps of 5000 each, every corp having seven standards. But I believe this did not quite tally with the information in the hands of the Intelligence Branch.

In the evening Colonel —— called and said I should have "no end of work" to do on the morrow. There was a brief night alarm caused, I believe, by some stray camels approaching the camp, and several volleys were fired.   G. P. caught up his sword and ran out with the rest, and returned much the worse from the exposure to the night air.

March 27.—No convoys went out to-day, not because they were not ready, but because the Colonels of the different Regiments struck work, and represented that their men were getting quite done up, and required a rest after the continual marching backwards and forwards of the last few days.   Poor fellows, they have certainly had a hard time of it, and already there have been many cases of sunstroke. I could not get any rest myself, and was hard at work all day and most of the night preparing the water convoy for the morrow.   Got it off at daybreak, and back to camp very tired.

March 28.—Rested part of the morning and had a visit from Colonel ——, who asked me to be with him early to-morrow, as great preparations are being made for a general advance.   One thing has troubled my mind much, and that is the knowledge that some of the enemy's wounded have been shot in cold blood.   I first heard of this at the zareba, though I could scarcely credit it of English troops; but it was unfortunately too true, and I was told by those I could not doubt that the same thing was repeated during the skirmishes with the convoys, and that even an officer had been seen to empty his revolver at a man writhing on the ground. It is most painful to me to have to allude to this subject, but I do so that we may never have to reproach ourselves with anything of the kind again. I was very anxious at the time to get some officer of senior rank to myself to bring the matter to the General's notice, but to my deep disappointment I found some among my friends who were little shocked at the practice, while a few seemed actually to uphold it, saying, in short, that the wounded Arabs were so retentive of life and so actuated by bitter hate that they would struggle up and stab any man who approached them, even when they were desperately wounded, and that it was better some of them should be killed in this way, than that our men should suffer.

Now, even supposing this to be the case, I cannot possibly admit that it is worthy of the troops of a great and civilized nation like England, to bring the barbarous customs of savages into our warfare with them ; it is for us, on the contrary, to teach them that we are nobler and more generous foes. War is quite horrible enough of necessity, and it should be the earnest endeavour of every civilized Power to introduce as much humanity as possible into its treatment of a fallen adversary, even though this chivalry may occasionally cost a life. The Russian Cossacks were regarded with horror because they speared the wounded on the ground, and, however great the provocation, we who wear the Queen's uniform should strain every nerve to guard against similar excesses on the part of our own troops. They should be rendered impossible by the most stringent regulations promulgated throughout the length and breadth of the Service, and I feel certain that it is only necessary to allude to the matter for the remedy to be found.   I do not say that a search party should not take every precaution, and point their rifles at a wounded man until he has been secured, if they suspect that he may try to injure them in his wild and ignorant belief that he is going to be handed over to torture or death ; but I do say that they should give him the benefit of the doubt, and not strengthen that belief by shooting wounded men at sight.   And if half a dozen armed and hale men cannot manage to disarm and secure one wounded and disabled adversary, I do not think much of their manhood.   A foe once fallen deserves our greatest compassion, and the more wounded prisoners that can be brought in and kindly tended, the more influence shall we gain over the people against whom we are fighting, for if there be only one grateful man in a hundred (and I think well enough of even savage nature to believe there are many more) he will be a living example to his fellows, when we allow him to return home, that we are not the cruel monsters our adversaries of the Osman Digma type try to paint us, while it is needless to point out that the most valuable information may frequently be obtained from wounded prisoners.   To strike a man when he is down is repugnant to true English feeling, and our national honour demands that the strictest regulations shall be enforced to prevent anything of the kind happening in future campaigns.   So deeply did I feel on this subject that I determined to speak to the General myself before further fighting took place.

March 29, Sunday.—The Australians landed to-day amid much enthusiasm, and hearty indeed was the welcome we were prepared to give them. There is something very touching in this ready assistance tendered by the children to the parent nation that stirs our better feelings, and is worthy of the best traditions of the English race, breathing, as it does, of patriotism and loyalty and unselfishness,— homely virtues that appear sometimes almost to be forgotten in the strife of party, the race for wealth, and the tacit recognition of self-indulgence as one of the main objects of life. I feel inclined to quote Tennyson's lines on Peace and War in "Maud" when I think of these things ; but the kindly critics who reviewed a former work of mine hinted I was too much given, like Mr. Silas Weg, to "dropping into poetry," so I have put a strong curb on my Pegasus in this journal, and

> In spite of all temptations
> To indulge in neat quotations,

I refrain. By the way, this reminds me of the navvy and the Army Chaplain at Quarantine Island. It is a story which has been repeated a hundred times and will be repeated again, but it was true this time, which is more than can be said of every story we hear out here.

The principal Army Chaplain was quartered near the navvies' huts on Quarantine Island, and was so scandalized at the language they used, that one day, like the bold and worthy man he is, he went into their shed when they were all collected at dinner, and said, " My lads, I cannot sleep at night for thinking of the awful language you use. I know you do not mean it, but when I lie in my bed and listen to the dreadful way you swear about the smallest thing, it makes me quite unhappy and destroys my sleep." Thereupon a gigantic navvy rose up and, striking his horny fist on the table, said, " Show us the man who

done it, sir, and dash my eyes if me and my mates
don't smash his blanked head for him,—dashed if we
won't." And here followed a volley of expletives
that nearly blew the poor Chaplain out of the hut.
Yet the honest fellow was speaking in all good faith,
and trying to be his champion.

I fear the Army Chaplains had rather a hard time
of it when first they landed, for, somehow, no particular place in the camp had been assigned to them,
and the first night or two they slept in a lonely tent
all by themselves, from which the Arabs might have
carried them off with ease. They had one revolver
among three of them, and sat up all night listening
to the firing and doubting whether they would be
justified in using it, a doubt which was presently
settled by their discovering they had no ammunition.
However, the Arabs, who at that time harassed our
lines, did not discover them, and next morning the
Chaplains went in a body to Colonel ———, at Headquarters, to complain of their unprotected condition ;
that officer, who did not happen to belong to their
persuasion and was fond of a joke, rather cruelly
remarked, "But surely, gentlemen, you have the whole
armour of God, the shield of Faith, and the helmet
of Salvation: what more can you want?" "It is true,
quite true," replied the senior Chaplain, so humbly
that the officer felt rather ashamed of himself, though
one of the younger Chaplains was heard to mutter,
" The shield of Faith is all very well, but with these
Hadendowas about I should like a few sentries."

To return to the Australians: Nothing could have
been finer than the physique of the men ; broad
shouldered, brown bearded, blue eyed, most of them
over thirty, they only needed the stiffening of continuous drill to mould them into a force it would
gladden the heart of any soldier to look upon, after

the pale and weedy boys we too often see in our
ranks. General Graham rode down and addressed
them in frank soldier-like words of welcome—" In
the name of the British army under my command,"
he said, " I heartily welcome you as comrades and
brothers-in-arms, sharing with us our perils and
toils,—we hope, our glories too. This expedition is a
proud one. In our common country English hearts
beat high when Englishmen heard of the noble
loyalty of Australia, which is welding the widely-
divided parts of the Empire together. We honour
you for leaving your hearths and homes to share our
desert campaign, abounding, as it does, in privations
and dangers. I feel sure that your discipline will
equal your patriotic courage. England and all her
Colonies—indeed, the whole civilized world—are
watching you. Once more, I repeat, I am proud to
command you, and certain that you will do honour
to your country and race."

The sun was very hot, and I was busy all day
again organizing the water transport. I am thankful to say I at last got the matter of the wounded
Arabs off my mind, and took an opportunity of
speaking to the General when he rode down to the
water depôt. At home in society one usually thinks
of a General as a gray-haired genial man of the
world, whom everybody likes and nobody is afraid
of ; but a General on the war-path is quite a different
thing, he is in fact a king in a small way, and I have
known grizzled Colonels who would rather face a
shower of Hadendowa spears, than run the chance
of a rebuke from "the Chief." However, I took
my courage in both hands, as the French say, and,
having asked permission to speak to him, plunged
at once into the subject. "I wish to report, sir,
that it appears that many of the enemy's wounded

have been shot in cold blood during the recent engagements, and I am certain I need only mention
the fact to you for it to be put a stop to." A slight
look of suprise came into his eyes as he said, " There
has been strong provocation, I believe ?" " Yes, sir,
but even so, such a practice is contrary to the usages
of war and civilized nations." General Graham's
answer was only what I had expected, and had
the true ring of the gentleman and soldier as he
replied frankly, " Thank you ; it is a practice I have
the greatest objection to, and I shall see that it is put
a stop to in the future." I saluted and withdrew,
with a heart far lighter than it had been for the last
few days.

I got back to camp after dark very tired, having
been working with hardly a moment's rest from
7.30 A.M. to 8 P.M.; then I found I had to sit up till
10 writing a report on Tofrek, though I could hardly
keep my eyes open. Sunday is not a day of rest
here.

March 30.—Had a consultation with Colonel
——— at 6.30 A.M., after which snatched a few
moments to write letters, as the mail is going out.
Went down with P——— in the afternoon to see G. P.,
who has now been removed on board the hospital ship
Bulimba, as the camp is to be struck when the
advance on Tamai takes place. Poor old fellow,
he was looking very much pulled down, and so
feeble he could hardly move. There was some nice
lemonade by his bunk, but he said he had no one
to talk to since 9 A.M., and there was no electric bell
in the cabin. It seems as though on board this ship,
unless a patient has very strong lungs, he might die
before he could get any one to come to him. G. P.
gave an account of the way he was carried down
from camp by native dhoolie-bearers, who did not

know where to take him, and, as he could not explain to them in Hindustanee, kept carrying him from pillar to post for nearly two hours. Certainly a non-commissioned officer should always be detailed to go with patients sent into hospital to see that they get there. I was away on duty when he was taken off, or I would have gone myself.

March 31.—Much packing-up going on in camp preparatory to the advance on Tamai, which has been fixed for April 1, a rather ominous date. The greater part of the camp will be struck before we advance, and all superfluous stores moved into the town. I am waiting for final orders; there is a council of war sitting.

Telegraphing on this date the *Times* correspondent says, "Yesterday the final preparations had been made for the march of almost the entire force to the advanced zareba. Ever since the fight on Sunday week, the troops had been incessantly occupied in pouring into the zareba convoys laden with the greatest and most essential of our necessities—water. It is impossible to overestimate the enormous difficulties attending the formation of this zareba depôt in the bush." Now, however, we are all looking forward to reaping the reward of our exertions and advancing once more against the enemy; but, as the morning passes, a sinister rumour spreads through the camp that Osman Digma and his force have vanished; that a white flag has been seen near Tofrek, and another near Hasheen; that the Arabs have dispersed, presumably into the mountains, and there will be no fight at all. Consequently it has been a boot and saddle day, and Cavalry have been scouring all over the place : some have gone to reconnoitre Hasheen; others, the Mounted Infantry and Bengal Lancers, to Tofrek, from which they will push on to-morrow towards Tamai. The "All fool's day" advance has been postponed, and General Graham this afternoon reviewed the Australians, who have been busy exchanging the pretty scarlet jackets they arrived in, for the more workmanlike khakee. I am told the smell at the zareba is something awful, but Sir J. M'Neill sticks manfully to his post, and says he was never better in his life ; perhaps, like Vitellius at Bedriacum, he finds "the smell of a dead enemy is sweet." The Berkshire Regiment, with fine spirit, declined to be relieved from their guard at this unpleasant spot. I heard a story, which of course was *not* true, of an officer who had been sent with a convoy of water to Tofrek. He had a habit of stammering if any one spoke suddenly to him, which was sometimes most provoking, and on this occasion the General, not approving of the way he was managing his convoy when it arrived at the zareba, rode up to him and said, "Captain ——, you are making a great mess of it, sir." "I-I m-m-ay be, sir," replied poor —— meekly, with his worst stammer on him, " b-b-but I'm n-not the o-o-only one that has b-b-been in a m-m-mess here."

April 1.—The mail came in. Nothing settled yet about the advance, so cantered down to Quarantine Island, got a boat, and took G. P. his letters. As soon as I reached the ship I heard that Osman Digma, who was yesterday supposed to have retired, had done nothing. of the sort, and that the flag of truce had turned out to be an old biscuit box with the sun shining on it. Galloped back to Headquarters, therefore, *ventre à terre*, but could get no definite instructions till 1 P.M., when I was told to have a convoy with over 14,000 gallons of water ready to march from the Right Water Fort at 3

A.M.   Galloped back to the depôt, the notice being
very short, but was ready to begin loading the
camels at midnight, and reached the rendezvous
punctually at 3 A.M., where a force of no less than
7188 officers and men, had been ordered to parade
at the same time, but, owing to the darkness, the
real advance did not commence till 5.30.   This is
according to my journal.   General Graham's despatch of the 8th April says : " The square moved
off at four o'clock, and were joined by the Cavalry
and G Battery B Brigade Royal Horse Artillery,
which had paraded at daybreak ;" but, as according
to the Soudan almanack the sun only rose at 6.3
A.M., it is difficult to reconcile these statements ;
however, it is a matter of little consequence.   While
the darkness lasted the enemy's fires were visible in
the distance on the Hasheen hills, and everybody
was in hopes that this day, or the next at latest,
we should fight our great battle ; for the reconnaissance of the 1st April, reported that the enemy were
still occupying Tamai.   The officers of the Intelligence Branch, I believe, were not at all certain of
this, being aware that Osman's forces were dispersing, but they kept their own counsel, and preserved
what is called in diplomatic circles an air of dignified
reserve.

Of course we moved off in square, or rather
oblong, for the front face of the formation was only
200 yards wide, while the sides measured 500 yards.
This enormous parallelogram contained 1639 camels,
930 mules, with 1773 followers, besides the Hospital
equipment, consisting of eight Ambulance waggons
and two Field Hospitals.   The Balloon Detachment,
Horse Artillery, Royal Artillery, two seven-pounder
mountain guns on mules, two do. in draught, the Rocket
Troop, four Gardner guns, regimental water-carts,

dhoolie bearers, etc., all packed so closely together
that it was with the greatest difficulty one could make
a way through them.   The front face of the square
was formed by three companies of the Coldstream
Guards, and the rear by the Sikhs.   The right flank
consisted of the Scots Guards, the East Surrey
Regiment, and 28th Bombay Native Infantry; and
the left of five companies of the Coldstreams, the
Marines, and Shropshire Regiment.   Four companies of the New South Wales Contingent were
held in reserve, inside the right and left flanks of
the square, but were afterwards brought into line.
Besides these troops, there were two companies of
the Royal Engineers, 200 men of the Commissariat
and Transport Corps, and 324 men of the Royal
Horse Artillery and Royal Artillery accompanying
the guns.   The Cavalry Brigade scouted on Front
and flanks, and the Headquarter Staff, numbering
forty officers, accompanied the force, which presented
quite an imposing appearance as the sun rose and
gleamed on the arms and accoutrements.

   The greater part of our camp at Suakin was
struck before we started, and the lines, which only a
day before presented such a scene of busy life, were
soon to revert to a howling wilderness of sand, with
nothing but a few broken bottles to denote the
former presence of an English army.   The garrison
left to protect the town consisted of about 3000
men, the 17th Native Infantry being the only entire
Regiment, and the rest details from all the other
Battalions.   Four screw mountain guns and the
Australian Artillery were also left at Suakin, all
the remainder of the Field Force being either on
the war-path or at Tofrek.

   As we advance, we find that a clearing about
200 yards wide has been cut through the bush

during the last few days, which greatly facilitates
our march as far as the zareba. Every here and
there human legs, or hands, or heads, can be seen
peeping out of the sand, ghastly remains of the
engagement of the 22d. Carrion birds flutter away
at our approach, and, notwithstanding the short
time that has elapsed, many a limb has been picked
clean, so that only the skeleton of it remains. A
fortnight ago these bleached bones belonged to men
in the prime of life ! It is very strange the contrast
between the much we think of ourselves while we
are alive, and the little that remains of us after we
are dead.

When we reach the zareba, the smell all round is
disgusting in the extreme, all the more that we are
drawn up on the open ground to the left where so
many of the Transport were killed. It is now 9 A.M.,
and we halt for an hour and a quarter to rest the
men and let them have food and water. Major
Templar's balloon is meanwhile unpacked and he
proceeds to have it inflated, for on leaving the
zareba we shall plunge once more into thick bush.

At 10.15 we advance again, our force being now
augmented by the Mounted Infantry, the Grenadier
Guards, the Berkshire Regiment, a company of Engineers, and a troop of the 9th Bengal Cavalry,
which was engaged in the reconnaissance towards
Tamai yesterday ; while the 28th Bombay Native
Infantry are left in the zareba. Our total strength
is now 8175 officers and men, with 1361 horses, a
goodly army to "smash" Osman Digma, if he will
only show fight.

The bush beyond the zareba is very thick and
we have to make frequent halts to preserve our
formation, but, considering the great size of the
square and the enormous convoy it contains, the

advance is made with wonderful steadiness, though the dust, of course, is suffocating and the pace dreadfully slow. What a change to the Guards this plodding through deep sand must be, from the shady side of Pall Mall. The dust and heat are pretty trying for those riding on horseback at the head of the square, but this must be "caviare" to what the poor fellows trudging on foot at the flanks and in rear experience.

The wind has risen and it is soon apparent that the balloon is in difficulties. Major Templar, who has devoted many years of his life to advancing the art of military ballooning, looks anxious and watches every motion of the cart to which the balloon is attached with almost maternal solicitude; but it is no good, the thin gold-beaters' skin has given way, a rift shows itself near the bottom of the balloon, which soon grows larger, and, at 11 A.M. it has to be hauled down and packed up; but it has already served to discover parties of the enemy some miles to our front. Our direction, which is guided by an officer of the Intelligence Branch, who was out reconnoitring with the Cavalry yesterday, at first inclines slightly towards the seashore, to avoid the very thick bush immediately in front of Tofrek, but as the country gets more open, we work back again into the straight line between Suakin and Tamai.

At 12.15 the Cavalry and Mounted Infantry, who are scouting well in advance of the square, report scattered groups of the enemy, some on camels, but the greater portion on foot, moving through the bush and apparently coming towards us, but they fall back slowly as the Cavalry approach. Half an hour later there is a brief halt, and at 1.30 the enemy are reported to be retiring on the Teselah hills and Tamai.

We pass an Arab cipher in a small sandy gully; it consists of pieces of camel dung carefully arranged in a single row, a certain number of pieces are placed close together, then an interval and a different number of pieces, followed by another interval, and so on, very much on the principle of our Morse alphabet. No doubt it conveys a message to any Arabs who may pass this way.

At 2 P.M. we have reached to within about three miles of Teselah hills, two miles from Tamai, where it is intended we shall bivouac for the night, and the force is halted for food and water; while the 9th Bengal Cavalry are pushed forward to reconnoitre the position, supported by the Mounted Infantry in echelon of companies.

Teselah is a half-moon shaped group of bare basaltic hills about a hundred feet high, but practicable for guns. The enemy are at first reported as lining these, and seem inclined to show fight, their dark forms being clearly visible against the skyline through our field-glasses; and it is a matter of interesting speculation whether we shall have to fight for the position before dark. Our force has been under arms for over eleven hours and displayed wonderful endurance, considering the trying nature of the ground and the heat of the sun, but there are now a few cases of exhaustion, though not more than six or seven—a very small percentage. The suspense is not long, for the enemy, seeing that flanking parties of the Cavalry are threatening to turn their position, continue their retreat towards Tamai, and at three o'clock the Teselah hills are occupied by the Bengal Lancers and Mounted Infantry, and heliographic communication with Suakin is quickly established, while the square slowly advances, only reaching the hills at 5 P.M. As soon as the convoy

has halted within the semicircle, fatigue parties are
told off to build a zareba and strengthen the ridges
of the hills with parapets of loose stones ; guns are
dragged up into position, and everybody is very
busy during the brief space that remains before
darkness will set in.

The position of our camping ground is naturally
a very strong one, and from the top of the hills
there is an excellent view of the scattered villages
of New Tamai, hardly two miles distant, lying between some low rocky ridges beyond our zareba,
and of the Khor Ghuob behind, a deep ravine flanked
by the precipitous spurs of the Guharai Aweb range,
from which it apparently drains the water in the
wet season ; the country beyond being exceedingly
mountainous.

The Mounted Infantry were ordered to push on
through the villages, if possible, and water their
horses at the wells in the Khor Ghuob, but, when a
company had advanced about a mile south through
one of the villages, it was fired upon by the enemy,
who occupied another village beyond, and also some
of the ridges near the Khor, so the Mounted Infantry
fell back on the Teselah hills, and were then ordered
to return with the Cavalry to Tofrek for the night.

Meanwhile a large zareba, some 300 yards square,
had been formed in the centre of the group of
Teselah hills, and the surrounding crests fortified by
the Engineers and Madras Sappers, and so well had
the men worked, notwithstanding their long and
exhausting march, that by the time darkness set in,
about an hour after our arrival, all the arrangements
had been completed. It was now my duty to see
that water was served out to the whole of the force,
which, including followers, numbered nearly 10,000
men ; a work that had to be performed by the aid

of a flickering candle, for the darkness was profound, and which occupied all my energies till ten o'clock. At last, however, this task was completed, and thoroughly tired out, after twenty-two hours' continuous work, I sought the General to give him the detail of the amount of water still remaining in store. I was told he was on the crest of one of the hills, and, after much stumbling about among the sleeping forms of exhausted officers and men, succeeded in finding a sentry who could show me the spot where he lay, wrapped in his cloak on a barren rocky slope with some of his personal staff around him ; but he did not move when I stood over him, and seemed slumbering so peacefully that I had not the heart to wake him, so returned to the zareba where I was soon stretched in slumber myself.

I presently became aware that bullets were flying not far above my head and heard their sharp splashing sound as they cut into the ground or struck a pile of biscuit boxes hard by ; but there was no call to arms, and I was so dead tired that I dozed off again tranquilly, though the whizz and thud of the bullets as they occasionally dropped into the zareba mixed themselves up with my dreams. Some of the enemy's riflemen had occupied a ridge of rock about 800 or 1000 yards away and amused themselves by dropping long shots into our square, which, as the moon had risen, was now clearly visible. This was about one o'clock. One man was killed and two wounded, besides a camel and a mule being hit, while some of the sleepers had a rather narrow escape. To put an end to this nuisance, the Gardner guns on one of the hills were ordered to fire a volley, and one of the guns of the Horse Artillery also discharged a shell, after which the firing ceased, but whether the enemy suffered any loss could not be ascertained.

April 3.—At 4.30 A.M. the " Rouse " sounded, and
we all sprang to our feet.   Another day had begun
which was to decide whether Osman Digma would
hazard the issue of a battle or not.   My first care
was to see that all the men going with the fighting
square had their morning allowance of water and
their bottles filled; this occupied me till seven o'clock,
when, feeling very decidedly in want of something
to eat, I asked A——, an officer of the Bengal Staff
Corps, who had helped me before, to be good enough
to attend to my duties for a few minutes and answer
questions; for in this country so great was the anxiety
about the water, that I was constantly besieged by
inquiries concerning it.   Now it was the doctors who
wanted to know if they could have an extra allowance
for their patients, which of course was granted, then it
was the newspaper correspondents asking if they
were not entitled to a special tin full, again a Staff
officer wanted to make interest for a drink for his
horse, or a General came by and said that every drop
of the precious fluid was worth its weight in gold,
and he hoped I was not permitting a soul to have
more than the strict allowance, etc. etc.

I had just sat down beside some comrades who
were having their breakfast, and lifted a sardine
to my lips, when Capt. F—— came hastily up
and told me that there was an officer dancing
with rage on the water tins and calling for
me, and, he added in a whisper, " I think by the
nature of the language he is using he must be a
very big swell."   So I put the sardine down untasted,
and went off to see what was the matter.   True
enough somebody was there, and I could perceive a
large solar topé bobbing above the water depôt like an
agitated mushroom ; its owner was a small man, and
to secure a more commanding position had mounted

on a pile of empty tins, from which post of vantage he fired off his remarks like sharpnel shell. " Look here," he said, as soon as I came within range, " did you give orders for the mules to have water ? " " Certainly not, sir ; animals are only to be watered when the wells have been captured." " Very well, here is your representative, the officer! (with withering scorn) you leave in charge, breaking the orders and watering mules." Here the luckless A—— was understood to say that he was not doing anything of the sort, but was only *looking* at a paper on which some one had written a request for water for mules. " I don't care, sir ; I saw you with my own eyes take this paper in your hand, and if you were not going to water the mules what were you doing with it ? " " Pardon me, sir," remarked A—— meekly, " but if you are not careful those tins will come down," for he saw the pile beginning to tremble beneath his superior's wrath. Down jumped the other as if they were red-hot, but as soon as he found himself on firm ground, continued the attack. " I'll tell you what it is, sir," he said, " this water is as precious as our life's blood, and there is only one thing to do to prevent its being squandered, we must make an example of an officer." Here he fixed his glance sternly on poor A——, whose enormous big eyes and somewhat cadaverous face gave him a most melancholy expression. " He must," continued he slowly, " *be taken outside the zareba and shot.*" " Why, certainly, sir, a very good thing too," I replied cheerfully ; but, just for decency sake before consigning my friend to an early death, I added, " If you will trust me, I will be responsible that the mules get no water, and there is still a large reserve in store." I did not dare to look at A——, who, notwithstanding his solemn face, was perceptibly shaking with internal spasms of

suppressed mirth which threatened at any moment
to be too much for him, though he pulled himself
together and managed to look as sober as a criminal
at the bar, when the other replied severely, " I am
glad to hear you say so, and I will trust you, but,"—
and here he again fixed A——— with his eye before
turning away, as though regretting his leniency,—
" mark my words, if that officer attempts to give
water to the mules he must be taken outside the
zareba and shot." " You evidently are not good
enough, my dear fellow, to be shot inside the zareba,"
I said to A———, as bidding him prosper at his post
I returned to my breakfast. I fear I have described
this scene very feebly, but there was a fine old-
fashioned flavour about the idea of casually shooting
an officer before breakfast that tickled me immensely.

At 7.20 the Mounted Infantry and Cavalry arrived from Tofrek, and at 8 the fighting square was
formed outside the zareba. It consisted of all the
troops except the Shropshire and East Surrey Regiments, which, with the Gardner guns, were left to
defend the zareba under Sir John M'Neill,—the
Transport, of course, remaining with them.

The ground between the zareba and the Khor
Ghuob consisted of three ridges, between which the
clusters of huts and enclosures of New Tamai were
situate ; and, to quote General Graham's despatch of
the 8th April, " It was soon evident that the enemy
were unable to oppose any serious resistance to the
advance of the force.

" Fire was opened on the Mounted Infantry and
9th Bengal Cavalry about 8.45 A.M. from the East
side of the ravine, and soon afterwards from the
gullies to the South.

" The advance of the force was continued through
the villages, which were found to have been recently

deserted, the lines of the leading Brigade occasionally forming fours deep, or advancing by fours from a flank to pass through the bushes and huts, until, at 9.30 A.M., the crest of the North side of the Khor Ghuob was gained.

"The Mounted Infantry and 9th Bengal Cavalry were at this time engaged with the enemy on the right flank, but were unable to draw them from their positions.

"I now ordered the leading (Second) Brigade, under General Hudson, to descend the Khor, inclining to the right, so as to avoid a steep hill immediately in front, which was occupied by a company of the 15th Sikhs.

"The Brigade moved to its right, advanced across the Khor, which was at this point about 100 feet deep and 400 yards wide, and descended the hill on the opposite bank. The Berkshire Regiment was posted on the highest point in the centre, the Marines on the right, with their right thrown back, while the 15th Sikhs crowned the heights on detached hills to the left front and left.

"The Berkshire Regiment opened fire on the enemy, marksmen were thrown out about 30 yards in front of the Marines, and the Scots Guards, who had advanced into the Khor in reserve, threw out a company to fire up the Khor on their right. The Guards Brigade and New South Wales Battalion moved forward in support of the Second Brigade, crowning the ridges on the North side of the Khor.

"The G Battery, B Brigade Royal Horse Artillery came into action on the left flank of the First Brigade, at the position shown, and opened fire on some parties of the enemy.

"During these operations the enemy were keeping up a distant fire, which resulted in the casualties I

have already reported by telegraph, viz. :— 1 man
killed, 1 officer and 15 men wounded. The enemy's
numbers and loss it is impossible to estimate with
accuracy ; but a steady well-aimed fire was kept up
on such bodies as showed themselves, and the effect
of the fire was to overcome any opposition they may
have intended to make.

" On descending to the bed of the Khor, I found
that at the spot where last year we had found running water, there were no signs of water beyond a
little moisture, and well holes partially filled in. By
digging about four feet down a small supply of
brackish water could have been obtained, and at a
short distance there was a shallow pool of water on
a bed of black fetid mud.

" In view, therefore, of the retirement of the enemy,
and their evident inability or indisposition to meet
the force under my command, it appeared to me to
be best to withdraw, as it would have been fruit-
less to attempt to follow Osman Digma into the
mountainous country with no water for my Transport animals.

" At 10.20 A.M. I, therefore, ordered the withdrawal of the force, by alternate Brigades, from the
position which had been taken up. By 10.40 A.M.
the troops had recrossed the Khor, the movement
being covered by two Horse Artillery guns on the
ridge to the North, which fired a few rounds of
shrapnel at detached parties of the enemy. I
ordered New Tamai to be destroyed, and it was fired
as the troops retired through it. Considerable quantities of ammunition were destroyed, and Osman
Digma's residence is believed to have been among
the number of huts burnt.

" At 12 noon the force reached No. 2 zareba at
the Teselah hill."

An officer who was in the front line told me he did not think there were more than thirty Arabs engaged against us during the operation, and, notwithstanding this big demonstration, and that we fired away, counting the volley of last night, 3217 cartridges and 36 shells, I believe there was no evidence to prove that one of the enemy was killed. As soon as the troops got back to the zareba, I had for the third time to endeavour to quench the thirst of some 9000 tired and dusty men, and the rush for a drink was tremendous. Poor Colonel Gordon of the 93d, who afterwards died in my cabin on the *Ganges,* helped me to preserve order. There was now a plethora of water, for the quantity I had brought out (14,500 gallons) equalled three days' supply for the whole force, at the rate of half a gallon per man, a very fair allowance for troops on a flying column, and there was also a reserve of nearly 30,000 gallons stored at Tofrek, so that, had it only been a question of supplying the men, there would have been no difficulty in pushing farther into the mountains, but, as Sir Gerald Graham's despatch shows, the supply at the wells, which had been relied on for the cattle, was inadequate, though last year, when a British force was at Tamai, a running stream was found somewhere in this neighbourhood. Under these circumstances, and considering the improbability that Osman would consent to give us battle if we followed him into the mountains, it was no doubt a wise decision to return to Suakin.

As soon as the men had enjoyed a brief rest and a meal, the whole force started on the homeward march, the greater part of the Cavalry, accompanied by Sir Gerald Graham, riding straight back to Suakin, and the Infantry and Transport, with the sick and wounded, making for Tofrek, where they were to halt for the night. We took a line rather more to the West than that we had come by, and, when we were about a couple of miles from Tofrek, Sir J. M'Neill told me to ride forward, as soon as we got a little nearer the zareba, and order an opening to be made in the hedge and a ramp across the ditch for the cattle to enter by. The square was then halting, and when I saw it in motion again I galloped forward on this errand. It was my first ride entirely alone through the bush, which was very thick here, and for a few minutes I saw an imaginary Hadendowa lurking under every tree; however, after a smart gallop, the unmistakable smell of dead bodies told me that I was close to the zareba, for on this side there were many of the enemy's slain among the outlying bush, who had not been discovered and buried, and, emerging from a hollow, I saw the heliograph tower just before me.

It was nearly dark by the time the square arrived, and everybody was very glad to bivouac for the night, for the force had been under arms for sixteen hours yesterday, and over thirteen to-day, having marched altogether about twenty-six miles through bush and deep sand at a slow pace under a very hot sun, besides which they had constructed a zareba, fought a small engagement, and had their rest broken by the firing on the previous night. Sir Gerald Graham bears testimony to the pluck and stamina of the men in his despatch, and says : " The number of men who fell out on the march was only eleven, which fact bears witness to the spirit and physical capabilities of the troops, while the number (thirty-three) on the sick list at the end of the operations is very small, considering the largeness of the force and the great fatigue and privations which had to be undergone by all."

April 4.—We passed a quiet night in the old zareba, which has been much changed and strengthened since the day of the fight, and early this morning were all on our way back to Suakin. I noticed the graves of the officers and men who were killed on the 22d have been neatly covered with loose stones, arranged in ornamental patterns ; but I fear when the place is abandoned the sand will soon drift over them.   Rode forward, and arrived at Suakin about four miles ahead of the square, and then went down to No. 5 pier to attend to my duties.

This is the end of our abortive efforts to force Osman Digma to fight ; to-morrow the really practical work of pushing forward the railway will be commenced in earnest.

CHAPTER IX.

WE OCCUPY TAMBOUK.

APRIL 5 — (Easter Sunday). — Attended church parade in the early morning. This is only the second service I have been able to be present at since our arrival, so continuous has been the course of duty even on Sundays. Had a long consultation afterwards with Colonels R——, W——, P——, etc., as a new series of operations are to be commenced tomorrow at daybreak, and an advanced zareba established five miles on the road to Handoub, to cover the head of the railway, which will now be pushed up to it as fast as possible. This station is to be called " No. 1 Post," and a block-house will be built and a fresh zareba then established at Handoub, five miles beyond. Covering parties will protect the head of the line as it advances.

They say a spy has come in from Erkowit, and reports that Osman's followers are deserting him wholesale, and that he has now only 900 men at a place called Shakateb, between Sinkat and Erkowit. Two women have also come in and say that Osman had 100 men with him last week at Tamai, and there is great discontent among his followers, the women and children mourning the loss of husbands, fathers, brothers, and lovers, poor things. It appears Osman told his people our bullets would only fall

like drops of refreshing water on them, and that
the British troops would quickly run away; but now
they know better.

The Australians bore the hardships of the late
march wonderfully well ; but were unfortunate in
having two of their number wounded. A doctor
told me he heard a bullet rattle against the head of
a man he was riding beside ; it was a spent ball,
and, though it cut through the helmet, only stunned
the man, who must have had a strong skull. All
the doctors speak much of Professor Ogsden of
Aberdeen University, who has come out here to
study gunshot wounds, and they say has been greatly
interested in some of the operations. One was an
attempt to save a limb from amputation by cutting
out the shattered portion of bone, and stitching the
two ends together with silver wire, in the hope they
would unite as in an ordinary fracture, so that the
patient might only have his limb shorter than before,
instead of losing it. In this case the man had not
sufficient stamina to recover the shock of his wound,
and died, but there was reason to believe that had
he been of stronger physique, the operation would
have been quite successful. What a change from
the old days of the Peninsular War, when the surgeon
stood with his shirt sleeves tucked up to the elbows
beside a rude table on trestles, and cut off arms and
legs almost as quickly as the wounded were brought
in from the battle-field ; now the whole aim of
military surgery is conservative, to save, not to cut
away. Truly the sick and wounded are better off
now than they were fifty years ago, when, as Doctor
Quain has said, there were " no anæsthetics to induce
insensibility to pain, no antiseptic to promote the
healing of a wound, no chloral to procure sleep, no
antipyretic in general use to control fever;" and if the

art of killing has been successfully developed, so
has the art of healing. The surgeons are still mostly
Irish, as in the days Charles Lever tells so pleasantly
of in his novels, and I have often wondered why
military surgery should have such a charm for Irish-
men, but the " Linseed Lancers " of to-day are rather
quiet people, and no longer rattle out racy stories,
or sing convivial songs in a mellifluous brogue over
the punch bowl. I may add that their general
kindness and the excellence of their medical arrangements are beyond all praise.

One of our transports, the *Arafat*, was wrecked
the other day along the coast, but the crew escaped.
The Arabs were reported to be looting her, and the
Carysfort was sent out to see ; she, however, returned
yesterday, having found the ship's deck under water
and nobody in sight.

Got to bed very late, as W—— came in and
had a long confabulation. At 3.30 A.M. word came
up from the water depôt that mules had been sent
instead of camels for to-morrow's convoy, and the
loads were naturally not fitted for them. Some of
the Transport officers kicked at my rule of having all
animals for convoy duty paraded at sunset, and got
permission to send them down in the morning.
This is the result, but, as I see Colonel ——
shivering in pyjamas in the moonlight, I expect
to-morrow we shall revert to the old regulation.
P—— got out of bed and sent down camels very
smartly, waking up his men and starting them in
less than twenty minutes.

April 6.—Up at sunrise to see the convoy off ; it
is going with the troops that are to form No. 1 Post;
I shall follow to-morrow with another convoy, and
proceed the next day to Handoub, to establish a
water depôt ; there is a chance that we may have a

brush with the enemy when we reach the mountains, as some of Osman's men were seen moving towards Hasheen on Friday.

Notwithstanding our demonstration at Tamai, the enemy fired for three hours into the Tofrek zareba last night, wounding one man and two mules. To-day it has been abandoned, and a convoy of 3500 transport animals, under strong escort, went out this morning to bring away the stores; it returned in the evening with the garrison, after setting fire to the zareba. Sir J. M'Neill was in command.

April 7.—General Fremantle with the Coldstreams and Australians, some Engineers, screw guns, etc., established No. 1 Post yesterday without opposition. Only half a dozen of the enemy were seen, who retreated on camels towards Handoub; the Mounted Infantry exchanged a few long shots with them, but no harm was done. The day was one of the hottest we have had, and one Australian and four of the Guards fell out from heat exhaustion. At 1 P.M. I started with the Scots Guards and a convoy of water for No. 1 Post; the country was quite open, and we met with no adventures. The railway appeared to be making rapid progress. General Fremantle told me when I arrived that some new indiarubber bags, which had been tried for the first time yesterday, gave a most unpleasant taste to the water; I found it remained clear in them, but savoured horribly of indiarubber, and soon got very hot; moreover, they showed a tendency to burst at the seams from the jostling of the camels, while it was impossible to prevent the native drivers pricking holes in them to steal the water; therefore, I would recommend that these bags should not be generally used in the future.

Slept under the eave of the General's tent, and had a quiet night, no firing.

April 8.—At 3.30 A.M. we were all up and ready for the advance, which had been timed for 5, but we did not get away till 7, as we had to wait for the Mounted Infantry from Suakin. Our Force consisted of the Australians and Coldstreams, the Scots Guards being left at the zareba. A broad clearing had been made through the bush the previous day for some distance beyond No. 1 Post, and when we came to the end of this, the troops were halted and set to work to continue it, cutting down and burning the bush, which was rather thick, with great rapidity. We could see some of the enemy on a hill above Handoub, and columns of dust moving away as if they were retreating. Mahmoud Ali, a friendly chief of the Amarars, commonly known .as "the Great Baboon," from his monkey-like face, accompanied us; he was a thin old gentleman mounted on a white camel, and had a numerous retinue bearing his tribal standard, for he hopes to induce those of his tribe who have joined Osman Digma to come in and submit, when they see us established at Handoub.

During the march the correspondent of the *Standard*, whom I had never met before, rode up and showed me a copy of the telegram he had just sent home, correcting his statement about the empty water tins. He spoke very frankly and nicely, saying the error had been committed in good faith, which indeed I never doubted. About noon we arrived at the foot of the mountains that form, as it were, the gate of the Handoub valley; a broad shingly plain encircled by rugged hills. This plain is traversed by a Khor or dry water-course, 175 yards wide, which runs for some distance in a North-

Easterly direction along the foot of the Waratab
range, and then bends round to the East as it
emerges from the mountains and enters the plain
between them and Suakin, where its course to the
sea may be easily traced by the greater verdure of
the scrub and bush above it.   At the foot of a rocky
hill on the right bank of this lost river was an old
Arab graveyard, and on the left, nearly opposite, the
deserted huts of the village of Handoub ; miserable
shanties constructed of branches and grass round
mimosa trees, the spreading tops of which served to
form part of the roof.   The bed of the Khor was
about two feet below the level of the plain, and
covered with deep sand and shingle, bearing evident
traces of the action of running water, and in this dry
bed were the marks of many old wells, mere holes
scraped in the shingle.   We found water at a depth
of two feet below the surface, and a hole containing
as nearly as possible a cubic foot of water, yielded
two gallons a minute ; indeed, there seemed practically no limit to the amount of water that could be
obtained by increasing the number of wells.

The water was extremely soft, slightly saline in
taste, but not very unpalatable.   The Arabs and
cattle drank it freely, but owing to the numerous
caravans that for centuries have halted at this spot,
there is a great deal of organic matter mixed with
the sand of the Khor, and when the doctors afterwards
analyzed a sample of the water which I brought
them in a bottle, they found it contained so large a
percentage of salts in solution that they would not
allow the troops to drink from these wells.   Nevertheless, it is certain that large numbers of the Arabs
have done so from time immemorial, and when I
passed Handoub twelve years ago, on my way from
Berber, I drank the water freely without suffering

any ill effects.   No doubt there is a hard bed of
rock below the Khor, on which the water that pours
down from the mountains, during the severe thunderstorms that occasionally visit this region, lies all the
summer ; and the mineral salts it holds in solution
are absorbed from the sand of the Khor.

No sooner had we reached Handoub, than the
busy Engineers at once set to work to fortify the
crests of two rocky hills, between which the Khor
passes, and under the shelter of the larger of these on
the North side of the wells, a zareba was constructed.
There was an old well near it, about 200 yards from
the edge of the Khor, sunk in the solid earth ; it was
six feet deep, four feet in circumference, and the water
rose to within three feet of the surface, but it filled
much more slowly than the wells scraped in the Khor
itself.   The plain beyond the zareba was bounded
on the left by the Waratab and Abdarak ranges,
forming a rude semicircle extending nearly as· far
as Otao, some eight miles distant, while on the right
it was bounded by what was called the North range,
for want of a better name.   The general appearance
of the country was a broad expanse of nearly level
sand and shingle, about ten miles in circumference,
completely encircled by barren hills, and its surface
somewhat thinly covered with mimosa bush and light
scrub, while here and there isolated piles of boulders
rose from the plain, presenting useful landmarks.

I well remember crossing this plain twelve years
ago on the 22d of June, but then the mimosa trees
were covered with delicate green leaves, and large
herds of gazelles were cropping the young herbage,
which had sprung up as if by magic after the violent
tropical thunderstorms that usually burst over the
mountains about that season.   I had ridden over
from Berber, whither I had travelled by river from

Khartoum, after a shooting trip in Abyssinia ; and I remember the country looked quite pleasantly green to my eyes, in comparison with the vast tracts of sandy desert I had previously passed through.   At that time Gordon's name was as yet unknown in the Soudan, and Ishmael Ayoub Pasha ruled at Khartoum ; they say he was a bad governor, but, if so, he successfully concealed the fact during the few days I spent with him ; and though I often heard him answering petitions and settling matters of difficulty, I personally never saw him do a harsh act—in fact, he treated many of the poor people who came to him with a good-natured patience and consideration that impressed me favourably.   This may have been acting, but I can only say that at that time I was able to travel safely by day and night, attended by a single servant and a native guide, through the whole length and breadth of the country East of the Nile ; that at the Arab villages where I halted, the people seemed well fed and were always courteous and trustworthy, though I had a portmanteau full of dollars on my baggage camel, and my silver-mounted hunting knife, revolver, rifle, etc., were objects that might well have excited their cupidity.

I little thought at that time, as I rode beneath the bright starlit sky and breathed the pure air of these wide plains, delighting in my independence, that I should ever see a British army at Handoub, and that a couple of hundred men, armed with all the appliances of modern warfare, would be unable to venture three days' march from the camp without running the risk of being cut to pieces.   That thousands of Arabs would have been slaughtered, and it would be certain death for an Englishman to approach alone any of these villages, where before milk and sheep were readily offered to the passing stranger. Yet such has been the result of only three years of uncertain policy, and famine and murder now stalk hand in hand through this country where, as a boy of twenty-two, I travelled so gaily, thinking myself quite secure in the possession of a single rifle and revolver.

True, the slave-trade existed then, but not unchecked as it does now ; and I believe it could have been got rid of with little danger to the peace of the country, had the simple policy been followed of levying a heavy tax on slaves, and offering a yearly remission of taxes as compensation to those who chose voluntarily to emancipate them. The Eastern mind would not have regarded a new tax in the light of confiscation, because it recognizes the right of those in power to levy taxes ; but to escape the new tax and obtain relief from the old ones, there is little doubt many of the Arabs would have voluntarily emancipated their slaves, as a matter of form, knowing well that they could still retain their services ; and the slaves once emancipated, would have been placed on an equality with their masters before the law, and soon ceased to be saleable. The foundation of the whole system would thus have been undermined by the voluntary efforts of the people to escape taxation, without any violent disruption of the social traditions, and the way been gradually prepared for the total abolition of slavery at a later date.

D——, who had come out with us, told me he was going to ride back to No. 1 Post with the *Standard* correspondent, without waiting for an escort, as he was pressed for time, for to-morrow he sails for England to return to his Parliamentary duties. So the two started off together, D—— on his camel, the correspondent on his horse ; but they had not gone far before a dozen of the enemy, who had been watching our movements from some safe place of concealment, started in pursuit, creeping through the bush in their usual snake-like manner with the object of cutting them off. The look-out at the signal tower, or " crow's nest," as it is called, at No. 1 Post, however, saw their movements ; and great was the excitement at the zareba when it was known that D—— and his companion might be attacked. The gun was at once manned ready to throw a shell, and I believe some men got ready to go out to their assistance ; but luckily the travellers kept in the centre of the broad clearing that had been cut through the bush, and when the Arabs, who by this time had crept almost alongside of them, perceived the gun trailed in their direction, they did not venture to break cover, and abandoned their prey ; while the two friends jogged contentedly into the zareba, quite unconscious of the little drama that had been enacting around them.

About 2 P.M. General Graham rode into Handoub, and the camels were ordered to return to Suakin under escort of a troop of the Bengal Lancers. This was a great change from always moving in a square of Infantry, as they had hitherto done, and we got along at a good pace. I believe 200 of the enemy were seen from the crow's nest watching us from behind a spur of one of the hills, but they did not decide to make a dash at us, and, as most of the drivers were mounted on the unladen camels, I expect they would have been able to show them a clean pair of heels if they had.

We reached Suakin before sunset, and heard that the Headquarter camp had been fired into on the previous night.

April 9 to 16.—An uneventful week of con-

stant work sending out water to the advanced posts.
An Indian camel-driver called Haroo, who fell into
the hands of the enemy at Hasheen on the 20th
March and was made prisoner, has come into camp.
He says that he got separated from the troops and
was pursued by a prowling party of Hadendowas,
who cut off his retreat as he was trying to escape
towards Suakin. Knowing they generally gave no
quarter, he thought his last hour was come ; but
luckily he spoke Arabic, and had the happy thought
to call out as he fell on his knees, that he was a
" Seyed," or descendant of Mahomet ;—an awful lie,
but it served his purpose, for the Arabs, not liking
to kill a relative of the Prophet, dropped the points
of their spears, and, after asking him a few questions,
decided to spare his life, and made him prisoner.
He was then sent under a guard to the neighbourhood of Hasheen, where 2000 of the enemy were
encamped ; and while he was there two other Indian
camp-followers were brought in. Whether they also
pretended to be descendants of the Prophet, I do
not know. According to a correspondent who
interviewed him, " Haroo witnessed the departure
of the flower of Osman Digma's army for the attack
upon M'Neill's zareba, and the return of the broken-
spirited survivors of that terrible day." This would
imply that a portion of the force that surrounded us
at Tofrek hailed from near Hasheen, and was part
of that concentration of 8000 men I have before
alluded to. After a few days he was taken across
the hills to Tamai, where he found that the enemy
had spared the lives of ten Indian camel-drivers who
attempted to escape to Suakin when the stampede
of the convoy at Tofrek took place. They were all
kept prisoners in the hills behind Tamai. He said
that there were only 200 of the enemy at Tamai,

and that, though Osman Digma's followers had plenty of arms, they were very short of food and much discouraged. He was generally closely watched, but at last managed to slip away unperceived, and ran nearly the whole way into camp.

The Headquarter camp has now been moved close to the railway, a little in rear of West Redoubt, and as I lay in bed last Sunday morning, I almost thought I was back again at dear old Winton, for the hour was being tolled on a big gong belonging to a Regiment near, which sounded just like the cathedral bell, while the trains went puffing past as they do through the cutting beside the barrack square, and to add to the illusion, the Guards' band was playing "Christ Church Bells," the tune to which the Rifles always muster for Church parade.

The Field Force orders of the 1st inst. said "Captain De Cosson's office will be near that of the Director of Transport," but that was a little 1st-of-April joke, and my office really consists of half a tent, a camp-bed, and a three-legged table. Everybody at Headquarters is doubled up except the G. O. C., and I am living with Major —— of the Intelligence Department, a most gallant soldier and pleasant companion, who, however, makes me feel quite ashamed of going to sleep when I see him sitting up writing, as he often does, far into the small hours of the morning. We have got a regular Mess now, under the care of an Italian, to whom we each pay 5s. a day, and it is a great improvement on the old way the Staff used to Mess, when each man walked to table with his own tin plate under his arm. Indeed, we look quite civilized with table-cloths, glass, china, etc., and a real German waiter called Otto, with a shock head of yellow hair brushed straight up from his forehead, who, after the manner of his kind, speaks a few broken words of half a dozen languages, but seems to have mastered no one in particular, not even his own.   We have tried him with English, French, Italian, German, Arabic, and even Russian, and he will answer in all, but his German is not much better than his French, and his French only a little purer than his English ; however, he is a capital fellow, and his alacrity remains unimpaired notwithstanding the intense heat that has set in.   He seems to have implicit faith in his shock head of hair as a covering, and dashes out into the noonday sun without ever troubling to put on a hat, in spite of our repeated warnings.   Our breakfast consists of the inevitable eggs and bacon familiar to English eyes, occasionally varied by bacon without the eggs.   The bacon is pale and sinewy, and visions of long lean German swine rise before us as we eat it ; as for the eggs, they come from Russia, and have been rubbed with paraffine to make them keep ; no doubt they were very nice eggs in their youth, but that must have been long, long ago ; when the bacon appears without the eggs, Otto says, " Les œufs sont trop mauvais this morning, sar;" they are always mauvais, but sometimes they are *trop* mauvais.   Our cook is a very fat man, and usually stands and gasps, in a helpless sort of way before his fire, so do a score of unfortunate chickens which creep about with gaping beaks and drooping wings, picking up occasional crumbs, and waiting their turn to nourish Her Majesty's officers ; they are like a chicken I once ate in the Tyrol at a wayside inn, which was served lying on its breast, because its back was the fattest part of it.

There are few members of the Mess under Field rank, and their pleasant sunburned faces and slightly grizzled hair always carry my thoughts to Clubland when I see them at table, and I find myself wondering why so many amiable middle-aged gentlemen should be perspiring here in a sandy desert, instead of sitting comfortably in their arm-chairs behind the morning papers at the Rag or Senior.   One thing impairs the serenity of our lives, the crumpled rose-leaf, as it were, among the other delights of the Soudan, and that is the plague of flies which swarm round us in hundreds and millions, mixing themselves with our food, or committing *felo-de-se* in our drinks with reckless persistency ; to carry a fly whisp is to be a public nuisance, for if one man attempts to chase the flies from around him, he only drives them into the face of his opposite neighbour, who, probably getting exasperated, sends them back again, so they go buzzing from side to side like a new game of battledore and shuttlecock, and to bear the evil patiently is the best policy in the long run.

Though the heat is now increasing rapidly, they say that at Handoub the thermometer has fallen as low as 47 degrees at night.   General Graham has issued a proclamation to the enemy calling on them to submit.   I am afraid when they read it they will be tempted to do whatever is the Arab equivalent to putting their thumbs unto their noses and spreading their fingers out, unless we are prepared to promise a permanent occupation.   A very curious book might be written on the scornful and derisive gestures of all nations, their origin, history, etc.   To how many stories of rejected love might be traced the first origin of those expressions of scorn common to the feminine portion of the population, what exciting tales of desperate combats may be connected with the history of those of the male ?   It is a subject well worthy of research.   I remember the author of

the Breitmann ballads telling me he intended some
day to write a great work on the oaths of all nations,
but how much more interesting would be the legends
of their gestures and expressions. Who was the
first maiden who invented the art of pouting, and
for what reason? Why do the Germans think it
insulting to imitate the action of scraping a carrot
with the finger? why in Spain is it considered an
affront to touch the elbows? and why in Italy was
biting the thumb supposed to be a provocation to
the drawing of swords, as Shakespeare tells us?
what subtle irony first lurked in the action of taking
a sight, now so dear to the street arab? and who
was the first "duffer," and how did he obtain that
name? What curious insight into the esoteric
mysteries of ironic gesture might not be obtained by
the student who would be bold enough to penetrate
into the *halles centrales*, or our own Billingsgate market,
and study the manners of the fair denizens thereof;
but the subject would take a book to itself, and I
merely suggest it to students of an inquiring mind.

Our proclamation offers payment for food and
cattle brought in, which may produce some good
effect; but as I understand the Arabs, though they
would like to be privately paid for their goods, they
would rather be outwardly coerced, so that they may
plead compulsion to Osman Digma, when they come
to us, and thus avoid his avenging himself on any
of their relatives who may be in his power. "Hedg-
ing" is an art of the greatest antiquity, and it is
universally practised in the East, where the whole
aim and object of the weaker tribes is to keep safe
with the winning side; and at present they are not
at all certain that we shall win, because they think
we shall go away as we have done before, nor can
we blame them.

On the 11th, a reconnaissance was made to
Hasheen, which was found deserted. There has been
a case of glanders, which gave us rather a fright, but
every precaution has now been taken to stamp it out
among the horses. The friendly Amarars, directed
by officers of the Intelligence Department, went out
on the 12th, and intercepted some cattle that were
being sent to Osman Digma, so now the camp at
Handoub is full of goats, which are to be bought for a
rupee each, and everybody is revelling in fresh milk.

Sir Gerald Graham telegraphed to Lord Hartington this day—"General Fremantle sent message
last night from Handoub that a Sheik of Amarars
had just come in, and that he had counterordered
advance to Otao. This Sheik and others are waver-
ing, but they say that they would come in if assured
of further protection against Osman, or of English
not going away as last year. May I ask how far I
am justified in giving such assurance?" The answer,
which was sent to Lord Wolseley on the 15th, ran
as follows:—"Proposed Suakin policy. Construction
of railway for any considerable distance to be suspended pending further consideration. Suakin to
be held for present, and any position in neighbourhood necessary for protection from constant attack,
as last year. Report on point to which railway
should proceed, and instruct Graham, with reference
to his message of 12th, not to enter into engagements with tribes inconsistent with this policy."

On the 13th a reconnaissance was made from
Handoub to Otao, eight miles nearer Berber, without
opposition; the route across the gravelly plain
proved quite easy for railway laying, and two wells
were found at Otao, with a constant supply of water
$3\frac{1}{2}$ feet below the surface. As usual where wells are
found there was a sandy Khor, where more water

could be obtained, and near the wells was a knoll
100 feet high, on which a fort will be placed
when the troops advance.   On the 14th the Indian
Contingent had their Gimkhana, or sports, which were
well attended ; I could not go myself.   On the 15th
the Mounted Infantry rode through the hills beyond
Hasheen to Deberet, and brought in forty prisoners,
many of them women and children, and over 500
sheep : they were apparently on their way to join
Osman Digma when we surprised them.   There was
no fighting, and most of the men, who wore the
Mahdi's caps, bolted, which was not very gallant
to their womankind.   The women and children
were of course taken good care of, and afterwards
liberated.

To-day the 16th, a mounted R.E. division,
which arrived from Cairo on the 8th inst., went out
to Handoub with a company of the Guards Mounted
Infantry.   This, I believe, is the first time Mounted
Engineers have been sent to serve with a force in
the field ; the division was mounted on Arab horses
and equipped for pioneer work.

The utility of Mounted Infantry drawn from various
branches of the service is rapidly becoming so important a feature in military operations, that the attention
of the authorities should be directed to the formation
of some regular plan for placing such a force in the
field, the moment hostilities commence.   Infantry Battalions might pass a certain number of men through
the riding school every year, and the complete equipment for one mounted company per Battalion be
always kept in store, while the general principles
of Mounted Infantry drill ought to be learned by
every young officer, and a certain proportion of the
men who know how to ride, exercised in it from
time to time, on horses borrowed from the Cavalry

depôts. A sabre, not to be worn by the man, but attached to the saddle, as in some of the Indian Cavalry regiments, might also be added to the equipment, and the bayonet discarded on mounted duty ; for to arm a mounted man with a bayonet is absurd, and, as at present armed, the Mounted Infantry would be at a great disadvantage if surprised and pursued by Cavalry. If it is feared that to give them sabres would have a tendency to convert them into Cavalry and destroy their true character, they should at least be provided with revolvers and taught how to use them, for a mounted man who knows how to shoot, with a good revolver in his hand, has little to fear from either lance or sword.

The Scots Guards, with two guns, a squadron of Cavalry, and a company of Engineers, went to-day from Handoub to Otao, and formed an advanced post there.

April 17.—There are fresh demands on the water transport owing to the advance of the troops to Otao, for, though the water is better there than at Handoub, the doctors will not yet let them drink it, and we are not able to make use of the railway, which is fully employed transporting the permanent way, owing to the deficiency of engines.

Rode to Handoub alone, and spent a long day making arrangements ; got back to Headquarters at sunset very tired. The sun is gaining power every day, and the twenty-mile ride across the plain and back is scorching work. The camp at Handoub is also a regular trap to catch a sunbeam, for the surrounding hills shut off the air and reflect the heat. As our spies report that Osman still instructs his followers to waylay isolated parties, the authorities discourage the practice of riding from Suakin to Handoub, except with the daily convoys that go under escort ;

but practically many officers have to do it, and
sometimes in the early morning, parties of them go
out shooting sand-grouse a long distance from the
lines.   These little birds are found in great numbers
among the low scrub just after sunrise, and prove
capital eating, but they are already beginning to get
shy, and the sportsmen have to go farther a-field
every day to find them.

Poor P——— sailed yesterday in the *Deccan*, invalided ; he was very loath to go, but there was no
hope of his recovery in this climate, which, the
doctors say, is peculiar from the fact that patients
experience no rebound in their condition, and are apt
to sink steadily unless they are sent away.   There
is only one plan to follow ; if a man is seriously ill,
ship him off at once and he will probably recover,
but if you try to keep him here, he will die.   On
board the *Deccan* are thirty-six invalids who have
been ordered a sea cruise, after which they are
to return, but the plan of bringing them back is not
one to be recommended, because at least six months
are required to recover from the exhausting effects
of the climate.

I saw a sad instance of this later.   One of the
invalids ordered to go for a sea trip was a young
officer in the Guards' division of the Mounted
Infantry, and he seemed so much better after the
voyage that he was returned to duty.   I met him
shortly after his return, at a Board that had assembled
to value some of my outfit which had been captured
by the enemy at Tofrek, and as he had formerly
been in the same Militia regiment with myself, we
soon began chatting of times past and present, for
there are few pleasures so great as that of meeting
a familiar face far from home.   I remember he
complained that, notwithstanding his voyage, he

could not rally his strength, and that the heat of the sun, to which on vedette duty he was sometimes exposed for twelve hours without shelter, tried him very much. A few days later, I was shocked to hear that he was lying dangerously ill at H. Redoubt, and on the first opportunity rode down there, but was told he was too weak to see any one. The tent where he lay was a beautifully cool hospital marquee, and a portion of it had been curtained off for his sole use. From time to time the nursing Sister, in her red cape and snowy apron, came to peep at him and stole away on tiptoe. I sat for some time talking to a sick Staff officer who lay in the other half of the tent; but poor Sutton never rallied, and a few days afterwards, as a last chance, he was carried on board a ship, where he died before she had gone many leagues on her homeward voyage.

This was only one case of many that began to sadden our lives about this time, for death now came, not in the heat of battle heralded by the roar of rifles and the gleam of steel, but creeping silently through the camp like a thief in the night, so that of two men sleeping in a tent, the one would be taken and the other spared. When next a British force is sent to Suakin, I trust it may be understood that the sand of the plain, for a radius of at least two miles round the town, has been actually poisoned by the many camps that have been established on it during the late expeditions, and that it is teeming with the seeds of dysentery, enteric fever, and all the germs bred of decaying camels and other matter, which, though it may be reduced to dust, has not been purified or rendered inoculous, as it would have been by fresh earth. The only way, therefore, to preserve the health of the troops, is to get them up as soon as possible to fresh untainted camping grounds near the mountains. It was not, however, the fault of the authorities on the spot that we remained for five weary weeks in this unhealthy situation, because the telegram of the 15th April, I have quoted a few pages back, naturally paralyzed their movements, "pending further consideration" by the Government.

A deserter is said to have come in, who declares Osman is at Tamai with a hundred men, and that he has five of the Indian camp-followers with him, whom he keeps hard at work and treats badly. I believe some attempts have been made to ransom these men. The deserter has lost his hand, and says Osman cut it off because he complained of want of food. That is how he treats an Arab Oliver Twist! The tribes are anxious to come in, but Osman still points to our ships lying in the offing, and says we are going away as we did last year, and that then the Mahdi will revenge himself on them if they do.

April 18.—The grand event of to-day was a reconnaissance made to Deberet and the valley of Khor Aberet. It started at 5 A.M., and was composed of the 15th Sikhs, two Regiments of Cavalry, Horse Artillery, and fifty Mounted Infantry. Another column from Handoub, composed of the Australians, some guns, and Mounted Infantry, co-operated with it, advancing on Deberet through the Waratab Hills; while a third column from Otao, composed of Mounted Infantry, supported by half a Battalion of the Scots Guards, operated from Otao towards the same point. The Cavalry scouting in front reached Deberet at 9 A.M., where a few half-filled wells were found, with water three feet below the

surface.   The column from Handoub occupied the
mouth of the pass, and that from Otao the low hills
near Khor Aberet.   Some parties of the enemy
were seen retiring, but no cattle were found, so
probably the Arabs had got wind of the movement.
On their way back the troops burned the village of
Hasheen, which showed signs of recent occupation.

These combined operations were well designed,
and, had the enemy been found, would no doubt
have proved very successful.   It was, in fact, just
the kind of movement we ought to have executed
at the commencement of the campaign, had we
seized Handoub and Otao, instead of wandering
after Osman Digma through waterless bush.

The troops during this reconnaissance displayed
great endurance considering the heat of the weather,
the Scots Guards from Otao, marching twenty miles
without a single man falling out.   The Australians
from Handoub, marched for nine hours, covering a
distance of about fourteen miles, through a rough and
difficult pass, and had only one man falling out;
while the Sikhs from Suakin, marched twenty miles,
three men falling out.

April 19, *Sunday.*—I had hoped for a quiet day,
but there was no such luck, for at sunrise I had to
see a convoy off, which kept me from Church parade,
and then got orders to attend a Board assembled to
condemn nearly 500 leaky water tins, which obliged
us to stand in the full glare of the tropical sun
from 10.30 till half-past twelve; though why
Sunday and such an hour should have been selected
for work of this nature it is difficult to determine,
unless it is thought desirable to thin off a few of the
officers.   When I got back to Headquarters feeling
very sick, there was the usual pile of telegrams from
the front to answer, and wearisome administrative

details to go into, which engaged me till Mess time ;
so the two hours' gallop in the cool of the evening,
which is our one relaxation and tonic, had to be
abandoned.

I hate grumbling, and am fully convinced that
the habitual grumbler never makes a good soldier,
but it *does* relieve one's mind sometimes, and I should
like to see a little more consideration shown to
Sunday in the camp, when no overwhelming military
necessity intervenes.   Not only is it morally good
to observe Sunday as a day of rest, but the physical
advantage is great to the health and minds of officers
and men, if they know that one day in every seven
they will be left in comparative peace.   It is something to look forward to, a pause in the continual
round of duty ; that does more than anything else to
give fresh elasticity to mind and body for the labours
of the coming week.   Yet in the history of warfare
how many battles have been fought on Sunday ?
And since we have been here, it is not too much to
say that no real attempt has been made to render
Sunday a day of rest to the mass of the troops.   I
venture to think that if officers were instructed
that they may work their men without stint every
day in the week, but should endeavour to order their
operations in such a way that nothing but the
absolutely necessary routine of duty should be required on Sunday, it would prove a distinct gain to
the health and *morale* of all ranks.   Of course, in
the face of serious military combinations, this rule
could not be observed, but there have been many
cases where it might have been without the slightest
detriment to the service ; and it should be accepted
as an important principle in economizing the physical
powers of a force in the field.

To-day the Scots Guards, with two guns and a

company of Engineers, were sent to Tambouk, six miles beyond Otao, to occupy the wells ; no signs of the enemy were seen, and the water supply appeared abundant and of much better quality than at the other stations. My experience is that it goes on improving the farther the road is pursued, and that if Es Sibil were reached, no more condensed water would be required between that station and Ariab. There was a report in the bazaars that Osman had been stabbed ; if bazaar reports could have killed him he would not have given us much trouble.

April 20.—Rode to Handoub with Colonel B——, who gave me an account of a shipwreck he was in. The vessel came in collision with another and sank very quickly, but B—— had time to place his wife with other ladies in a boat, and then, thinking she was quite safe, and being a strong swimmer, he secured a plank and jumped into the sea to wait his chance of being picked up. The plank kept tilting out of the water and throwing him off every time he tried to sit on it, and he was rather amused at the tricks it played him, when, on drifting to the other side of the sinking vessel, he was horrified to see his wife struggling in the sea and nearly exhausted, the boat in which she was placed having capsized, and all its other occupants been drowned. He reached her just in time, and supported her on his plank till they were eventually rescued, if I remember right, the only survivors of the wreck. It was strange this meeting together again of husband and wife in the ocean, when the chances were so great against it.

A little beyond the crow's nest at No. 1 Post, we found a horse writhing in great agony beside the line ; its rider had been thrown, and his revolver falling out had gone off and wounded the horse in

a terrible manner, but he dared not destroy it, because, until a veterinary surgeon had reported on
the case, and a Board condemned the horse, he might
have been obliged to pay its value, had he done so ;
he had, therefore, gone forward with the troops,
leaving the poor beast in its agony.   The appealing
look of the dying horse lying in the burning sun
with the flies clustering round its wound, and the
vultures hovering near, went to my heart ; and I
asked Colonel B—— if he had any objection to its
being put out of its misery, as a soldier standing
near said that if I would lend him my revolver and
give the order, he would shoot it.   B—— said it was
a risky thing to do, so tight are the strings of red
tapeism, but he was too humane a man to hold out
long, considering the wound was incurable, so we
had the poor beast quietly put out of its pain, and
it 'remained for many a day a well-known object
beside the rail.

I was again feeling the sun, and nearly fainted
when we reached Handoub, where there was a good
deal to do arranging for the water to be sent up by
rail, as the line had now reached this station, and
for keeping the advanced posts at Otao and Tambouk supplied by convoys.   For the first time I had
to apply to the doctors, who gave me " a pick-me-
up," which enabled me to get through my work, but
they would not let me ride home, and told me to
send back my horse and take the rail in the cool of
the evening.   About sunset General Graham, who
had been on to Tambouk, came in, and we returned
together by train to Headquarters, where I found
F——, the Staff surgeon, waiting to meet me.   He
said he had very nearly brought a stretcher with
him, some foolish story of my being ill having gone
home, and he insisted on my drinking a huge tumbler

of whisky and soda water ; no bad medicine either.
After that, chicken-broth and bed.

April 21.—Ordered to remain in tent all day.

April 22.—Rode down early to inspect the depôt
at No. 5 pier. It is wonderful what arrears of work
even a single day's rest will throw on one's hands,
for the doctors will not allow the men to drink anything but condensed water from the base, and, as
the troops keep moving from post to post, it is
necessary to keep a most careful watch on the requirements of each station to prevent it being drunk
dry. My assistants are working splendidly, but they
have not all the threads of the scheme in their
hands, and do not know what movements are going
to be made as I do, or should do at Headquarters,
for I sometimes do not get notice till the last
moment.

In the afternoon the news spread like wildfire
through the camp that the expedition was brought
to a close, and that we should all quickly re-embark.
Nearly everybody I met was dancing and singing
for joy, because, now that sickness is increasing so
rapidly, and it is known that there is no intention of
letting us fight our way to Bérber, there are few who
are not longing to get away. Some are already
turning their eyes eagerly towards India, and the
question every one asks is, " Where are we going.
To India, Cyprus, or England ? " I rode into the
town in the evening and found the streets thronged
with officers buying souvenirs. The native population
are waking up to the fact that money is to be made,
and the women and children offering their silver
bangles for sale ; shields and swords have run up
to £5 a piece, and spears to £2 or £3. There is a
little Italian who keeps a curiosity shop, a sort of
niche in a wall, and he has new spears manufactured

every day. They say an armourer on one of the
ships turned an honest penny by making a lot of
spear-heads and having them mounted, and that a
batch of "real Soudan spears" has already been
sent out from Birmingham. Only the store-keepers
look gloomy, for they see their days of prosperity
are coming to an end ; one of them, who keeps a
sort of restaurant, gave £2000 only a few days ago
for the business, which he bought from the last pro-
prietor, who had made a fortune in it since the
expedition came out.

This rumour of the withdrawal of the force,
which, however, was not fulfilled for some time, was,
in consequence of Mr. Gladstone's statement in the
House, foreshadowed by Lord Hartington in his
message of the 20th April to Lord Wolseley :—
"Government will announce on Tuesday that it is
necessary to hold all military resources of empire,
including forces in the Soudan, available for service
wherever required. They will not, therefore, make
provision for further offensive operations in the
Soudan," etc.

On the 23d April, Lord Wolseley telegraphed to
Lord Hartington :—" I think it would be a very
good thing if I went to Suakin. . . . Please send
me definite orders when you wish me to begin to
act, with regard to stopping Graham's advance, progress of the railway," etc.

It will be seen from this, that as yet no orders had
reached us at Suakin to suspend operations, and
word was passed round that everything was to go
on as before. Indeed, so anxious were the authorities to prevent officers having their attention dis-
tracted by the rumours flying about, that the news
telegrams from home, to which we all subscribed,
and which were usually published every afternoon,

were stopped, and for a time we were kept in ignorance of what was going on in Europe. But in spite of this censorship, men knew well that the object of the expedition would never be fulfilled, and the long month of suspense which ensued was very trying to their health.

CHAPTER X.

WORK ALONG THE LINE.

APRIL 23.—Railed by early train to Handoub, then borrowed a horse and rode to Otao. On leaving Handoub a very large vein of white quartz can be seen on the side of one of the hills of the Abdarak range to the left of the route, about five and a half miles distant, and nearly due South-West of the wells. It looks to the naked eye like the smoke of a burning village, and the men of the New South Wales Contingent say it is exactly the kind of place where gold might be found, and declare that all the rocks in this neighbourhood present the characteristics they are accustomed to look for in a gold-mining district; in fact, I believe a few grains of gold have been discovered in the sand of the Khor at Handoub. For the first six miles, the route runs nearly West across a hard shingly plain sparsely covered with bush and scrub, then one of the spurs of the Abdarak range, which here trends Northwards to within a short distance of the track, is passed, and a soft sandy Khor entered that leads to Otao, about two and a half miles farther on. Rising in bold relief from the plain on the right are many isolated piles of large boulders, red, white, black, and gray; some are of red and white sandstone, others of granite, and nearly all of them bear traces of the action of water. Most noticeable among them is one great monolith called 'the tower rock," which forms an unmistakable landmark on the right of the route, as Otao is approached ; it is situate about two and a quarter miles N.E. of the wells, and consists of a rugged pile of rocks, from the summit of which one huge isolated boulder rises perpendicular to a considerable height, presenting at a little distance very much the appearance of the gray time-worn tower of a castle. When the railway afterwards passed this spot, some of the navvies painted on the tower rock the familiar inscription " Pears' soap is the best," in letters a yard long, and probably it remains to this day for the information of the Arab population ; but whether any of Osman Digma's dusky wives have written to the enterprising firm in question to say that they find it matchless for the hands and complexion, I do not know.

Many of these rocks are deeply stained with iron ore, while quartz veins are frequent in the fragments of stone that strew the ground. It is curious that the Australians should think gold exists in this country, because I remember twelve years ago the same idea struck me forcibly, when I was looking at some long ridges of quartz seamed with thin red veins which rise above the surface of the plain between Ariab and O Bak. How strange it would be if the greed for gold should some day cause the work on the railway to be completed, which our love of civilization has not been strong enough to accomplish, and a line to the gold fields of Suakin solve the Soudan problem !

Stranger things have come to pass. Twelve years ago when travelling along this route, I wrote in my journal, " In years to come, perhaps, a railway will traverse the African desert ; and the traveller, no

longer a tiny insect crawling across the plain, will
feel like some winged geni flying over it at forty
miles an hour." But I little thought then, that this
morning my dream would be realized, and I should
be transported from Suakin to the mountains in
about twenty minutes, instead of having to endure
four or five hours' weary camel-riding.

Presently Otao is reached, where I get a hospitable invitation to lunch with two officers of the
Intelligence Department, who are established there
with Mr. Brewster. Mahmoud Ali came in and had
a chat. I was pleased to see the thorough way in
which Brewster seemed to understand the feeling
and tone of thought of the Arabs, who have a strange
mixture of childishness and shrewd common sense
in their nature. I never had any sympathy with the
school that includes all coloured races in the general
category of "niggers," and thinks they should be
treated as such; and I believe these Soudanese
Arabs would display many fine qualities if they
could only be developed. Our great object of late
has been to induce the weaker tribes to federate
against the despotism of Osman Digma, but there
is no doubt the Hadendowas are the most warlike
race in these parts, and I do not think any of the
races along the Nile can equal the desperate courage
of their first charge. It is clear, therefore, that the
Amarars, Fadlabs, etc., will never be able to resist
them without English support, and now it is known
in the bazaars from Mr. Gladstone's statement that
we are not likely to give help, the prospect of getting
them to co-operate is practically at an end; though,
could we promise permanent occupation of Suakin
and continue our advance, there is no doubt the
tribes all along the line would come in, and Osman's
power be completely broken; the Arabs themselves

say there would be little more fighting if we went
on to Ariab. I do not think these Amarars are
treacherous or even untruthful, either from my past
or present experience of them, but they are afraid of
being made the victims of Osman's vengeance when
we leave, and, being the weaker party, wish to do
what is best for their own safety, and frankly avow
it. Of the two, they prefer us to Osman, who is a
tyrant, and it is probable they would be faithful to
us if we would be faithful to them ; but they see no
reason why they should run their necks into a halter,
lose their goods, and have their wives and children
sold into slavery for our amusement, if we will not
promise to give them support till Osman and the
Mahdi have been crushed, and in this they only
show their common sense.

After lunch I rode on to Tambouk with Templar,
who was taking his balloon detachment there to
assist in a reconnaissance that is to be made to-
morrow by the new Camel Corps, which Major James
has just organized. The object of the reconnaissance
is to explore the road to Es Sibil, or Dissibil as it
is sometimes called, twenty miles beyond Tambouk.
This Es Sibil appears to be the little valley I find
described in my old journal as—" a charming verdant
spot hidden away in the heart of the mountains, the
steep rocky sides of which formed an inaccessible
wall round it. A level lawn of the softest grass
spread like a green carpet under foot, while a variety
of beautiful trees afforded a pleasing shade from the
powerful rays of the sun." But it must not be supposed, as some people at home appear to think,
that there is any place suitable for the encampment
of a big force in the mountains, except Ariab. On
the other hand, there is nothing to prevent a large
force passing from Suakin to that place and estab-

lishing small posts on the route, because the local
water supply can be developed to any extent, and a
condensing engine is all that would be necessary at
Handoub, where the water is brackish.   This, I take
it, is because the sea originally extended to the foot
of the mountains and has left saline deposits ; indeed,
if excavations were made, I fancy a great portion of
the plain would prove to be coral reef.   Inland the
water would be found to be good till O Bak was
reached.

Beyond Otao the spurs of several surrounding
hills close in on the route, and the bush becomes
thicker, no doubt deriving sustenance from the
moisture below the bed of a Khor that traverses
the valley.   Otao is soon lost sight of, and, just
when we were in the thickest part of the bush, the
tremulous cry of the desert lark, which we remembered so well at Tofrek, rose up all round us.   The
balloon waggon was immediately halted, and we
closed round it determined to hold it till assistance
arrived, should an attack take place ; but this time
the larks were real and nothing happened, so we
continued our march, and presently emerged on more
open ground, from which we could see the signal
station at Tambouk perched on a hill above a broad
Khor twenty feet deep, which runs along the foot of
the mountains on the left.   Some steep rocky hills
on the right form the other side of the gate of the
valley of Tambouk, a stony mimosa-covered plain
similar to that of Handoub, but smaller.

These flat plains encircled by hills, through which
there is always a natural gate formed by the dry bed
of a river, follow each other in regular succession till
the mountains are passed and the open desert reached
that divides Ariab from Berber.

I found the Guards very comfortable in their

little zareba at Tambouk ; they had been fired into four or five times the previous night, but nobody was hurt. With characteristic neatness they had cleared the big stones from the approaches to the zareba and piled them on either side, making quite a tidy road ; the position of the camp was very strong and protected by three redoubts on the neighbouring hills. At dusk the Camel Corps arrived, accompanied by several of the Friendlies, and bivouacked for the night. The friendly Arabs are all supposed to wear red shirts, or some garment striped with red to distinguish them from our foes, a very necessary precaution. Most of them had rifles and belts full of cartridges ; they were not allowed inside the zareba, but encamped behind it under the shelter of the hills.

April 24.—I went out at daybreak with a rifle to try to find some gazelles, several of which have been shot in the valley, but was unsuccessful in my search. There is a story that Colonel ——— of the Scots Guards came upon six armed natives one morning when he was out shooting alone, and asked them if they were Mahmoud Ali's men, to which they promptly replied that they were, and immediately made off ; it was afterwards discovered that they were some of Osman's scouts. I returned to camp and found the Camel Corps preparing to start on their reconnaissance. The balloon was sent up to a great height, from which the country as far as Sinkat, twenty-six miles distant, could be seen. Templar afterwards made a young Friendly, who was remarkable for his keen sight, go up ; he had never been in a balloon before, but nevertheless stepped into the basket with the greatest coolness and began to sing as he ascended, his voice growing fainter and fainter like that of a lark till he could hardly be

heard on reaching a height of 800 feet.   He then
asked to be let up higher that he might get a better
view of the country, and 1000 feet more rope
was, therefore, paid out, when he said he could see
very well, and that the country was clear of the
enemy for twenty miles round ; he also discovered a
stray camel five miles away, and when he came
down and got out of the basket, immediately went
after it and returned on its back.   There were nearly
200 of his tribe watching the ascent, and I fear they
have lost all reverence for the balloon.

The balloon was kept inflated and anchored near
the zareba for five days.

I found the wells at Tambouk yielding only 600
gallons a day, but by the 27th their yield had been
increased to 3000 gallons, and there is no doubt
that, like all wells along this route, they could
have been still further developed.   The principal
well was 16 feet deep, its bottom being on sandstone
rock.   On the side of the black slaty hill, which
rose abruptly above it, was a tangle of delicate green
foliage, among the leaves of which fluttered two tiny
humming-birds of the most brilliant colours it is
possible to conceive.   One tree, the drooping
branches of which hung gracefully over the well, I
remember having seen at Es Sibil.   I believe it is
called by the Arabs " *Hebe*," and it bears clusters
of edible red berries like very small bunches of
grapes ; they taste something like a currant eaten
with the leaves of young mustard, being both pun-
gent and sweet, but are not disagreeable.   None of
the doctors could tell me the proper name of this
plant, and I had some trouble to get any one to
venture on tasting its fruit.

In this country the trees have habits of their
own, and the budding leaf, the full-blown flower, and

the curling seed-pod, may all be seen on the mimosas at the same time.

I galloped the six miles between Tambouk and Otao in twenty minutes ; the advancing spurs of the hills, so favourable to concealment, the thick bush and the trilling notes of the desert lark, rendering it a route a solitary horseman would not care to tarry on. Yet who would not ride a spirited charger on a summer morning through an enemy's country with a good sword at his side, feeling that there was just that spice of danger which gives zest to every exercise ? How the blood goes coursing through the veins as the horse bounds onward and the pure air of the hills blows in one's face ; how blue the sky looks overhead, with the glorious tropical sun shedding its radiance on the landscape ; and how pleasant is the sight of the friendly camp nestling below the fort-crowned hill, where a soldier's welcome awaits all who pass that way! Once in the saddle, the drudgery, the sickness, the many vexations of campaigning are forgotten, and nothing is felt but the joy of life, the zest of adventure.

From Otao I rode on to Handoub, and thence railed back to Headquarters.

April 25.—General Graham telegraphed to Lord Wolseley this day, strongly recommending the crushing of Osman Digma before our withdrawal, as we are now in a position to operate on Sinkat and Tamanieb, from Tambouk and Suakin ; so nobody knows if active operations are not about to recommence.

The Camel Corps only went half-way to Es Sibil yesterday, and then came back, as the Friendlies were afraid to remain out for the night. It seems Mahmoud Ali has a private feud with the chief at Es Sibil, and most of his men were in a great fright,

stopping to say their prayers all the way out. It is
believed about 500 of the enemy are between Tambouk and Es Sibil. The road, as far as the reconnaissance advanced, proved easy for the railway.
The camp at Tambouk was again fired into, and the
enemy's fires could be seen on the surrounding hills;
probably they have heard we are going away. They
say that on the 23d some of the Nurab tribe passed
Handoub and Otao, and established themselves near
Tambouk ; if so, they cannot have been far off when
Templar and I rode there on that day with the
balloon waggon. Some reports, however, say that
Osman is leading a wretched life, never sleeping
twice in the same place, and accompanied only by a
handful of his most devoted followers ; so everybody
hopes General Graham will get permission to make
a final effort to capture him before we leave.

April 26 to 29.—Nothing of any importance has
taken place. I have been ordered to have 28,000
gallons of water ready at a few hours' notice, in anticipation of fresh operations ; this, with the care of
the advanced posts which obliged me to go again to
Handoub, has kept me pretty busy.

I think Regimental officers have an easier time of
it than those on or attached to the Staff ; of course,
they have to work very hard, but as a rule they get
at least some hours of the day to themselves, and
the juniors are free from any very heavy strain of
responsibility. Staff officers, on the contrary, are
frequently given work that entails great personal
responsibility, and can hardly call an hour of the
day their own ; for if they leave the camp for even
a brief interval on any other errand than duty, the
chances are they will be wanted during their absence,
and the knowledge of this prevents them from being
able to enjoy any thorough rest or relaxation. On

the other hand, their work is of a more interesting nature than purely Regimental routine, and naturally there are many hours of the day when they are not actually engaged.   What should, therefore, be provided in a camp like this, is a large tent where the officers could keep their chairs and newspapers, and where they might go to read, rest, or chat, as in a club, when not actually at work, and yet still be within call of their various Chiefs, should they be wanted ; but there is nothing of the kind at Headquarters here, and for men to spend the greater part of each day in their own tents, is, I am certain, bad for their health.   The same principle applies to the non-commissioned officers and men, who should be provided in a camp which is established for any time, with two or three E.P. tents thrown into one, to form reading rooms, where, when not on duty, they could see the papers which the officers and the National Aid Society would willingly supply them with.

The news that Lord Wolseley will soon arrive is causing a general brush up all round, and it is wonderful how fast the beards have disappeared from many a hirsute chin, which erst used to grace our Mess, for it is understood that Lord Wolseley is an advocate of the razor ; those who have suddenly taken to shaving are called the sycophants, and an officer on being chaffed the other day replied pathetically, "One *has* to be a sycophant nowadays, you know."   I may here say that, though I did not shave myself, till the idea of another march after Osman Digma had been definitely abandoned, I think that, on the whole, it is better for one's health and comfort to shave during a campaign, if possible ; though during a desert march, where every pint of water is of value to the men, even if one does not

want it oneself, it would be almost criminal to do
so, but under ordinary circumstances, there is nothing
so refreshing, nothing that wakes one so effectually
in the morning, or that makes one feel so clean and
comfortable, after a long day's work, in the evening,
as a good shave.   The Arabs, it is true, have much
greater respect for a bearded man than for one with
a smooth chin, because they are rarely able to grow
beards themselves till they have reached the full
maturity of manhood, frequently not even then ; and
for this reason alone, it may be advisable that troops
engaged against them should cultivate their beards ;
but, though at sea a beard is no doubt a luxury, on
land it is a very troublesome thing to keep thoroughly
clean and free from dust, and much more time is
occupied in washing, trimming, and combing it, than
would be required for shaving.   Therefore, I say,
unless there is a special reason to the contrary, I
would advise those who go out campaigning not to
grow their beards.

On the night of the 26th, the enemy again fired
into the camps at Tambouk and Otao, wounding one
native follower ; they also cut the telegraph.   On
the 28th they scraped holes under some of the
sleepers of the railway near Handoub, and set fire
to them.   To-night, the 29th, an ambuscade is to be
set to watch the line, and to-morrow an armoured
train will begin patrolling after dark.

April 30.— Breakfasted with the Sappers at
Quarantine Island, as I had to arrange with them
for some work, and met B——, who accompanied
the party of thirty volunteers from the Shropshire
Regiment, who formed the ambuscade last night ;
they caught six of the enemy trying to injure the
line, and fired a volley at them, but captured none,
though traces of blood were found.

On returning to camp, I received a telegram from E——, who has just taken over the water depôt at Otao, to say there were only 500 gallons in the tanks that were supposed to contain 5000 ; a train was passing, so I gave my horse to an orderly and scrambled on to one of the trucks, where I found ——, who was also going to the head of the line. We sat on a pile of rails so hot from the sun that we could not touch them with our naked hands ; in fact, we felt very like chesnuts roasting on the hob. The head of the line is now within half a mile of Otao, so we walked the rest of the way. I was quite sorry to notice how the voice of the young warrant officer, who had been in charge of the missing water, shook when I questioned him about it. He is a keen soldier, married, with a rising family, and has been hoping to win a Quarter-Master's commission for his services,[1] but he could not explain how the water had disappeared, and declared he examined the tanks daily before reporting to me.

After arranging for a fresh supply, I borrowed a couple of horses, and galloped on with —— to Tambouk, to see how matters were going on there ; and then the mystery was solved, for one of the large canvas storage tanks had just been emptied, and on examination the bottom was found to be punctured with innumerable tiny rust holes, caused by the iron the water held in solution from passing through vessels of that metal. The precious liquid had escaped imperceptibly into the sand through these small perforations, and the only remedy was to get new tanks. These canvas tanks, which are otherwise very clean and portable, are subject to this defect ; and I would recommend

---

[1] He has since obtained it.

that instead of being covered all over, they should
be provided with a large opening in the centre of
the top, closed by a canvas flap, so that they may
be frequently cleaned and examined.

General Fremantle was acting as political officer
at Tambouk, assisted by Captain Clarke, R.E., and
there were a great many Friendlies, both at that
place and Otao, some of whom had only recently
come over from Osman Digma, still had their heads
shaved, and were unprovided with red shirts. As
they were all armed, it was rather puzzling when
meeting them in the surrounding bush to know
whether they were friends or foes. Some of these
natives would dearly have liked to take advantage
of our presence to prosecute their own private tribal
feuds ; but General Graham was strict in his injunc-
tions to old Mahmoud Ali to endeavour to win over
the tribes along the line of railway by friendly means
alone, and, had we been allowed to give any promise
of permanent protection, there is no doubt this policy
would have been entirely successful.

In his despatch of the 22d April, General Graham
says of Mahmoud Ali, " He was very clear on the
point that if we would promise protection, settled
government, and the re-establishment of the Prefec-
tures at Sinkat and Tokar, the tribes would come in
at once!" Apropos of the Friendlies, we were all
much puzzled by a story which got abroad one day
that some of them had brought a human hand into
Handoub, and offered it for sale to the Guards. I
afterwards heard that one of the School of say-
something-at-any-price writers at home, got hold
of this legend of the bloody hand, and tried to make
capital out of it, by hinting that we were not above
encouraging our native allies to mutilate the enemy,
and purchasing any odd limbs they brought in. I

have not seen what he did write, but I know the true story, and these were the facts.

Small numbers of the enemy hovered round our positions every night with a view to harassing them, cutting off stragglers, etc., and we used to send out parties of the Friendlies to watch their especial haunts, a work for which they were eminently fitted. Occasionally there was a little fight, though as a rule it did not end in much slaughter, for both parties fought warily behind their shields and knew each other's tactics. In the present case five Amarars engaged three of the enemy, and one of them tried to wrest a rifle out of the hands of his adversary, a slave of Osman's. The two men had a struggle, and another Amarar ran up and decided it by cutting off the slave's hand with a blow of his sword. The other two Osmanites then ran away, and the Amarars brought in the rifle and the hand to an officer of the Intelligence Department, who ordered it to be decently buried. Meanwhile, the wounded man fainted, but came to himself again, and was picked up by our Cavalry vedettes who brought him to Otao, where his wound was carefully tended, and so great is the vitality of these people, that he was soon walking about again as if nothing had happened; probably the sand stopped the bleeding of his wound when he fell.

We met Colonel T—— of the Guards, as we were riding back, and I noticed that he wore a pad down the front of his jacket, as well as the usual spine protector behind. I do not know what was the object of this. His subsequent fate was very sad, for though he reached England safely, and might have been supposed to have escaped all danger, for he was well enough to stand for Parliament, he died on the very day of polling, yet another victim of the exhausting effects of this treacherous climate.

It was getting dusk when we neared Otao, and
heard the whistle of the last train, so we galloped in
at racing pace, and flinging ourselves off our horses,
managed to scramble up on the engine just as it was
moving away.   The train had to collect parties of
navvies and coolies all along the line, who came
running up when they heard its whistle in a great
fright lest they should be left behind, and soon
clustered upon it in hundreds, overflowing the trucks
and hanging like a swarm of bees on every available
holding place outside.   —— and I hung on to the
engine, where we got the fresh air in front, though
the fire made it very warm work.   It was eight
o'clock and quite dark before we reached the camp,
though, as the line was all down hill, once the
workmen were collected, the train ran in very fast,
doing the ten miles between Handoub and West
Redoubt in about eighteen minutes.

The other day a navvy found one of the enemy
hidden under a pile of sleepers by the line ; the
Arab jumped up, but the navvy caught his spear
with one hand, and hit him such a straight blow
from the shoulder with the other, that the poor
Hadendowa was knocked completely " out of time,"
to use a sporting expression.   The navvies were
very proud at having captured this prisoner, but, as
a rule, they did not evince any martial spirit, and
had a wholesome dread of the enemy ; they were
such great strong-looking fellows, one would have
thought that, with their picks and shovels alone, they
could have thrashed twice their number of Arabs ;
but I suppose they argued that they had been
engaged to work and not to fight, and they rarely
ventured far from the covering parties.   A navvy
told me that one night when two rockets were sent
up at the Headquarter camp after Mess, none of the

men on Quarantine Island would go to bed, fearing the enemy were approaching.

May 1.—To satisfy those people at home, who still suppose a delightful hill station can be found somewhere near Suakin, the Headquarter Staff made a sort of pilgrimage this morning to the top of the highest mountain of the Waratab range, from which they telegraphed to Lord Hartington as follows :— "Top of Waratab Hill, 1600 feet above sea-level, eleven miles from Suakin in direct line. Arrived here after one and three quarter hours' hard climbing. Road inaccessible to mules. Peaks and narrow ridges of metamorphic rock. Unsuitable for sanatorium, unless road were made at enormous expense. Air fresh ; sun hot. Commanding view of country." Air fresh, sun hot, is delicious, and I think the party of gray-headed gentlemen who gallantly scrambled up 1600 feet of sharp metamorphic rock under a tropical sun to satisfy the Secretary of State for War, and then slid down again, for the slope was too steep for walking, deserved well of their country, and should at least have been awarded the blue ribbon of the Alpine Club. They all came into the Mess tent looking very burned and blistered after accomplishing this feat, and there was a great demand for ice and soda water.

In the evening after Mess, I went to see the new armoured train start to patrol the line. The engine was placed in the middle between trucks defended by a breastwork of iron plates, each truck being capable of holding forty men, who, besides their arms, were provided with picks and shovels for repairing the line. It appears that last night when the train was at Handoub, as many as six fires were seen, which the Arabs had made under the sleepers as before ; the train ran down at once and found the

rails red-hot in places ; some shots were fired at the
spot where the enemy was supposed to be, but with
no visible result, and it is certain a train of this kind
should be provided with a search light.   The moon
is now at the full, but the place where the Arabs
usually approach the line is near a dry water-course
running from a thick belt of bush, and there is a
deep shadow across the plain, under cover of which
they creep to their work unperceived.   The General,
the Chief of the Staff, and Colonel ——, commanding
the Grenadiers, were all present to see the train off.
Colonel —— asked me to dine with him on Sunday;
we were laughing about the sudden disappearance of
beards in the camp, and I asked him if the Guards
had taken to shaving.   " No, indeed," he replied ; " I
shall not let a beard come off till we have been
inspected by Her Majesty."   " You will surely let
me take off my Newgate fringe," said ——, a young
A.D.C. belonging to his regiment, whose beard did not
grow very luxuriantly.   " Oh no," he said, " people must
grow what they can ; but you will come and dine too,
Johnny ;" so it was arranged we should go together.
Poor ——, to see him looking so light-hearted and
well, one would never have guessed that his days
were already numbered, and that though he would
reach England it would only be to die ere the leaves
had fallen.

This night the enemy again fired into Otao.

I must now try to describe the work that has been
done on the famous Suakin Berber Railway, as this
was the last day of its construction, the terminus at
Otao nearly nineteen miles beyond Suakin, having
been reached at nightfall on the 30th April.

I have before said that only about two and half
miles were laid during March, and that the active
pushing forward of the line commenced on 6th April,

from which date to the 30th, sixteen miles of permanent way were put down, at the rate of about two-thirds of a mile per diem.   This was not very fast progress considering that the route followed presented no engineering difficulties whatever, but it must be remembered that the civil contractors had no previous experience of laying a line hampered by the requirements of troops in the field.   Had they been provided with piers or lighters of their own, for unloading a large quantity of material quickly, and formed an adequate depôt from which every requisite necessary for the line could have been supplied as required ; had they landed sufficient engines and rolling stock at the commencement, and ascertained that the fish plates sent from England fitted the rails and the fish bolts the fish plates ; had they taken care that the trains sent to the head of the line always carried their equipment and material complete in every detail, and had the railway been worked on the " line clear " system by help of the telegraph, so that two trains should never meet half-way between crossing stations and one have to run back ; had they punctually observed fixed hours for the departure of the trains carrying sections of the line and those required for the transport of Government stores to the front, so that they might not interfere with each other, etc. etc.,—the railway might have been constructed nearly twice as fast as it was.   No doubt the contractors laboured under great difficulties in having to take their chance of being able to use the military piers, which were frequently required for the unloading of Government stores, and also from having an insufficiency of rolling stock ; for engines had to be used for Commissariat trains, that were wanted to draw railway material.   No plan was adopted for signalling along the line, and two trains

would frequently be seen apparently charging each
other from opposite directions, and on one occasion
the drivers got down and wanted to fight out the
question who was to retire.   It was like the old
story of the two bagmen who met in a narrow
Devonshire lane and would neither of them back his
gig.   One pulled out a newspaper and began slowly
to read it from the first line to the last, while the
other lit his pipe and sat waiting with great com-
posure till he thought he was near the end, when he
said politely, " If you have *quite* done with that
paper, sir, perhaps you would not mind kindly passing
it to me."   History relates that the first bagman
collapsed after that ; but though such things may
occur in a Devonshire lane, they hardly answer on a
military railway.   Moreover, there was hardly a fish
plate that fitted the bolt holes properly, so the rails
were not very strongly clamped together ; a time-
table was made, but the trains did not attempt to
follow it, and the imaginary one that appeared in
Punch would have done just as well.   The engines
were not powerful enough, and often had to make
two or three runs at a gradient of 1 in 50 with a
load of only 40 tons before they could get up, or
else were obliged to pause and take a breath as it
were.   It was only at the last moment any proper
arrangements were made for watering the locomotives,
and they either had to stop work or use the
condensed water intended for the troops.

All these things caused delay, and were the
natural result of the want of experience of the
civil contractors who supplied the material and
administered the line, and were unprepared to com-
bine rapid work with the requirements of the military
force that had to use and protect it.   No doubt
they did their best, and it would be unfair to attach

blame to them, for, though they had vast experience
of railway-making at home, they had never been
called upon to construct a line under such conditions.

For this reason, I am strongly of opinion that it
is a mistake to bring civil enterprise into the construction of a military railway in a hostile country,
soldiers alone being in a position to form such an
organized system as shall meet the requirements
of a force in the field, without interfering with the
progress of the line.

The general principle on which the railway was
constructed, left little to be desired.   The direction
having been settled, every hundred yards was marked
out by pegs, and the ground smoothed off for six
feet on either side of the centre line ; bushes were
cleared away, elevations cut down, and hollows filled
up so as to make the track fairly level.   Where the
beds of dry water-courses were passed, they were
filled in with brushwood and ballast, separate divi-
sions being laid down at the larger ones, so as to
permit of bridges being constructed later.   No drain
pipes were put in at first, as that could be done
where necessary without stopping the traffic.   The
work of preparing the formation level of the permanent way was entirely performed by coolies assisted by
the Madras Sappers; and, as it progressed, a train with
sleepers, rails, and fixings, complete for one-eighth of
a mile, was run up as far as the line extended, and
unloaded by coolies and navvies, who put the sleepers
on Maltese carts drawn by two mules each, under
charge of the Transport Corps; they were then carried
to their proper position, where the coolies laid them
down across the track.   The rails were, meanwhile,
attached to chains and dragged forward by teams of
four horses, supplied by the R.H.A. and C. and T.
Corps, and placed on the sleepers, fished together

and spiked down by the navvies,—the coolies afterwards filling in the line with ballast at their leisure.   The tools, loose bolts, fish plates, spikes, etc., were kept on a trolly, which was pushed forward as the work progressed, and by the time a fresh train arrived from the base, the rails were ready for it to pass over, so that it could drop its material for the next eighth of a mile at the head of the line. Every five miles, temporary sidings were laid down to enable the trains to cross each other.

It was generally admitted that had the rolling stock been sufficient, and the relays of material punctually and properly supplied, there would have been little difficulty in making the railway on this system at the rate of two miles a day, for the first fifty miles at least ; but, as I have mentioned, there were many delays which, on another occasion, might be avoided.   The error was to place the administration of the line in civil hands, when it had practically to be constructed by Government labour, as every military surface-railway under such circumstances must be.   The line was laid out by a survey party of Engineers, the track was cleared and levelled by coolies, supplied by the Indian Government, working under English officers, and assisted by the Madras Sappers, and, after the cessation of active hostilities, by working parties of the European troops as well. Coolies unloaded the material from the ships, at piers constructed by the Government; they lifted, straightened, and boxed up the line under the superintendence of Engineer officers and the usual native head-man. Government horses, mules, and carts, were provided for the work, under charge of the Transport Corps. " The only work done by labour supplied by the contractors," says Capt. Kunhardt, writing to the *R. E. Journal*, "was the running of the trains, and the actual fishing and spiking down the rails, for which the navvies were receiving from 12s..to 15s. a day pay,—work which might have been done quite as well by the native plate-layers present on the spot for 1s. a day." The conclusion is obvious.

We now know that the eighteen and three-quarter miles of railway laid to Otao, cost £865,369. Had there been no civil contractors receiving a bonus and in administrative charge of the line, probably the military authorities, who practically made the railway, would have been able to lay it quicker, and at far less cost. Sir A. Hayter, speaking for Lord Hartington, in reply to Sir F. Milner, told the House that, "even if it had been desirable to construct the railway by means of Engineer officers and coolies, that course was not at the time practicable, Indian resources in skilled railway labour being fully employed in India." If that was so, it clearly points to the necessity of developing those resources in case of sudden emergency.

It is satisfactory to know that the nucleus of a Military Railway Corps has been formed by the conversion to such duties of the 8th and 10th companies of Royal Engineers, and that it is proposed to form a reserve force of Railway Artificers, a most desirable step, which will do away with the friction which arose in the Soudan from the fact that the navvies would take no orders except from the civil contractors, who themselves had perhaps little control over them. And, lastly, it is pleasant to know that 50 miles of light railway for military purposes are now kept in store, and will be retained with a view to contingencies. But I would suggest that these 50 miles ought to be increased to 150 to be of practical use, and, if it should unfortunately be discovered in the future that the possession of

Khartoum, with its arsenal and dockyard, is essential to prevent the Soudan from becoming a standing menace to the safety of Egypt, we shall then be able without delay to send a force to Ariab, which I hope to show in another chapter is the key to the military position in the Soudan.

There is little doubt that the metre gauge would have been better suited to the railway than the ordinary 4′ 8½″ gauge which was adopted, for it is cheaper, lighter, and better adapted to going round sharp curves, while it requires fewer men to put it down, and less labour to prepare the narrower bed on which it is laid. The rate at which the permanent way can be run up to the rail head is the same as on the broader line, for, as the gauge of the engine is greater or less, so is the weight of the rails, sleepers, etc., it has to transport ; and it is generally admitted that the metre gauge is capable of answering all ordinary military requirements, viz. a load of 120 tons, exclusive of the weight of rolling stock, can be carried on it over a line with a ruling gradient of 1 in 150 at a rate of from 15 to 18 miles an hour, which is all that is necessary to enable a Regiment of Infantry, or an ordinary supply of stores, to be forwarded to the front with reasonable despatch.

The route of the proposed railway was reconnoitred for 35 miles beyond Suakin, and presented no difficulty for the construction of the line, the gradient as far as Handoub being about 1 in 200, and from thence to Otao, 1 in 80. An English merchant at Suakin, who had been nineteen times over the route, said that the steepest portion was just beyond Tambouk in the Wady Mareg, where the gradient was in no place steeper than 1 in 40. My own recollections agree with this, and

reporting to the Intelligence Branch in 1884, I said :
" I am still of opinion the steepest gradient will
be found about 14 miles from Otao, between
elevations 2150 and 2300,[1] where there is a rise of
150 feet in 3 miles. I cannot agree with Major
Prout's report, published in the papers, that the most
difficult part of the route will be at Wady Haratri.
There is a rise of 219 feet there, but it is spread
over 6 miles, and I have no recollection of any
difficulty in the road, nor can I find anything in my
journal to indicate it." This opinion I still adhere
to, and all the information we were able to obtain
tends to bear it out. Though the actual reconnaissance was not carried more than 10 miles beyond
Tambouk, the country was seen from the balloon
anchored there for a much greater distance, and
there is little doubt that, till the desert is reached
beyond Ariab, the route presents no engineering
difficulty for railway construction, or for the passage
of carts and horses ; moreover, there is practically
an inexhaustible supply of water at fairly convenient
distances, and though the Norton tube did not find
water between Tambouk and Es Sibil during the
hurried reconnaissance that was made, the green
grass and damp appearance in the bed of the Khor
presented certain indications that it would have been
found if carefully searched for and wells sunk, the
Norton tube having been known more than once to
fail where water was afterwards discovered.

Probably the existing distance between the wells
could be divided, if necessary, anywhere between
Handoub and Ariab, as the road constantly follows
the bed of a Khor ; while from Ariab to Berber,
there appears to be an alternative route 19 miles
South of the ordinary track, by following which

[1] On the Intelligence Branch Sketch Map, No. 369.

the drift sand can be avoided and sufficient water obtained.

Briefly, the experience gained by our work on the railway, showed that its construction from Suakin to Berber would not only be practicable, but easily accomplished with proper organization, should the military necessity arise.

CHAPTER XI.

HOME, SWEET HOME.

MAY 2.—Lord Wolseley landed this afternoon, but continues to sleep on board ship ; a memorandum has been sent round that he does not wish officers to call on him, as he hopes to meet them on shore. Last month a trooper which had arrived from India with 1200 coolies for the railway, was ordered to go back to Bombay, now she has been telegraphed for to come here again. I pity those poor coolies travelling up and down the Red Sea in this weather ; but they are perhaps better off than we are on this baking plain of pestiferous sand, where the mere exertion of thinking sends you into a violent sweat, and you have to hang your jacket outside the tent in the sun every half hour to dry it, where the air burns your tongue as you breathe, and the doctors say you may get sunstroke by the reflected heat from the ground acting on the brain through the optic nerve.

May 3, *Sunday.*——The Chaplain preached a sermon on swearing, not before it was wanted, and told the men that the word " bloody," which is somewhat too frequently heard proceeding from their lips, is not a warlike or sanguinary expression, but simply a corruption of " By our Lady ;" I do not know if this is strictly correct, for " By our Lady " was used

in ancient days as an oath or ejaculation, while
Tommy Atkins uses " bloody " almost invariably as an
adjective ; but, whatever the derivation, it is a word
that might well be dispensed with from his vocabu-
lary.   I think it is my uncle Toby who said the
English Army first learned to swear in Flanders, and
I suppose the habit has never died out.   Even
among officers, it is curious to remark how men of
refined education will fall into the habit of slipping
out a " big big D," under the trials of a campaign,
who would not think of doing such a thing in their
own homes, and it seems strange that we, who live
on the brink of the grave as it were, should disregard
the bad example thus set to the men, the admission
of mental weakness implied in the inability to bear
annoyance without howling (for the relief to the
mind which no doubt is experienced by some people
after uttering an oath, is very nearly akin to the relief
experienced by those who cry out when they are
hurt), and the solemn injunction—" Swear not at
all."   I do not mean to say that officers swear at
their men,—far from it,—such a thing is hardly ever
done nowadays ; and it is of the little, useless, pur-
poseless, past participles, ejaculations and adjectives
that come into daily use, I am speaking now ; the
small oaths that are overheard by the servants and
bâtmen, and which render it illogical to find fault
with the men for following suit, even though their
expressions are naturally of a stronger and coarser
nature.   I admit that flesh is weak, that the climate
here is trying, and the habit is almost as catching as
yawning, also that there has been a vast improvement
within the last fifty years, and the tone of the modern
military Mess is nearly as quiet as that of a private
dinner-table, and sometimes rather duller ; still there
are occasional slips, and it would be interesting to

know whether if a poor-box were started in every
Mess, and each officer asked to sign an agreement
that he would put a shilling into it when he caught
himself swearing, there would be any money for
the soldiers' orphans at the end of the year.   I
should like to see it tried, even though I might be
a poorer man myself.

Having been warned that four days' supply of
water may be wanted any day for a strong force, I
have had a number of troughs put up by the
Engineers near West Redoubt for filling the tins,
which will save the camels a march of two miles. The
water is forced up through an iron pipe, which it was
originally intended should be laid the whole length
of the line, though for some reason it was never
carried beyond West Redoubt ; what there is of it
answers admirably, and the water rushing through
gains a vitality and sparkle that makes it much
more palatable than the flat unaërated water drawn
direct from the condensing ships.   I strolled as far
as these troughs with a couple of friends this afternoon, and we let a number of tired and dusty coolies,
who had been working on the line, have a drink ;
there is nothing the Indian coolie delights in like a
draught of pure water, and it is a luxury he gets very
little of here.   One man, after sucking down nearly
a gallon without pausing, lifted his eyes to heaven
and said in Hindustanee to my friend, a young Staff
officer, " It is not like water, Sahib; it is milk !" Poor
fellow, he had been accustomed to the brackish water
from the wells.   The very low-caste Indians must
have a happier time of it here than those of high
caste, for they can drink direct from a cup as we do,
while the high-caste natives have to suck the water
out of the hollow of their hands, which is both uncomfortable and wasteful.   It is very strange to see

these miserable-looking coolie workmen at 1s. a day, paying such strict regard to their caste rules.

The Guards gave us an excellent dinner, and the band played outside their Mess tent, which sounded very homelike. Little Captain Gioppi, the Italian Military Attaché, was there ; it is a marvel to us all how he manages to keep the light sky-blue tunic he always wears on such occasions so bright and spotless ; it is double-breasted, and he generally rides in tight trousers strapped over narrow black boots with high heels and very pointed toes. It must cost him great agony to preserve such a get-up in this climate, but he is an excellent fellow, and his politeness and amiability never leave him for a moment ; his great ambition is to be under fire, for he arrived too late for Tofrek, and I am told he sits up nearly all night writing voluminous reports in a beautiful Italian hand. When afterwards he fell ill and was taken to hospital, the poor little fellow said, " Ah ! I shall never return, perhaps I am going to die," but I am glad to say the prophecy was not fulfilled, and for once the climate spared its victim.

May 4.——Water on the brain all day, 15,000 gallons having been ordered for a proposed advance, which kept the men hard at work in a broiling sun till dusk. If the movement is countermanded, as has happened before, the water will have to be emptied out in a few days, and the sand will then be enriched by just £1875, for I am told that the condensed water costs one way and another half a crown a gallon.

May 5.——It has been decided that a small force is to proceed to-night to try and capture Mohammed Adam Sardoun, a lieutenant of Osman Digma's, who has established himself at Thakool, in the valley of the Abent beyond Hasheen. I cannot get an excuse to go, as I am ordered to hold myself ready for the general advance, but L——, the Naval A.D.C., with whom I am now living, is going, and at midnight he got up, buckled on his sword, and started.   It always gives me a strange feeling to see the friend one has been chatting with gaily a few minutes before, mount his horse and ride away perhaps to his death, and the little jokes that are sometimes bandied about at Mess, " Is there any small thing I can do for you, old fellow, if you should happen to be absent when they come back ?" or " I say, when the sale of your effects comes off, I mean to secure that hunting flask," etc., sound rather chill and hollow.

May 6.—There was a slight commotion in camp this morning, as it was reported that B——, who had been stationed on the top of the Dihilbat Hill with a company of the 28th Bombay N.I., for signalling purposes, had been surrounded by the enemy, and that we should have to send help out to him ; however, he presently heliographed that he was all right, as the Arabs, after climbing to within 300 yards of his eyrie, thought better of the adventure on receiving a volley from his escort, and went away.

In the afternoon L—— returned very sunburned, and said that the expedition had successfully destroyed the village of Thakool, though Sardoun had escaped, and that he had been fighting all the way home, as parties of the enemy hovered round the column in the bush keeping up a desultory fire, though they did not attempt to charge ; these men were reinforcements that Osman had despatched to assist Sardoun.

The force that paraded last night for this expedition consisted of the 9th Bengal Cavalry, the Guards

and R.E. Companies of Mounted Infantry, and the
Camel Corps, while another column composed of the
15th Sikhs, a company of Mounted Infantry, and
about 400 Friendlies, moved from Otao to co-operate
with it.   The two columns marched in such a way
as to arrive at Thakool, which is eighteen miles West
of Suakin, and ten South of Otao, about daybreak ;
and closed the entrances to the valley, where there
is a well, and Sardoun was supposed to be with 700
to 1.000 men of different tribes, and a number of
cattle.

Our force was very nearly successful in sur-
prising the enemy, who only had time to seize their
arms and run up the hills, from which some of them
opened fire, while others endeavoured to drive off
the flocks and herds.   There were a good many
women and children mixed up with the fugitives,
and the officer commanding the Mounted Infantry
from Otao restrained his men from firing, in order
to save them from being shot down ; but it was not
true that they were hemmed in, " nor were they,"
says General Graham in his despatch of the 21st
May, " to my knowledge fired on by the column
from Suakin with me."   He also says in the same
despatch, " with reference to Lieutenant Austin,
Shropshire Light Infantry, that officer nearly lost
his life owing to his humane endeavour to save an
Arab whom he imagined badly wounded.   The man
sprang up, and Austin received a severe wound in
the arm from his spear."   I believe this officer shot
the Arab through the head as he ran in on him, but
he did not fall until he had delivered his thrust.

The enemy made no stubborn resistance, and
after some volley firing, principally by the Mounted
Infantry and Camel Corps, were driven over the
crest of the hills, and by 7 A.M. the " cease fire " had

sounded, and the various branches of the valley were all completely in our hands. It was calculated that the enemy's loss was about 100, while ours was only 1 officer and 3 men wounded. Ten prisoners were captured, 3 flags, 3 war drums, and nearly 2000 sheep and goats, besides camels and donkeys, so that altogether it was a very successful little raid of the old borderer type. It was also the first engagement in which the Friendlies had taken an active part, 200 of them under Captain Clarke acting with the Mounted Infantry from Otao, and rendering good service. The troops breakfasted at Thakool, and were all on their homeward way by 10 A.M. Unfortunately some of them were not quite so careful as they might have been in guarding the cattle, several head of which were recaptured by a part of the enemy lying in ambush near Hasheen; but as a whole the operation was very well planned, and it was not the unnecessary piece of slaughter some people at home tried to make out, because Sardoun, who had been joined on the 3d May by another chief from the North, with the Irish sounding name of O'Noor, had established himself at Thakool, for the special purpose of harassing our line of communications, and intimidating the well-disposed Amarars, to the Abd-er-Rahmanab clan of which he himself belonged.

It was his people who fired nightly on Otao and Tambouk, and who burned the sleepers of the railway. It was from him Osman Digma drew a great part of his supplies, and being possessed of the only organized force in our neighbourhood, he was a constant menace to the safety of our outposts and allies, and, even for the purpose of carrying out the policy of evacuation, it was necessary his followers should be dispersed.

This evening I got a letter from the special correspondent of the *Times*, who is going away, asking me if I would take over his duties ; I confess I felt very flattered at this, but my military duty still engages every moment of my time, and is of course my first care, so I have had to decline, as no man can serve two masters. The General and the Chief of the Staff, with their usual kindness, would have been willing to give me the necessary permission, but I afterwards learned that there was a departmental rule which would have prevented me from being able to accept the post in any case, much as I should have liked it.

May 7 to 14.—The news of this week might be epitomized : Lord Wolseley went up the line, Lord Wolseley came down the line, Lord Wolseley held a review and inspected everything that could possibly be inspected.

The Indians had a Gimkhana on the 7th, and a sporting party of the enemy were reported to be watching the races, etc., from a respectful distance. The wrestling on horseback was very amusing, and the long hair of the Indians getting loose in the tussle, gave them a very wild appearance as they galloped about on their active little horses, naked to the waist, with their jet-black locks floating a yard behind them. In the sailor's race a poor coolie got knocked over, and I fear was hurt, Jack's riding being typical of the light-hearted recklessness of his disposition. I should like to have seen the Sikhs throwing the round steel disks they wear in their turbans, for I am told they can send them whirling through the air with marvellous accuracy and cut a stick in two at nearly 100 yards distance, but they made no exhibition of their skill. They say these disks were formerly used as a weapon, and against

Cavalry they may have proved rather effective. There is a native priest with the Indian Contingent who is quite a character, and his turban has become a marvellous structure, for year by year, as his holiness increased, he has added another story to it, twisting in a fresh disk, till now it stands nearly six feet high ; and according to popular report he never removes it even when he sleeps. His only weapon is a big stick, and his great ambition is to kill a Mohammedan with it as a crowning act of piety ; whether he will add another story to his turban after that, I do not know. Apart from this slight leaning to high hats and homicide he is a mild-mannered man, and may often be seen preaching in the evening to his co-religionists ; he was a soldier himself once.

On the 8th Lord Wolseley held a grand review of all the troops here, and it was a beautiful sight to see the Guards march past in their usual splendid fashion ; the Australians also did wonderfully well, considering how little time they must have had to practice parade marching ; but, after the Guards, I think the 15th Sikhs carried off the palm, the front of each company being level as a wall. The Cavalry and Camel Corps had a very brilliant appearance with the early morning sunshine glittering on their arms and accoutrements. English soldiers look even better in their fighting dress than they do in their bright uniforms at home. Though the parade was fixed for 6 A.M., and the morning was somewhat clouded for Suakin, the heat was intense, and no less than eleven men fell out.

The idea of making another expedition after Osman has at last been abandoned, though I was once actually under orders to start in the morning ; I expect this change of plan is owing to the report of the principal medical officer, referred to by Lord

Wolseley in his telegram to Lord Hartington of the
11th inst.—"I do not consider that British troops
ought to be subjected to the test of three days, or
even one day's march, in this climate. If they were
the mortality would probably be appalling."

It is a safe saying that, where Englishmen con-
gregate together, there will be racing ; and "the first
Suakin Divisional Race Meeting" is fixed for the
16th, and the second for the 18th, five races to be
run each day. L—— and myself are both Stewards,
and though the other night an invisible guest passed
through our tent, and in the morning L—— was
down with enteric fever, he persuaded himself till the
last moment he would be able to ride in the race.
Poor fellow, he was taken down this day, the 14th,
to the *Ganges* in a dhoolie ; his brother, a Sapper,
is also ill with enteric fever, and was brought down
by a train from Handoub the other evening ; my
servant is ill with the same disease.

It is very sad the way sickness is spreading, and
even the most high-spirited are beginning to get the
curl taken out of them when they think of the faces
missing from Mess. The doctors are in despair,
for every day the number of cases admitted to
hospital increases with leaps and bounds, and the dis-
eases of a febrile character show a marked tendency
to develop into typhoid. As I said before, the fact
is we are sleeping on poisoned ground, and at Headquarters we have suffered perhaps as much as any
Regiment ; indeed, there are few of us who have
not been struggling against the knowledge that our
health has been steadily breaking down for the last
few weeks. There was a heavy rain on the night
of the 9th, which brought out all the foul emanations
from the sand and swelled the sick list considerably.
On the 11th R——, notwithstanding his wonderful

vitality, had to go to hospital ; L—— has gone to-
day; almost all hope is given up of Sutton's recovery;
and they say Reuter's agent, Roberts, the only correspondent who is a member of the Headquarter
Mess, will hardly live through the night.   He is
only twenty-six, poor fellow!   I remember so well
his coming into my tent not long ago and saying
that he had a bad headache, and the doctors told
him it was fever.   He sat down in my easy-chair
and asked wearily if I could give him any scrap of
news for his telegram, but I was then living in a
tent belonging to the head of the Intelligence
Department, and had to tell him that I was the
last person he should come to, as, even if I had any
information, which I had not, it would be a breach
of trust for me to repeat it.   G—— just then came
in, and Roberts addressed his question to him, but
G—— could give him no help, so the poor fellow
tottered out of the dark tent into the bright sunlight beyond, saying his head was splitting, but he
must make up a telegram somehow.   That night he
was carried down to hospital in a dhoolie.

I asked for the Mess corporal the other day, and
the reply was, " He died last night, sir."   I rode
out across the camp, and met a cart full of dead
bodies ; I passed a quiet little hollow and found a
Chaplain reading the burial service.   On another
occasion I said I would go for a gallop to rouse my
drooping energy, but the breeze that blew from the
seashore wafted to my ears the solemn notes of
the " Dead March in Saul."   How the deep beat
of the drum in that most sad of all marches strikes
to the heart on such occasions, those only can tell
who have heard it in a foreign land with comrades
sickening all round !

May 15.—Orders have arrived at last for the

Guards to embark, and telegrams are flying all over
the place to recall troops from the front.   Tambouk
is to be evacuated to-morrow.   The long suspense
is over, and the beginning of the end has come.   Let
me here say one word in praise of the Signalling
and Telegraph Departments, for I have made constant use of them, and admirably have they done
their work.   It is not too much to say that wherever
the troops have moved, there a signal station has
been simultaneously established, and it has been as
easy to communicate with them by day or night as
if they were in the same camp, while the messages
have been delivered with much more promptitude
than they often are in London.   But I regret to see
so many young officers are ignorant of signalling,
and, considering the great importance of the knowledge, I hope in future all officers will be taught it
on first joining, so that wherever they may be, if a
signalling point can be found, they may be able to
transmit messages without having to employ orderlies
as messengers.   The advantage of a signalled message is that the enemy cannot possibly intercept it,
and, as it can be sent in cipher, it is perfectly safe.
Every officer employed at night should be provided
with a small portable lantern, which would answer
all practical purposes for signalling from advanced
posts, when the more elaborate apparatus could not
be provided.

A party of the Camelry, and Mounted Infantry,
was sent out to-day to bury some of our dead at
Tofrek, whom the jackals had uncovered.   They
were attacked by a small party of the enemy, and,
they say, lost two horses.

May 16.—How often have I listened to the
early morning sounds in camp, lying in my bed
watching for the dawn.   First comes the gobble,

gobble, gobble, of the turkeys which the General keeps for his table ; then the bugles begin to sound their calls ; then the drums and fifes of the Guards' band hard by, play a " Point of War ;" then comes the neighing of the horses, as they see the bâtmen moving about, and think of their corn ; I always think there is something intensely suggestive of approval in a horse's neigh—it is like the " hear, hear," in the House of Commons. After the neighing of the horses, the hum of voices begins to be heard, and the camp gradually awakens to life ; the gray dawn mellows into day ; the pickets come tramping steadily home, clad in their long greatcoats ; the voices of impatient officers, peeping out of their tent doors with unshaven faces and calling for their servants, may be heard all over the camp, and every man soon settles down to his individual work. But we shall not hear these familiar sounds much longer, for General Graham is going to embark to-night on board the *Deccan*, and has been busy all day bidding farewell to his troops.

May 17, *Sunday*.—Up at 4.30 A.M., and rode down to see the General off. Most of his Staff were lying still sound asleep on deck when we arrived, but they began to wake up when they saw Sir George Greaves. Then there were good-byes all round, every one looking so happy at getting away. The vessel sailed at six, and I mounted my horse and rode back through the sweltering sun to our pestiferous camp. The *Jumna* with the Guards also left to-day ; Lord Wolseley goes in the *Queen* on Tuesday, so there is a general exodus. He has issued an address to the troops, in which he says—" The deeds of the force in the Soudan have added one more chapter to the glorious record of our national prowess ; " but the proof of the plums in the military pudding must be looked for in the " Honours' Gazette." Poor Frank Roberts is dead, and was buried this evening.

May 18 *to* 21.—This is a soldier-servant's description of a lazy bâtman :—" Why, sir, he has nothing to do; he does it all day, and has not finished it when he goes to bed at night."

Now that the enemy are plucking up courage at the prospect of our prompt departure, and again prowling round our lines, dining out, if your friends live at any distance, is something like going to a party in the old garrotting days as depicted by Leech in *Punch.* I wanted to dine with some friends living about a mile and a half from our lines, at a big zareba which had been formed for parking the camels, and the question was how best to get back at night across the waste stretch of sandy plain between. " I advise you to take a revolver," said the Provost-Marshal, when he heard I was going alone. "Well, I am thinking of a sword and a lantern." " But that will show you to the Arabs if there are any about." " Yes ; but it will save me from the pickets, who, if I fire a shot in the dark, will take me for the enemy and let fly a volley at once. So, choosing the lesser of two evils, I paraded home with a drawn sword, peering into every bush and gully with tender solicitude. It is strange how different a country you are perfectly familiar with in the daytime looks at night, and what a number of funny, creeping, crawling, cracking, and rustling sounds may be heard then, by any one who chooses to stop and listen ; sounds which are quite inaudible in the daylight, when, even in lonely places, a sort of busy hum of life pervades the air. I have read somewhere in a fairy tale of a man who had such keen ears that he could hear the grass growing, the buds bursting, the rustle of the passing clouds ; this

is hardly an exaggeration ; the air is full of such
sounds, and every tiny insect that moves beneath
the sun helps to swell the chorus.

The Government is sending back the Australians
to Sydney in the *Arab*. There was some talk of
a portion of the Contingent going to England, but
the Colonial Secretary preferred that the whole force
should return together. They have presented us
with their Artillery horses, a very fine lot of animals,
which they valued at £10,000. Truly their loyalty
has been one of the pleasantest, and historically one
of the most important incidents of this campaign.
They say many of them left lucrative employ-
ments in the Colonies to serve as privates ; in a few
days a patriotic fund of over £50,000 was raised
in New South Wales, subscriptions of one and two
thousand pounds being offered in lump sums. When
the news arrived that England would accept Colonial
assistance, the Ministers were at a banquet 300
miles from Sydney, and cheer upon cheer rent the
air when somebody struck up " Rule Britannia " on
a piano in the room : I can imagine the scene.
They have been true and gallant comrades, thinking
as every good soldier should, that hardship is a
pleasure in the service of Queen and country, and
heartily do they deserve the thanks of England for
the patriotic example they set. Not that the other
Colonies were backward ; indeed, I believe that
there was great heartburning at the impossibility of
all their offers of service being accepted, and New
South Wales only won the blue ribbon because her
offer was received first.

We had another thunderstorm on the 20th; the
weather is breaking, but the heat has been steadily
increasing, and as far back as the 10th May it had
reached 108 in the tents. Huts are being erected

on a long pointed strip of coral reef that stretches
into the sea on the east side of the harbour, which is
called Graham's Spit. It is supposed it will be a
more healthy encampment for the troops left behind.
When Osman sees them there, he may well assert
that, if he has not quite driven us into the sea as
he threatened, we at least cannot go any farther
without falling into it. The enemy are now again
at Hasheen, and exchanged a few shots with our
vedettes yesterday. Otao was evacuated to-day,
the 21st ; Handoub will be evacuated to-morrow.
The scattered tribes are returning to Osman Digma,
and even some of the Friendlies are beginning to
go over to him.

May 22.—My work is over ; F—— has ordered
me on board the *Ganges;* he has threatened to do so
once or twice during the last few days, for I have
been far from well, but I tried hard to escape being
invalided till the last man had come in from the front.
To-day all the troops have been withdrawn from
Handoub, which is now in the hands of the enemy,
who quickly ran down from the mountains whence
they had been watching the proceedings, and fired a
few derisive shots after them. This, however, was
too much for the men of the gallant Berkshire, who
faced round and fired a volley that sent them flying ;
then the whistle sounded and the train brought the
Regiment back to Suakin. To-morrow the Headquarter camp will be struck and removed to Quarantine Island. My occupation is gone ; there is no
longer any need for a Field Water Service.

In the afternoon the dhoolie bearers brought their
ghastly litter to my tent door and carried me down to
the *Ganges.* I had often pitied the sick and wounded
being carried in dhoolies before, little knowing I should
lie in one myself. Colonel Gordon, the Provost-

Marshal, was carried down beside me in another dhoolie ; he is suffering from fever. The motion of a dhoolie is anything but pleasant, and I think some sort of spring mattress might be fitted to it to break the vibration of the long bamboo pole to which it is hung ; if the four bearers who carry it move perfectly in step it is not so bad, but should they once begin to shuffle the jar becomes horrible to a sick man. After a short delay at Quarantine Island, where the doctors kindly brought out chairs for us to sit on, we were transferred to a steam-launch and taken to the *Ganges*, where we were placed together in the same ward, a nice airy cabin with two large ports, and swing iron cots with punkahs above them ; the wooden side of the cabin next to the gangway had been knocked out and muslin stretched across in its place, so that our abode was beautifully cool, though somewhat transparent. We were treated with the greatest kindness, made to go to bed at once, given some soup and barley-water, and told by the doctor that he would pay his official visit later, but when he came we were sleeping the sleep of exhaustion, and he mercifully refrained from waking us.

May 23 *to* 25.—In the morning the doctor appeared in state attended by the Hospital Orderly who has charge of our cabin, and a nursing Sister in her neat red cape and white apron ; our cases, daily diet, etc., were written up on a couple of boards hung at the foot of our beds, and we are now fairly under treatment. The custom the doctors follow of making their first visit attended by a lady nurse is rather trying to a bashful man, and I have known several gallant soldiers who were fain to conceal important symptoms rather than give a catalogue of them in the presence of the Sister. The doctors and nurses

are so accustomed to sickness that they do not think
of this, but men little used to it, feel shy at the idea
of bothering a lady with a list of their ailments, and
it would be more merciful if the doctors began by
seeing their patients alone. I am only speaking of
the first visit, and would not for the world depreciate
the services of the nursing Sisters, for I know well
that the gentle care and the brightening influence
they exercise on the patients in hospital is of
inestimable value ; indeed, I am told that the men
watch their coming and going as they would look
for the visits of a ministering Angel.

How pleasant is the perfect cool and quiet of this
beautiful ship, where every comfort and even luxury
is provided for the sufferers! There is a most
excellent cook on board, but his *chefs d'œuvre* are
for the convalescent ; we, as yet, are only allowed a
bowl of soup twice a day and gruel. I heard an
amusing story of a sick officer who came to the
Ganges hoping he would get a good dinner, for he
had heard of the cook, and was suffering more from
want of properly prepared food than anything else ;
so when he arrived, he said he thought he could
manage the wing of a chicken and a pint of champagne, but to his dismay was promptly put to bed
and told he should have a nice comforting bowl of
water gruel.

There are one or two patients who frankly admit
they are delighted to be here, but most officers consider it their duty to go through a little comedy
before they arrive. They feel ill and struggle
manfully against it, till they are at last forced to call
in the doctor. He says at once, " My dear fellow,
you should have told me of this twenty-four hours
ago ; I will send you to hospital, *if you like.*" To
this the patient replies indignantly, " Nonsense, I

am not going to be invalided, I only want you to give me just a little something to pick me up and enable me to do my work." The doctor yields, and a few days pass during which the patient gets no better, then the doctor comes, looking severe, and says, " I tell you what it is, the *Ganges* is the right place for you, *I advise* you to go on board at once." In his secret heart the sufferer perhaps feels that the shady awning and perfect repose of the *Ganges* are like the oasis in the desert to the thirsty camel, but the instincts of his race make him revolt against the idea of giving in, and, resolved to make another struggle, he says, " No no, doctor, you must not invalid me ; I shall be all right again soon, if you will just give me something to stop these abominable symptoms ; I hate the idea of leaving my duty." So the doctor goes, another day or two passes and the patient is worse ; then the doctor grows cross and says, " I shall just *order* you into hospital, and leave you no choice in the matter." Then at last the patient feels that he is come to the end of his tether and says, " Well, doctor, of course if you *order* it, I must obey." So he is brought down to a region of soft beds, shady awning, quiet days, cool drinks, and tender care. All honour to those who provide so thoughtfully for our sick and wounded.

On the 24th the P.M.O. came on board, to hold a Board, and we were all ordered to England on three months' sick leave. Sir George Greaves visited the ship in the evening, and told me that the enemy had lifted up some hundred yards of the line bodily, and thrown it on one side of the track.

May 26.—This morning there were signs that we were preparing to depart, the *Ganges* having been ordered home ; she is now crowded with sick, mostly fever cases, and at the last moment Major D——

came on board from Headquarters, also with fever ;
he was placed in the next cabin to Gordon and myself ; which is pleasant, as we were all members of
the same Mess.   In the afternoon a terrific thunderstorm burst over Suakin, the rain falling in torrents,
and the thunder and lightning being continuous.
Brewster came on board and told me that Osman's
people had pounced on some of the Friendlies yesterday, and carried off their women and cattle.   It is a
great shame.

At 4 P.M. the anchor is lifted and we glide
swiftly away from Suakin, which soon fades in the
purple distance behind us.   " Thank God that I
have left it alive," cry more than one of our number
as they stand gazing over the taffrail at the little
cemetery by the sea with its thick cluster of crosses.

I have begged leave to lie on deck on one of the
long manilla chairs with which the ship is well provided, and as the pure curling waves part before the
sharp prow of the good P. and O. steamer on her
homeward voyage, my heart is very thankful.

It is not my intention to repeat the experiences
of a sea journey ; we were now retracing our way
along the same route we had traversed a few months
ago full of health and high ambition, but the ship
was the abode of sickness and suffering—no concerts
broke the stillness of the starlight nights ; the nurses
stole from ward to ward with noiseless step ; we
hardly dared to walk the decks for fear of disturbing
those below.   I was told that from the 1st March
to the 14th May, no less than 103 officers had
been admitted to hospital, of whom one had died,
and only 50 been returned to duty, while 2146
men had been received, of whom 1080 had returned to duty, and 21 died in hospital.   This did
not include all those who died before or after

reaching home, or over 1000 men of the Indian Contingent, who also fell sick, but whose record was kept separately by the Indian doctors; in other words, nearly one-fourth of the whole force must have passed through hospital in two and a half months.

"I always used to think the Red Sea hot," said D—— to me one day as we were lying side by side on deck chairs, "but now it seems so deliciously cool, almost chilly," and so it did after Suakin, though it was the 27th of May.

On the 30th we stopped in the Suez canal for the funeral of a Marine who died on board the previous night. He had fallen off the train that was bringing him back to Suakin to embark for home, and his leg had been cut off by the engine, the only accident, I believe, that happened on the line. They say that had he kept up his spirits he might have lived, but the shock of his bad luck was too much for him, and he declared at once they might just as well throw him overboard; so the poor fellow sank and died, and was carried down the side of the ship under the flag of his country and buried at Ismailia.

And now came for me the saddest part of all the journey. Poor Gordon, my cabin companion, had never been able to shake off the fever with which he came on board, though he fought against it with brave and patient spirit. Once or twice I noticed with uneasiness that his mind wandered at night, but in the daytime he spoke in his usual frank soldier-like manner, and did not appear alarmed at his condition; so we hoped for the best. He was most unselfish throughout, and on the night of the 30th, when I went into his cabin, said, "Oh! De Cosson, you must not sleep here; it is for your own sake, you know." The doctor had already asked me not to do so, as the nurses would be passing in and out all night, and I had my blankets carried on deck, for the other wards were all full. On the morning of the 31st, Sunday, I thought he looked worse, though at 1 P.M. when I was in his cabin, he was still quite conscious, and spoke to me in his usual voice. I had noticed him in the early morning listening very attentively to the Communion service that was being read in the Sisters' day cabin, which was next to ours, and after lunch I was just telling the Chaplain that I thought he would like him to read with him, when the doctor came up and said, " the Colonel is dying," so we went down together and then the end came very quickly. Another brave soldier had given his life without a murmur in the service of Queen and country.

June 1.—We buried poor Gordon this morning in the cemetery at Port Said, where we arrived last night. The Egyptian Governor sent his military band to play the Dead March, not that in Saul, but a strange wailing Turkish air, that rose and fell with wild pathetic cadence, as we marched sadly through the narrow streets. An Italian man-of-war also sent her band and a strong contingent of officers, while the English gun-boat, *Coquette,* furnished a firing party of blue-jackets. All the convalescent officers from the *Ganges* and the officers of the Turkish corvette attended. The coffin was covered with the flag Gordon loved so well, and placed on a hearse drawn by two horses. I walked beside it as his personal friend, for D—— was too ill to be allowed to come. Just two days ago I posted Gordon's letters for him at Suez, no doubt announcing his return ; how little those to whom he is dear at home know that this bright, sunny morning he is being borne to his rest.

The wailing of the Turkish dirge brought the people of Port Said to their windows, many of them half-dressed, to witness the unwonted sight of a British officer's funeral. We lingered in the pretty little cemetery till the grave had been filled in, and then returned to our ship, having performed the last sad duty soldiers can do for each other. At five we sailed, and in the evening I returned to my cabin, where it was sad to see the empty berth. I believe poor Gordon had thought of leaving Suakin a fortnight before, when he was well and strong, but a sense of duty made him remain till it was just too late.

And now the breeze blew fresher, the sun was no longer scorching, the sea turned from a lovely lapis-lazuli blue, to soft cool green, and one by one, with pale pinched faces, the convalescents were able to creep on deck and drink in the life-inspiring air of the North. Once again the screw stopped in the early morning, and another of our number, a poor fellow who died of fever, was reverently consigned to his grave, this time in the deep sea ; but that was our last loss. Every passing vessel dipped its flag as it saw the red cross at our mast-head, and one steamer of the British India Line signalled to ask if we knew the winner of the Derby ; we did know, for in sickness or health Englishmen are sportsmen to the end.

So the days slipped by, the weather favouring our homeward passage, and one fine morning in June, the fair woodlands and meadows of the Isle of Wight hove in sight ; we were home again, some perhaps only to die, but even so in dear old England with loving friends and fresh green fields around them.

" I have only one wish," said an officer standing

beside me, " and that is to sit still and gaze on green meadows and shady trees for the next month."

As we steamed into Portsmouth harbour, the band of the training ship struck up, " See the Conquering Hero comes." Perhaps the familiar tune with which soldiers are welcomed home struck somewhat sadly on our ears, but as Lord Salisbury said, when proposing the vote of thanks, " We failed to fulfil the main purpose for which we were sent out through no fault of our own ;" and the strains of " Home, Sweet Home," which followed, were sweet indeed.

The thoughtful and gracious messages that our Queen had sent us on more than one occasion during the operations, and which are so highly prized by those who serve her, told us that she knew we had been true to our duty ; wounds and sickness were forgotten in the knowledge that we had won her approbation, and it was with light hearts, if with somewhat enfeebled frames, that we left the hospital ship *Ganges*, and felt the soil of England once more beneath us.

CHAPTER XII.

THE ROAD TO KHARTOUM.

WHEN a campaign is over, the question naturally arises, What has it taught us? The late campaign in the Soudan taught us, among other things, that our young soldiers of to-day, are fully equal in pluck and endurance to their glorious predecessors of sixty years ago; but there are also three questions connected with it that are worthy of careful consideration.

First, Was our failure to reach Khartoum in time to save Gordon, owing to fortuitous circumstances, or because the advance up the Nile was a strategical mistake? Secondly, Would the Suakin route, if it had been adopted, have offered a greater probability of our being able to rescue him? Thirdly, Should events in Egypt render it necessary to take Khartoum in the future, which route ought to be followed by a force invading the Soudan with that object? To arrive at a proper solution of these questions, it is first necessary to examine the statements of officers who took part in the Nile expedition.

In his despatch of the 6th March 1885 Lord Wolseley said—" I take this opportunity of congratulating Her Majesty's Government upon having adopted the Nile route as the line of advance for this force on Khartoum. Had this army been despatched from Suakin as a base, and upon arrival at, or near, Berber, learnt that Khartoum had fallen, it could not possibly have transferred its base to the Mediterranean, for it could not have been fed under those circumstances in this part of the Nile valley. The Province of Dongola would have been at the enemy's mercy, and the frontiers of Egypt would have been open to his attack." [1]

The construction of this paragraph is somewhat involved, but it may be taken to imply that, had a force on reaching Berber from Suakin, learnt that Khartoum had fallen, the province of Dongola would have been at the enemy's mercy, and the British army forced to transfer its base to the Mediterranean. With regard to the first point, there is grave doubt if an Arab force would have ventured a descent on Egypt with the British troops established at Berber in their rear. And with regard to the second, it may be urged that the reverse proved to be the case; for the Nile Column, after the fall of Khartoum, found it would be dangerous to continue the campaign with its base on the Mediterranean alone, and that it would be practically necessary to transfer it to the Red Sea—hence the Suakin expedition.

To quote Lord Wolseley's words, when advocating the construction of the Suakin line, in the same despatch—" In the campaign before us the construction of this railway even as far as Ariab will, in case of necessity, secure us a second and alternative line of communication, by which supplies may be obtained, and sick and wounded taken to the coast for embarkation. It will also give to our operations an appearance of irresistible strength, which the possession of only one line of supply, and that along 1400 miles of river, would never afford."

[1] Egypt, 13.   No. 7.

Telegraphing to Sir E. Baring on the 29th February 1884, General Gordon said—" Should you wish to intervene, send 200 British troops to Wady Halfa and Adjutants to inspect Dongola, and then open up Suakin-Berber road by Indian Moslem troops. This will cause immediate collapse of revolt." [1]

Instead of following this counsel, and making merely a demonstration at Dongola, while the real advance struck direct at Berber from the Red Sea, the Government decided on pushing the whole British force up 1400 miles of painful navigation ; and, as Lord Wolseley has congratulated them on their policy, it is presumable they acted under his advice. I feel great diffidence at differing from so eminent an authority, but let us compare the two routes.

It should first be understood that it is not now a question whether the expedition was decided on late in the day, for the duty of the expedition from a military point of view, was simply to do the best it could from the date it was decided on—to achieve, if possible, its primary object, viz.—" To bring away General Gordon and Colonel Stewart from Khartoum." It cannot be supposed that those who planned the Nile expedition were not fully aware that time was a matter of vital importance, for Gordon himself more than once laughed such an idea to scorn, and, writing in his *Journal* on 23d September 1884, said, " Now I really think if Egerton was to turn over the ' archives ' (a delicious word) of his office, he would see we had been in difficulties for provisions for some months."

It was certain then, that the endurance of Khartoum was limited ; and yet the plan adopted for an advance to its relief, was one where the rate of movement was the principal element of uncertainty.

[1] General Gordon's *Journal*, page 103.

Now it is an open secret that the Government believed that if they adopted the Nile route not a man would be lost in battle, and the campaign would prove a bloodless regatta up the Nile, like the Red River expedition ; while if they chose the Suakin route, there would be much fighting, and the water alone required for the force, would cost over £100,000 to provide. But perhaps the best proof of the optimist view the Government were led to take of the Nile route, may be found in the small vote of credit proposed to Parliament, viz. £300,000.

I well remember a conversation I had about this time with an officer, then holding a high position in that department of the War Office which is specially devoted to the culling and culture of intelligence. I had been pointing out to him that nearly every African traveller who had any practical knowledge of the Eastern Soudan, was distinctly adverse to the Nile as a line of advance ; when he replied, " Yes, but we think you African travellers know nothing whatever about it ; now several of us are old sportsmen who are accustomed to Canadian rivers, and we believe that you overestimate the difficulties of the Nile cataracts." " No doubt," I said, " skilful boatmen may enable you to overcome the rapids, but that is not everything : you have to consider the time it will take, the climate you have to face, the difficulty of obtaining fresh supplies, or land transport, once you are started, and the certainty that you will be in a grave dilemma if any hitch occurs." " Oh yes," he said gaily, " if there is a hitch, but no hitch will occur." I fear it will be found, on examination, that the expedition was undertaken somewhat in this spirit ; no allowance was made for a hitch.

However this may be, the result of it is best summed up in Lord Hartington's speech at Grimsby on 21st October 1885. When referring to the late Suakin expedition, he said, " It was necessary, in the then condition of our knowledge, that provision should be made against what, for all we knew, might occur, viz. the invasion of Egypt by a victorious and fanatical horde of Arabs flushed by the capture of Khartoum. It was necessary even as a measure of precaution *to ensure the safety of Lord Wolseley's army which was on the Nile.*"

These words, coming from the late Secretary of State for War, are a sufficient answer to any attempt to prove that the army on the Nile was not in a perilous strategical position. Had it been otherwise, the costly expedition to Suakin could not have been politically justified.

Writing to the *Times* as far back as the 25th August 1884, I concluded a long letter, in which I endeavoured to point out certain disadvantages of the Nile route which are now manifest, thus—"It was bad economy to send General Gordon alone to Khartoum, as we have now to send an expedition to relieve him, but it would be worse economy to send that expedition by a route which might entail the necessity of sending another expedition to relieve the relieving force." I only quote this, to save myself from the charge that it is easy to prophesy after the event.

Let us now look at the situation of the force on the Nile, and see whether it was the fault of the route adopted, that as fine a body of men as ever served their Queen, found themselves not only unable to reach Khartoum in time to save Gordon's life, but so unfortunately circumstanced that a reluctant Government was obliged to despatch at enormous cost another expedition to Suakin, to ensure their safety.

The Nile expedition was decided on early in August, but, as it was found necessary to have a fleet of boats specially constructed for the navigation of the river, to send for voyageurs from Canada, and kroomen from the West coast of Africa, a certain amount of valuable time was lost in these preparations. On the 31st of August, Lord Wolseley left London to assume command of the expedition, but only reached Korti on the 16th of December, and it was not till the 1st of January 1885 that the first boats of the Black Watch arrived at that place, and a forward movement was possible. He then found himself confronted with the dilemma which those who advised against the Nile route had long foreseen ; for he had received a letter from General Gordon dated 4th November, which said, "We can hold out for forty days with ease, after that it will be difficult." Yet here was the British force only just assembling at Korti, though more than fifty days had elapsed since the date of that letter. Before the troops there were still over 500 miles of river to Khartoum, 140 miles of which was broken by difficult cataracts, and Berber had to be taken on the way.

General Buller calculated that a River Column could not even reach Shendy, a hundred miles below Khartoum, before the 5th March, and then only on the supposition that no serious opposition would be met before Berber, and that Abu Hamed would be reached about the 10th February.[1]   In point of fact, when the experiment was tried, the River Column was still twenty-six miles below Abu Hamed on the 24th February, with a cataract before it, while it was in want of supplies, had already fought one serious battle, and was anticipating further opposition at Abu Hamed.[2]

[1] *From Korti to Khartoum*, p. 304.   [2] *The River Column*, p. 251.

But even under the original calculation, it was clear the Nile route could not be depended on. General Brackenbury, writing on the 24th December 1884, says, "The exact nature of Lord Wolseley's plans was not then known to me ; but I knew that his original idea of moving the whole force by river to Berber and thence to Khartoum had necessarily to be abandoned, and that, if Gordon were to be rescued within the period we had reason to hope he could hold out for, troops must be sent across the desert. This was a more or less desperate venture," etc. In short, the original idea of the campaign had proved impracticable, and a more or less desperate venture had to be made to retrieve the situation.

The alternative was a desert march of 176 miles to Matammeh on the Nile, 98 miles below Khartoum, where Gordon's steamers were supposed to be waiting ; and it was hoped that "a dash across the desert" might get us out of the difficulty. But, as it was clear that it would be dangerous to leave Berber in the rear, and that public opinion would require Stewart's murderers to be punished, the force, never a very large one, had to be split into three parts ; one to remain at Korti and keep open the long line of communications, another to go up the river towards Berber, and the third to cross the desert to Matammeh.

On the 31st December, an echo of Gordon's voice reached the General from Khartoum, in the shape of a verbal message brought by an Arab who had left the beleaguered city on the 29th of October ; it said, among other things, "The food we still have is little. . . . We want you to come quickly. Do not scatter your troops," and lastly, it warned us not to let rumours of the direction by which we were approaching spread abroad. But the very day before this message arrived, Sir Herbert Stewart had been sent to occupy Gakdul wells, though the relieving force would not be ready to advance till the 8th January.

Sir C. Wilson says, " From the Emir of Berber's letter it is evident that the concentration of Arabs to fight us at Abou Klea took place after, and was consequent upon, Stewart's occupation of Gakdul ; so that if he had gone straight across, as at one time intended, he would have met with no opposition in the desert, and probably not much at Matammeh. The original plan had to be given up for want of transport. Another thousand camels, which might have been easily got in November, would have done the business. Gordon's message by his last messenger was emphatic : " Come by way of Matammeh or Berber ; only by these two roads. Do this without letting rumours of your approach spread abroad." And here we had told every one, by our occupation of Gakdul, that we were moving by the Matammeh road. Stewart's first march was a complete surprise. The Arabs did not know of it till the morning he started ; and Omdurman not having then fallen, the Mahdi could not have sent down so many troops, even if he had had time to do so."

The want of transport which led to this error of policy, and perhaps precipitated the fall of Khartoum, was principally owing to the too great confidence that had been placed in the scheme of sending up relief to Gordon in whale-boats. Sir C. Wilson says, writing on 13th January, " The supply of camels is much too small, and we are already beginning to feel the effect of the fast and loose game played with regard to the purchase of camels in October, November, and December." The River Column had also to suffer, and, as General Bracken-

bury points out, "depend for food upon the supplies we could take with us from Abu Dom, upon
whatever we could buy or capture in the country we
were about to enter, and upon the promised convoy
from Korosko, which was to meet us at Abu Hamed."
It must be remembered that the despatch of a convoy
to Abu Hamed, depended greatly on the supposition
that General Earle would meet no serious resistance
before Berber. On the 9th January, General Buller
wrote to him—"Every endeavour will be made to
complete the Infantry of your force up to 100
days' rations per man before they start ; but it is
possible the difficulties of transport may make it
almost impossible to do this within reasonable time."

The Mudir, as might have been expected, was
meanwhile playing fast and loose.[1]   Gordon was in
his death-struggle with famine at Khartoum. "From
Christmas day 1884," says Sir C. Wilson, "to the
26th January 1885, the garrison lived on coarse bread
made from the pith of the palm-tree, on gum, and
on a little tobacco." Yet here was the first week of
January past and our force only just beginning to
move from Korti, and hampered at every point by
difficulties of transport, because our base was 1400
miles away, and the river alone had been depended
on as the means of communication.

That Lord Wolseley began to realize the gravity
of the position, is evident from the remark in his
instructions to Sir C. Wilson of the 7th January—
"You are aware of the great difficulty of feeding this
army at such a great distance from the sea." It
seems almost unnecessary to put such a truism into
a letter of instructions, for the difficulty had been
apparent to all who knew the country before the
troops left England.

[1] *River Column*, footnote, p. 15.

Still Lord Wolseley hoped against hope that when the Mahdi realized that English troops were approaching Khartoum, he would retreat and thus raise the siege, as if the Mahdi would not know our difficulties of transport just as well as we did ; but in the same hopeful vein he said (supposing the siege to be raised), "No British troops would be sent to Khartoum beyond a few redcoats in steamers for the purpose of impressing on the inhabitants the fact that it was to the presence of our army they owed their safety.

"The siege of Khartoum being thus raised, all our military arrangements would be made with a view to the immediate occupation of Berber, and a march across the desert to Ariab, on the Suakin road."

We are not told how it was proposed that a force already short of supplies and transport, should operate across over a hundred miles of barren desert against Osman Digma in the mountains, unless the idea of a Suakin expedition was already in contemplation ; but it is evident that, even at this date, Lord Wolseley had begun to see the vital importance of the road to Suakin as a line of communication.

There was no second fleet of whalers with its attendant voyageurs and kroomen ready to bring him fresh supplies up the river, which moreover was falling every day, while the advancing season would soon prevent all chance of effective succour by the Korosko route, even if it could be opened.

It is not necessary to descant on the fall of Khartoum, for it was almost a moral impossibility that a force approaching by the Nile could reach it in time to save the city from that worst of all enemies, famine.   Sir C. Wilson has clearly shown that the presence of "a few redcoats" some days sooner, would have made no difference ; in fact it is perhaps fortunate that they did not arrive in time, for Gordon would never have fled from the place, and their lives also might have been sacrificed. Gordon himself seems to have been mistaken in his estimate, when he said, " I ask for no more than 200 men," as the handling we received at Abou Klea clearly proved. Nothing but the appearance of a British force sufficiently strong to beat the Mahdi's hordes on their own ground outside Khartoum, and raise the siege, could have saved him ; and to do this, that force would have had to arrive before the 10th January and be able to bring supplies to the garrison.

Sir C. Wilson says, " I thought at the time that, if we had reached Khartoum before it fell, the presence of two armed steamers with a small detachment of British soldiers (twenty) might have turned the scale in General Gordon's favour. The fuller knowledge which I now possess of the condition of the garrison, and of the determination of the Mahdi to attack Khartoum before the English arrived, leads me to believe that if the steamers had left Gubat a week earlier, the result would have been the same ; and that even if it had been possible for them to have reached Khartoum on the 25th January, their presence would not have averted the fall of the city."

Even supposing Khartoum could have held out a little longer, buoyed up by the hope of succour, what prospect of succour would the force at Gubat have afforded ? It did not even take Matammeh. Sir C. Wilson has truly remarked—" The original programme had failed. It was that Stewart was to occupy Matammeh ; then that Beresford was to man the steamers with his Naval Brigade, and take me to Khartoum, and that I was to leave Burnaby in command. Burnaby was dead, Stewart dangerously

wounded, all the officers of the Naval Brigade killed
or wounded except Beresford, who was ill, and could
not walk without assistance.   The force had lost
more than one-tenth of its numbers, and was encumbered by over a hundred wounded.   It was absolutely necessary to send a convoy off for provisions
as soon as the camels could travel, and the horses
of the 19th Hussars were too much done up to
reconnoitre any distance from camp.   I had every
reason to believe that forces of the enemy were
advancing against us from the North and South."

How could the British force in such a condition
have fought its way up to Khartoum, or gone up
piece-meal in "penny steamers," under perpetual
fire?   The large masses of the enemy that came
down upon it at Abou Klea were despatched before
Khartoum had fallen, yet the siege was not relaxed.
What succour could our troops have offered to
Gordon's garrison, even if they reached it in time,
when they could hardly feed themselves and were
already short of ammunition?   What support could
Lord Wolseley have given them with what General
Brackenbury terms his "handful of men at Korti,"
when his Transport was already exhausted and no
more to be obtained?   There was no prospect of
Brackenbury being able to reach Gubat before April,
even if he did not stick fast at Berber.   In short,
the position at Gubat was untenable, even had
Khartoum held out a fortnight longer, and for all
effective assistance our troops could render the
garrison they might as well have been in London.

One more extract and I have done: it is dated
the 24th February, and describes General Brackenbury's position after the fall of Khartoum, when he
learned that Buller had been obliged to evacuate
Gubat.   "The conditions in which I found myself

gave no reasonable excuse for pressing on. And lightly as the message touched upon General Buller's difficulties, there was sufficient in it to give cause for anxiety as to the result of his retreat. That he had not retired an hour before it was necessary to do so was a certainty. If his troops should be surrounded by vast numbers of the late besiegers of Khartoum, who had already had three weeks within which to collect to oppose him, his situation might be full of peril. I knew Lord Wolseley could have but a handful of men at Korti ; and the flower of the force was here in the River Column. I had but one course open to me—to make my way to Abu Dom with all possible speed."

Our troops we know behaved admirably and were victorious in every encounter with the enemy ; yet the Nile expedition not only failed in rescuing Gordon, but was obliged to retreat at all points, while another army had to be despatched in hot haste to Suakin, to hold Osman in check and cover its perilous position. I leave my readers to decide whether this state of things was the result of fortuitous circumstances, and of Khartoum having fallen only two days before Sir C. Wilson reached it ; or only the natural and logical consequence of our having placed ourselves in a defective strategical position, and adopted a line of advance. that offered no reasonable prospect of supplying succour to Gordon in time to save him.

Let us now turn to the Suakin route, and see whether it was impracticable, or that the idea of laying a railway along it was a chimerical scheme, as the public have been led to believe. I do not say that the state of Eastern affairs in May did not demand the withdrawal of the force on the Red Sea Littoral, or that Lord Wolseley was not quite right in stopping further military operations, considering the time of year and that he knew the troops would not in any case be allowed to remain.   But I do say that, when the order first came to suspend operations, all difficulty in opening the line had been practically overcome, and that there was nothing to prevent our force from advancing on Berber, had it been required to do so.   All the experience we had gained of the route tended to show that it was quite practicable as a line of advance, and our military position at the time was most favourable.

We were not, like the Nile force, in difficulty as to supplies and Transport ; nor was it possible we should be, neither was our force separated or threatened by any concentration of the enemy. Osman Digma's power had completely collapsed, his followers were demoralized and scattered ; as Sir Gerald Graham said in his despatch of the 30th May, " At the period at which the evacuation of the advanced posts commenced, the political question was practically solved.   A large number of the Amarars had placed themselves unconditionally at my disposal, and a movement in our favour, which even embraced some of the Hadendowa clans, was on foot."[1]

Again, writing on the 22d April, he said, " I have every hope that the Amarars and other tribes on the line of advance towards Berber may not only refrain from opposing our movements, but may be induced to bring in supplies, and to take service for the protection of the railway."[2]   In point of fact, 5000 Friendlies were ready to join their fortunes to ours, who, once they *felt* their numbers, would have fought just as well as any of the enemy, except perhaps Osman Digma's Ghazis, and they had been beaten at Tofrek.

[1] Egypt, 18, enclosure 28.   [2] Egypt, 13, No. 64.

We had ascertained beyond a doubt that the natural features of the country presented no obstacle whatever to the rapid construction of a surface line ; that the supply of water as far as Ariab was practically inexhaustible, and probably capable of development at many points where wells do not now exist ; that with every mile the force advanced, it would be entering a more healthy region, and there was every probability that Ariab would prove the key to Berber, the possession of which is the first step to the dominion of the Nile Valley.

Lord Wolseley received his instructions for the Nile expedition on the 9th August 1884 : let us suppose the Suakin route had been decided on instead. Experience shows that a force similar in composition to that which actually went to Suakin in 1885, could have been assembled at that Port and ready to commence operations a month later.[1] Its first step should have been to occupy Handoub ; and, allowing a fortnight for this and the laying of the first twelve miles of railway, the 23d September would have seen our troops stationed at Handoub with the line behind them, and ready to advance to the relief of Khartoum.

Suakin would only have retained its normal garrison, because, had Osman attempted a descent on it, the force at Handoub could have intercepted his retreat, and it is not likely he would have ventured into such a trap. It is more probable he would have come down and attacked us somewhere between Handoub and Tambouk, because, once we reached that place, we should have commanded the road to Sinkat and many of his sources of supply. When he attacked us, the result would, humanly speaking,

[1] General Graham was appointed to the command of the Suakin expedition on the 11th February. By the 11th March the principal part of his force had assembled at Suakin.

have been the same as at Tofrek, viz. the destruction of his best troops, with this difference, that we should probably have lost fewer men, being unencumbered by an unwidely Transport and in a country where there is little thick bush, while the surrounding hills would have afforded look-out posts to guard against the chance of surprise.

During the progress of the railway, raids would have been made by our troops on Hasheen, Deberet, etc., and the force at Handoub and Otao might have been supplied with condensed water, either by a pipe along the line, which could have been laid at the rate of three miles a day, or by condensing engines placed at those two stations ; beyond Otao no condensed water would have been required. As soon as Handoub was occupied and the rail established to it, a Battalion would have been sent on to Otao, another to Tambouk, and this system of always occupying two stations beyond the head of the line, would have been continued as far as Ariab. The main portion of the Camel Transport would have remained at the head of the line, advancing station by station as it progressed, and leaving a depôt of stores at each post to be maintained by the railway ; but a certain number of camels would always have accompanied the Battalion occupying the station next beyond the head of the line, for furnishing convoys to the advanced zareba. The duty of each post would, therefore, have been confined to supplying the one beyond it, so as to avoid all long journeys to the camels. This plan answered perfectly in 1885 ; thus ·Handoub, drawing its supplies by rail, furnished Otao by convoy till the line reached it, and Otao furnished convoys to Tambouk ; had the operations continued, the Transport depôt would have moved on with the line to Otao and supplied

Tambouk, which would have supplied Es Sibil or
the next station, had an intermediate one been
established, and so on. The question of supply
might by this means have been reduced to a mathe-
matical certainty, and it must be remembered that,
working from Suakin as a base, it was just as easy
for us to procure 10,000 camels as ten, since they
could be drawn direct from India and Aden. Indeed, the unlimited command of Transport and
supplies, would have rendered the force to a great
extent independent of the rate at which the railway
progressed, for it would have been nearly as easy on
the telescopic system to supply four or five stations
beyond the head of the line, as two ; the fact that
the railway was following in rear and could replenish
the stores at each station as it advanced, being
sufficient to obviate all difficulty or anxiety as to
the future.

The permanent way would have been laid in the
manner before described, and protected by block-
houses or redoubts, within signalling distance of each
other. As each station was established, a Battalion
of Infantry would have advanced and formed a
temporary zareba, half-way between it and the next
station, to furnish covering parties for the workmen
engaged on the line. When the railway reached the
next station it would have occupied it, and the
Battalion already quartered there moved forward for
covering duty, so that each might perform it in turn.
Thus three Battalions would have been engaged at
the advanced zarebas and covering the line, while
the remainder of the force moved steadily with the
railway, halting at each station till a sufficient
quantity of supplies had been accumulated at the
next, and holding itself in readiness to engage the
enemy at any point threatened, besides furnishing

detachments to garrison the redoubts at the various stations, making Cavalry raids on neighbouring villages, if occupied by the enemy, destroying wells on the flank of the line of advance, etc.

The railway should have been under military administration, and of the metre gauge, which I have elsewhere explained is best suited to the country and rapid construction ; but if sufficient metre-gauge plant was not to be obtained, the broad gauge could have been laid almost as quickly, with proper organization.   Military engineers at Suakin were of opinion that there should have been no difficulty in laying the permanent way through such a country at the rate of two miles a day for the first fifty miles, and that this would not have interfered with the transport of necessary supplies.   It must be remembered that a steam-engine is not like a camel or a man rowing in a boat, for it can work all night, as well as all day, without getting tired, and only a limited number of men need be kept to look after it.   The stores, therefore, could all have been transported by night, if necessary, and in that case, the line might perhaps have been laid even faster ; while the constant use of it after dark, would have been the best safeguard against its being injured.

Supposing the actual advance had commenced from Handoub on the 23d of September, the railway, progressing at the average rate of two miles a day, should have reached the wells at Wady Haratri (57 miles) by the 22d October ; but we will give it another week to allow for unforeseen circumstances, and say that it reached Wady Haratri on the 29th of the month, and only progressed at the rate of *one* mile a day beyond that place.   By the end of November it would have been at Abdel Hab, 31 miles farther on, where there are plenty of wells

and fresh herbage for the Transport animals. Our
advanced Battalion would in the meantime have been
pushed forward to Ariab (31 miles), a fertile spot
which is only separated from Abdel Hab by a
perfectly open gravelly plain lying in the Amarar
country, across which convoys could have been
pushed without danger, under charge of the Friendlies alone. The railway would have reached Ariab
on the 1st January in due course, but by the end of
November, when it was still at Abdel Hab, the
moment would have arrived for straining every
nerve to reach Gordon.

On the 30th November, therefore, three Battalions
of Infantry, and a thousand Camelry, with some
Machine guns and a Mule Battery on camels, would
have joined our advanced post at Ariab, and this
force with a convoy of 2000 camels, a detachment
of Royal Engineers, Transport, and Medical details,
etc., would have started on the 1st December to
march across the desert that lies between Ariab and
Berber. There would have been no need for it to
move in square, for the country is perfectly open,
and from the top of any of the isolated hills that
rise above the plain, a view for twenty miles round
could have been obtained. The Camel Corps should
have been mounted on Indian camels with saddles
for two riders, but instead of the second rider, each
camel should have had two 8-gallon indiarubber
water bags attached to it. I have condemned these
bags for general transport purposes, but for Camelry
they would be useful, the weight of the two bags
when full being only 170 lbs., and the 1000
camel men would thus have been able to carry a
reserve of 16,000 gallons of water, or sufficient, at
an allowance of half a gallon per day, to provide the
whole force of 4000 men for eight days, inde-

pendently of the water carried by the convoy. [I suggest this as a measure of precaution.] If men became exhausted on the march, the water could have been emptied out of the bags, which only weigh 5 lbs. each, and a man taken up behind instead.

Leaving Ariab then, on the 1st December, the force would probably have reached the wells of O Bak (53 miles) on the 3d, where they would have halted to water their beasts. I found the water in these wells somewhat brackish when I passed them in June, but in December it would probably have been of better quality, and in any case, a little citric acid would have neutralised the unpleasant taste, and so far as my experience goes, prevented the water from having any deleterious effect. There seems also little doubt that the supply at these wells could be largely developed, as at all the other wells on this route.

There is no probability that the enemy would have attempted to make a stand at O Bak, as the country round is absolutely without shelter for them in case of defeat. A guard would have been left at O Bak, and the troops continued their march on the 4th December, reaching the wells at Bir Mahobeh (52 miles) on the 6th. That is supposing the Column marched at about the same rate as Sir Herbert Stewart's did from Korti to Abou Klea. It is possible the enemy would have attempted to fight at Bir Mahobeh ; though, as it is nearly certain the tribes would by this time have come in all along the line of advance, and the news of Osman Digma's collapse reached Berber [where we always had sympathizers] before us, it is by no means certain that they would have done so. If, however, they had decided to oppose us, the country is still perfectly open, and a battle would have been all in our favour.

On occupying the wells of Bir Mahobeh, a zareba
would have been formed, and the force halted for
two days' rest, after which it would have advanced
on the 8th to Berber, five miles beyond, and established itself on the rising ground above the town, if
it proved too strong to be taken at once by assault.
There it would have been perfectly secure, while
reinforcements and supplies were being pushed forward from Ariab.

In the meanwhile a detachment of Engineers
with Norton tubes would have been sent forward to
Wady Laemeb, twenty-five miles from Ariab, to try
for water in the Khor, with instructions, if they
failed, to return to Ariab; but it is probable an
intermediate water station would thus have been
established between Ariab and O Bak, as herbage is
found at this point.   Another detachment would
have gone from Bir Mahobeh to try for water in the
Wady Abou Kolod, about half-way between that
well and O Bak, where there is no doubt water could
be found; and a regular system of convoys would
have been established between Ariab and our camp
at Berber, the 5000 Friendlies being principally employed on this duty.

Allowing twelve days for the concentration of
supplies and the capture of Berber, we ought to
have been in a position to start a force up the East
bank of the Nile to relieve Khartoum, on the 20th
December.   General Gordon's message to Lord
Wolseley said, " Do not leave Berber in your rear ;
keep the enemy in your front ; when you take
Berber send me word, and come by the East bank."

In allowing seven days at Abdel Hab, two at
Bir Mahobeh, and twelve at Berber, it will be seen
that I have given three weeks for delays which
might not have proved necessary, and with good

fortune, it is quite possible the force would have been in a position to advance from Berber a fortnight earlier ; but it is always wise to leave a margin for possible hitches, which must occur even in the best regulated armies.   It is not necessary in a mere sketch of operations like the present, to go minutely into the composition of the force engaged ; but on the 30th December its general distribution might roughly be taken to have been as follows :—Two Battalions of Infantry and one Regiment of Cavalry at Suakin.   Two Battalions of Infantry occupying the twelve or fourteen redoubts at the stations between Handoub and Ariab, and a similar number of blockhouses between each station.   One Battalion of Infantry and one Regiment of Cavalry established, first at Es Sibil, and later at Ariab, to reinforce the line at any point, or operate against any reported concentration of the tribes.   One Battalion of Infantry covering the head of the line, or, if the railway was not pushed beyond Ariab, guarding the line of communication across the desert, and three Battalions of Infantry and 1000 Camelry at Berber,—total, nine Battalions of Infantry, 1000 Camelry, and two regiments of Cavalry, with a proper proportion of Departmental details.   To these should have been added three or four companies of Mounted Infantry, and a company of Mounted Engineers ; but it would not have been advisable to push the Mounted Infantry across the desert until the intermediate wells had been established.   I have left out the Artillery, as their numbers, like that of the Engineers employed on the line, would have been a matter for special calculation.   Gordon has more than once expressed his opinion that Artillery are a mistake in the open desert.   He says, " I do hope you will not drag on that Artillery ; it can only produce delay and do little good. I can say I owe the defeats in this country to having Artillery with me, which delayed me much, and it was the Artillery with Hicks which, in my opinion, did for him." Again, " The fighting force can take the guns of the steamers if they need artillery ; they are very good guns and have field carriages with limbers." At Suakin, and in the mountains between Handoub and Ariab, Artillery would have been most useful, but the force crossing the desert should only have been accompanied by Machine guns and a Mule Battery on camels.

Leaving one Battalion at Berber, the relieving force, consisting of two Battalions of Infantry and the Camelry, would have started from Berber on the 20th of December, and following the East bank of the Nile, reached Khartoum on the 4th January ; the date when the South Staffordshire Regiment actually passed the Gerendid Cataract, and Sir H. Stewart was still at Korti preparing for his ill-fated advance. On that date Omdurman had not yet fallen, and the Mahdi would have been able to spare no force to send against us. Gordon's steamers would have been communicated with, and utilized either to tow up the Infantry in nuggars, or to bring up stores in rear of the force. Besides the stores that would probably have been captured at Berber, supplies would have been rapidly accumulating at Ariab, now within ten miles of the railway, and a regular system of convoys would have been established to the front. Even supposing half the Camelry, with the native troops from Gordon's steamers, had to be left at Shendy, and on the line of communication, Gordon's heart would have been gladdened, on the morning of the 5th January at latest, by the sight of 2500 British troops on whose courage he could rely, and with such a force at his disposal, the raising of the siege would have been a certainty, and that accomplished, his steamers would have brought up supplies from Berber in any quantity.

How his gallant spirit would have rejoiced at finding himself once more with soldiers, instead of "hens," as he calls his Egyptian troops, it is not for me to tell ; at least we should have been saved the shame of having our General's head exposed in the public market-place on a butcher's hook.

That we should have had to strain every nerve to carry out this programme, I admit ; but, I think, if the two routes are compared, it will be seen that the one afforded a reasonable prospect of reaching Gordon in time, of securing a strong strategical position on the Nile, and the practical command of unlimited supplies, both by the Suakin and Korosko routes, without which no effectual succour could have been offered to the beleaguered city ; while the other presented no possibility of our being able to reach Gordon in time, and placed our force in a weak strategical position, where its offensive power was completely crippled by its inability to command those supplies and means of transport which are the very sinews of war; besides entailing the despatch of another expedition to Suakin, costly in life and treasure, "to ensure," as Lord Hartington has said, "the safety of Lord Wolseley's army which was on the Nile."

Clearly, if two expeditions were necessary for the protection of Egypt, it is manifest that the *relieving* force should have proceeded by Suakin to save Gordon, seize Berber, and open the direct route to the heart of the country; while the *defensive* force, should have followed by river to Dongola. To reverse the process, and send an army to Suakin after Khartoum had fallen, was very like putting the cart before the horse.

There now remains the third question. If it should unfortunately be found that Khartoum, with its arsenals and commanding position, has become a standing menace to the safety of Egypt while in hostile hands, and that it is absolutely necessary to retake it, either with Turkish or European troops: what route should the attacking force proceed by in the future? I think those who have had patience to read these pages will be able to decide for themselves, when they reflect that, though the life of a gallant countryman has no longer to be saved, time is always a factor of importance in such a climate. That the first objective of any force advancing on Khartoum must always be the capture of Berber, which cannot be safely left in its rear, and the possession of which practically ensures the command of the Korosko route, and the dominion of the Nile valley on either side of it. That the principal difficulty of any force advancing on Khartoum, will always be the length of the line of communications and the impossibility of procuring sufficient land transport, should the river route be followed, and that it is not practicable to feed an army from local supplies. That the heart of the Soudan will always remain inaccessible until the direct and natural route from the Red Sea to the Nile has been opened, and that the experience of the last campaign clearly pointed to the fact that there would be no engineering difficulty in constructing a line from Suakin.

Briefly, it should be clearly understood that, if in the future Khartoum is considered worth capturing, the line from Suakin is worth making, for until that route is opened, Khartoum can never be held or a settled state of government established in the Eastern Soudan. In conclusion, I cannot do better than quote Lord Wolseley's own opinion, expressed after the fall of Khartoum, and when he had gained practical experience of the country :—" In addition to the commercial advantages which it will eventually confer, this railway cannot fail to have the greatest political influence upon the Soudan, whilst its strategic importance cannot be overestimated. At present this country is cut off from the civilized world by hundreds of miles of desert on all sides, and if the Power ruling at Khartoum has to be assisted from without, it is both very difficult and very costly to send troops to its aid. A railway would do away with this isolation. Had Berber been joined to Suakin by a line of rail when the Mahdi first took up arms against the Egyptian Government, his power would long since have been disposed of."

THE END.